LIVING QUIXOTE

Performing Latin American and Caribbean Identities

KATHRYN BISHOP-SANCHEZ, *series editor*

This series is a forum for scholarship that recognizes the critical role of performance in social, cultural, and political life. Geographically focused on the Caribbean and Latin America (including Latinidad in the United States) but wide-ranging in thematic scope, the series highlights how understandings of desire, gender, sexuality, race, the postcolonial, human rights, and citizenship, among other issues, have been explored and continue to evolve. Books in the series will examine performances by a variety of actors with under-represented and marginalized peoples getting particular (though not exclusive) focus. Studies of spectators or audiences are equally welcome as those of actors—whether literally performers or others whose behaviors can be interpreted that way. In order to create a rich dialogue, the series will include a variety of disciplinary approaches and methods as well as studies of diverse media, genres, and time periods.

Performing Latin American and Caribbean Identities is designed to appeal to scholars and students of these geographic regions who recognize that through the lens of performance (or what may alternatively be described as spectacle, ceremony, or collective ritual, among other descriptors) we can better understand pressing societal issues.

LIVING QUIXOTE

*Performative Activism in Contemporary
Brazil and the Americas*

ROGELIO MIÑANA

VANDERBILT UNIVERSITY PRESS
Nashville, Tennessee

© 2020 by Vanderbilt University Press
Nashville, Tennessee 37235
All rights reserved
First printing 2020

This study was funded in part by the College of Arts and Sciences at Drexel University

LIBRARY OF CONGRESS CATALOGING-IN-PUBLICATION DATA

Names: Miñana, Rogelio, 1972– author.
Title: Living Quixote : performative activism in contemporary Brazil and the Americas / Rogelio Miñana.
Other titles: Performing Latin American and Caribbean identities.
Description: Nashville : Vanderbilt University Press, 2020. | Series: Performing Latin American and Caribbean identities; Book 2 | Includes bibliographical references and index. | Summary: "Examines contemporary appropriations of Miguel de Cervantes's masterpiece in political and social justice movements in the Americas, particularly in Brazil. The author examines long-term, Quixote-inspired activist efforts at the ground level, offering an applied model for cultural activism or, as he calls it, performative activism"- Provided by publisher.
Identifiers: LCCN 2019026478 (print) | LCCN 2019026479 (ebook) | ISBN 9780826522689 (Hardcover) | ISBN 9780826522696 (Paperback) | ISBN 9780826522702 (eBook)
Subjects: LCSH: Theater and society—America. | Social problems—America. | Cervantes Saavedra, Miguel de, 1547-1616. Don Quixote—Adaptations.
Classification: LCC PN2219.3 .M56 2020 (print) | LCC PN2219.3 (ebook) | DDC 791.0981—dc23
LC record available at https://lccn.loc.gov/2019026478
LC ebook record available at https://lccn.loc.gov/2019026479

CONTENTS

ACKNOWLEDGMENTS VII

INTRODUCTION: Living Quixote in the Americas 1

PART I: Transatlantic Quixotes: Brazilian Transculturations of *Don Quixote*

1. "Transforming People through Art": Transculturating *Don Quixote* in Brazil 23
2. American Quixotes: The Afterlife of *Don Quixote* in the Americas 46

PART II: Don Quixote of the Streets: The Performative Approach to *Don Quixote* in Brazil

3. Don Quixote of the Streets: Marginality and Metatheater in Brazilian *Don Quixote* Stage Adaptations 71
4. The Performative Approach: The Brazilian Third Way of Reading *Don Quixote* 99

PART III: Urban Quixotes: Performative Activism and Citizenship in Contemporary Brazil

5. "A Place of Hope": Performing Citizenship in Contemporary Brazil 125
6. "Quixotinhos Urbanos": Performative Activism and Urban Transformation in São Paulo 153

CONCLUSION: Don Quixote Lives On: Performative Activism in the Americas 193

NOTES 207
WORKS CITED 225
INDEX 243

ACKNOWLEDGMENTS

This book, which represents a significant methodological and cultural departure from my previous scholarship on seventeenth-century Spanish prose, is the product of a collective effort. First and foremost, María Elena Cepeda was and continues to be my greatest support and my main source of professional inspiration. She encouraged me to pursue this project from the beginning, despite my methodological and linguistic limitations. A phenomenal writer and editor herself, she patiently took my written English to a place of relative stylistic solvency. As an interdisciplinary scholar of contemporary Latinx Studies, she guided me as I acquired the methodological tools that I needed to undertake the study of twenty-first-century Quixote-inspired cultural activism. In every way, the professional re-invention that this project required of me would have never happened without María Elena, and for that reason this book is hers as much as it is mine.

Of course, I owe this book to the activists and theater companies that have taken *Don Quixote* to the streets of Brazil, Colombia, Mexico, and the United States, to name only the countries that I study here. The intelligence, care, courage, and commitment that these literary and community activists display in their appropriations of *Don Quixote* never cease to amaze me. For a Cervantes scholar, this project is a dream come true, for it deals with activist applications at the local level of arguably the greatest piece of literature ever written. *Don Quixote* is a living entity today, and I have had the privilege to meet in person and work with people who are living and practicing it in the everyday. My heartfelt gratitude to Márcio Meirelles, Chica Carelli, Valéria di Pietro, Telma Dias, Andreia de Almeida, César Badillo, Graziela Bedoian, Auro Lescher, Stephen Haff, and their teams, not only for the access they granted me but most importantly for the Quixote-inspired work they do. The conviction that their projects had to be studied as an activist and intellectual exercise of the tallest order gave me the motivation and strength to finish this project.

I have not had the pleasure to meet in person the following individuals, although their Quixote-inspired activism is also prominently featured throughout my book: Peterson Xavier (formerly at Instituto Religare) and Silvio Galvão and Sandro Rodrigues (Cooperaacs) in São Paulo, Brazil; Bill George and Lisa Jordan (Touchstone Theater) in Bethlehem, Pennsylvania; and Arturo Morell (*Don Quijote, un grito de libertad*) in Miami and Mexico. To all of them, again, my most sincere gratitude. Laura Calejón, Maria Augusta da Costa Vieira, Javier Escudero, and Arturo Steely have accompanied me in different ways in my Brazilian travels; each one of them has been instrumental in my personal journey into Brazilian Quixote-inspired activism.

Very early and partial versions of some of the material dispersed throughout this book have been published as "Righting Wrongs: *Don Quixote*'s 'Other History' in Brazilian Youth Theater," in Don Quixote: *Interdisciplinary Connections*, edited by James A. Parr and Matthew Warshawsky, Juan de la Cuesta, 2013, pp. 203–22; "The 'Don Quixote of the Streets': Social Justice Theater in São Paulo, Brazil," *Cervantes* vol. 31, no.1, 2011, pp. 159–70; "*Don Quixote* among Brazilians: *Um tal de Dom Quixote* (Márcio Meirelles and Cleise Mendes, 1998)," in "*Los cielos se agotaron de prodigios*": *Essays in Honor of Frederick A. de Armas*, edited by Christopher B. Weimer et al., Juan de la Cuesta, 2017, pp. 323–32; "Don Quixote Never Dies in Brazil: Performative Appropriations of *Don Quixote* II.74 in Contemporary Brazilian Theater," in *A Novel without Boundaries: Sensing* Don Quixote *400 Years Later*, edited by Carmen García de la Rasilla and Jorge Abril Sánchez, Juan de la Cuesta, 2016, pp. 199–216; and "Don Quijote de las Américas: Activismo, teatro y el hidalgo Quijano en el Brasil contemporáneo," in *El Quijote desde América* (Segunda parte), edited by Ignacio Arellano, Duilio Ayalamacedo, and James Iffland, Idea, 2016, pp. 247–60. I thank the publishers for kindly giving me permission to reprint fragments of those early studies as part of this book.

I received early encouragement and meaningful suggestions from Robert Bayliss, Frederick de Armas, James Iffland, and many other scholars who heard presentations about different aspects of my book. Sydney Donnell told me about the *Don Quixote of Bethlehem* project by Touchstone Theater. My thesis advisor, Frederick A. de Armas, remains to this day my most reliable mentor, together with Edward H. Friedman. Several grants from Mount Holyoke College, Drexel University, and the American Philosophical Society helped me with travel and research expenses at various stages of this project.

My editors at Vanderbilt University Press, Zack Gresham, Beth Kressel Itkin, and Kathryn Bishop Sanchez, diligently shepherded this project toward its conclusion. In particular, Kathryn Bishop Sanchez gave me many recommendations that enabled me to fill in some gaps in my understanding of Brazilian cultural history and helped me organize my manuscript in a clearer and more succinct way. My second external reviewer anonymously offered me the most detailed and helpful report I could have ever hoped for. I am most grateful to the four of them.

My mother, María Luisa; my late father, José; and my late aunt, María, always believed in me and gave me the gift of family and the love for education, languages, culture, and travel. Paraphrasing Don Quixote himself, I am who I am and I know who I can be thanks primarily to them.

Last but not least, this book only makes sense because of the thousands of children and youth, many of them from disadvantaged backgrounds, who have attended or participated in the activities and performances of Quixote-inspired activist organizations. Beyond academia and the cultural elites, the present and future of *Don Quixote* belongs primarily to them.

INTRODUCTION

Living Quixote in the Americas

This book examines contemporary appropriations of Miguel de Cervantes' *Don Quixote* in social justice theater and community activism in Brazil and the Americas. Beyond literary and academic contexts, Cervantes' masterpiece constitutes a most prominent example worldwide of a fictional book's influence in public discourse. The four-hundredth-anniversary commemoration of part I (1605) and part II (1615) of the novel spawned a *Don Quixote* revival of global proportions in the first two decades of the twenty-first century. A Nobel Institute-sponsored poll conducted in 2002 amply documented *Don Quixote*'s global clout even before the celebrations got underway. By more than a 50 percent margin, Cervantes' masterpiece was chosen by one hundred leading world authors, including John LeCarré, Nadine Gordimer, Toni Morrison, and Salman Rushdie, as the best work of fiction ever written ("*Don Quixote* gets authors' votes"). For the 2005 anniversary, the Spanish government alone earmarked forty million euros to celebrate Cervantes' cultural legacy through a myriad of events. Outside Spain, many Latin American countries organized grand acts of *Don Quixote* remembrance, such as Venezuela's free distribution of two million copies in what the late president Hugo Chávez labeled Operación Dulcinea, after the novel's famed female protagonist. With varying levels of governmental support, and often with none at all, celebratory acts promoted by local entities and cultural organizations (lectures, conferences, exhibitions, concerts, plays, performances) multiplied the effects of the *Don Quixote* craze and extended its reach to places and peoples traditionally overlooked by the official cultural apparatus. Below the shiny surface of institutional acts of remembrance, I examine long-term, Quixote-inspired activist efforts at the ground level, mostly in Brazil but also in the Americas at large.[1]

In chapter 1 of *Don Quixote*, an unremarkable *hidalgo* (a low nobleman with few possessions and no political influence) whose name, ancestry, and hometown the narrator fails to provide, embarks on a transformative process to become a fictional hero of his own invention, the knight-errant Don Quixote. Throughout the entire book, this dual protagonist tirelessly fights on to further his literary metamorphosis, a transformative project that he abandons only on his deathbed. Much like Don Quixote, the character striving to construct his literary identity, Cervantes' *Don Quixote* (the book) remains equally entangled in a constant process of becoming. In a never-ending cycle, successive generations of readers, theatergoers, and consumers of its public imagery (comics, commercial brands, movies, and merchandising) re-interpret its meaning. In Jorge Luis Borges' "Pierre Menard, author of the *Quixote*" short story, originally published in the literary journal *Sur* in 1939, the Argentinian writer precisely captured this continuous process of appropriation that keeps *Don Quixote* (or any work of fiction for that matter) alive. In Borges' cunning tale, the fictional French writer Pierre Menard authors a "new" *Don Quixote* by copying it word for word. As each letter of the book is recast in Menard's contemporary moment, Cervantes' original language takes on new meanings. With his deceptively simple literary proposal, Borges asserts that the mere act of reading, viewing, discussing, or even copying a fictional story perpetually brings it to life anew, infusing it with novel interpretations.

Widely branded for commercial purposes, heralded as an icon of the Spanish language and its many cultures, and required reading in school curricula across many countries, *Don Quixote* remains remarkably alive four hundred years after its original publication. On this premise, the title *Living Quixote* references the extraordinary public sway of Cervantes' literary classic in the early twenty-first century, a 1605 masterpiece that still lives on in the everyday imaginary of millions of people. In its ability to infiltrate political, commercial, and activist contexts, particularly but not exclusively in the Spanish- and Portuguese-speaking worlds, *Don Quixote* asserts its living condition. With each commercial brand, stage adaptation, piece of merchandising, and new edition or version, *Don Quixote* is infused with new life not only in literary circles, but also in everyday contexts, at the street level. In this regard, Cervantes' protagonists experience what Portuguese critic Carlos Reis defines as *sobrevida*, or afterlife, through which "a personagem prevalece sobre a ficção e vive uma vida para além dela" (a character prevails over fiction and lives a life beyond it;

"Pessoas de livro" 54). As its vast presence in public discourse, commerce, and school curricula demonstrates, *Don Quixote* indeed functions today as a living entity.

Most importantly for this project, however, the adjective *living* is also meant to be read in the title of this book as an action verb, as in the practice of actually "living" or putting *Don Quixote* into practice in daily life. Like Cervantes' story itself, my study reflects on the everyday act of rewriting and performing individual and societal roles, an appropriation of a fictional character that Reis does not contemplate in his concept of *sobrevida*, mainly centered on the commercial, artistic, and iconographic iterations of a fictional character. *Living Quixote* translates in the streets of São Paulo and other Brazilian urban centers into the practice of rescripting and performing one's role in society in the likeness of the hidalgo who embraces reading and acting as the driving force of his self-transformation. Consequently, for the most part in these pages I do not foreground my own close reading of Cervantes' masterpiece, but instead I investigate how others interpret and practice *Don Quixote* today. In contemporary Brazilian theatrical and activist endeavors, participants in Quixote-inspired projects are encouraged to imitate the reader Quijano in his unbreakable commitment to performing a heroic knight-errant by means of his own imagination and his courage to confront the status quo. *Living Quixote* thus reveals itself as a fundamentally activist process, one that employs literature as a model for rewriting and performing social roles in everyday life. In this most quixotic of spirits, I will probe the efforts of a variety of individuals and organizations in the Americas, but mostly in Brazil, that "live" *Don Quixote* in order to rewrite not only Cervantes' classic, but society itself.

Don Quixote in the Americas: Transculturation and Performative Activism

The appropriations of *Don Quixote* in Brazil and the Americas that I examine here inscribe themselves within a neocolonial, transatlantic, and activist context that distinguishes American readings from traditional, Eurocentric approaches to Cervantes. A book published in Spain at the peak of its imperial expansion, *Don Quixote*'s imprint in Brazil can only be fully assessed if we take into account the book's transatlantic journey to a former Portuguese colony. In doing so, I adhere to James Clifford's emphasis on the mobile nature of cultural exchange: "Everywhere individuals and groups improvise local performances from (re)collected pasts, drawing on foreign media, symbols, and languages" (14). Rather than regarding this process as a degradation of some theoretically pure indigenous culture, Clifford joins Aimé Césaire and others in celebrating the "pollination . . . and (historical) transplanting" that characterizes hybrid cultures (15). When examining the pollinizing quality of hybridization, however, power dynamics governed by the (neo)colonial contexts within which these exchanges occur cannot be ignored. In the case of Cervantes' cultural footprint in the Brazilian imaginary, for instance, what are the implications of Brazil's colonial past and relationship to the Iberian empire as it appropriates *Don Quixote* today as an icon for social change? In other words, how does a Spanish literary classic translate into contemporary Brazilian activism?

To address these questions, the concept of transculturation, and specifically how an artistic or literary work moves across cultures and across different groups within a culture, will be central to my analysis. First formulated by Cuban anthropologist Fernando Ortiz some eighty years ago, transculturation has evolved over the decades in ways I detail in Chapter 1. Suffice it to say for now that the concept initially came about as a means to explain how the new Latin American nations that emerged from the nineteenth-century wars of independence sought to differentiate themselves from both their European colonizers and indigenous populations. Instead of probing elitist nationwide efforts to define a new Latin American identity, however, here I analyze Brazilian transculturations of the Spanish-language classic deployed at the community level for activist purposes. My ultimate goal is to better understand how Brazilian activism appropriates Cervantes' masterpiece in community-engaged and underprivileged contexts, rather than as part of typically elitist nation-building projects.

Before we delve into the everyday experience of transculturating *Don Quixote* in Brazil, however, a more obvious question must be addressed: Why has *Don Quixote*, written in Spain four hundred years ago, found such fertile soil in Latin American public discourse (politics, activism, art, commerce) both historically and in the contemporary context? The answer likely lies well beyond the bonding quality of a shared common language across Spain's former colonies, for Portuguese- and English-speaking countries in the Americas, such as Brazil and the United States, have also embraced Cervantes' classic in significant ways. The reasons for *Don Quixote*'s remarkable imprint on this side of the Atlantic may indeed run deeper and perhaps even hinge on a biographical connection to the Spanish writer himself. Before publishing part I in 1605, Miguel de Cervantes unsuccessfully requested administrative posts in the "new world" on a number of occasions. Frustrated by the impossibility of starting anew in the American colonies, the Spaniard instead engendered a truly new world via an obscure old villager who, infected with literary madness, transformed his social persona from unremarkable hidalgo into heroic knight-errant. In this regard, Cervantes' literary project broadly aligns with the view of the American continent as a giant laboratory for social experimentation that inspired founding fathers, revolutionary leaders, and community activists across the Western Hemisphere. In other words, there is a very American quality to *Don Quixote* in its bid to rewrite the individual's very position within social hierarchies and norms. As a living entity, *Don Quixote* has influenced and continues to affect today a variety of artistic and activist efforts to articulate a new social order in the American new world.

Not surprisingly then, although little known, most founding fathers and revolutionary leaders across the Americas (all males and mostly white) sought inspiration from *Don Quixote* as the primary fictional source for their new societal models. George Washington, John Adams, and Thomas Jefferson, the first three presidents of the United States, regularly read and discussed *Don Quixote* (Jefferson even learned Spanish to read the novel in its original language). As if seeking guidance for the newly born country he was about to lead, Washington bought his own English-language copy of Cervantes' classic right after the Continental Congress approved the new Constitution on September 17, 1787 (Wood 3; Stavans 144–46). Two other foundational American figures shared this presidential fervor for *Don Quixote*: Benjamin Franklin and Alexander Hamilton. In South America and the Caribbean respectively, Simón Bolívar, also known as the *Libertador* (liberator), and José Martí, both leading figures in the independence of Latin America from the Spanish empire, kept Cervantes' classic at their bedside table. More recently, leftist Latin American commanders including Ernesto "Che" Guevara, Fidel Castro, Hugo Chávez, and Subcomandante Marcos have also employed *Don Quixote* as a primary source of revolutionary inspiration, at times in grand public gestures such as Chávez's aforementioned Operación Dulcinea.

However, this book is not concerned with grand national or revolutionary stories, but rather with the rewriting and enactment of new social narratives at the community level. Here I examine the practice of "living Quixote" mostly at the street level, in public squares, and in neighborhood stages as performed by independent theater companies and relatively small non-governmental organizations (NGOs). For this reason, my account of *Don Quixote*'s reach into contemporary community activism will include a consideration of broader gender, generational, class, and ethno-racial factors, as Cervantes' classic walks alongside real people in their daily life struggles.

To analyze this sort of practiced, applied quixotism (I use the term in the broadest sense to refer to *Don Quixote*-inspired ideology or behavior), I draw on the social justice-oriented tradition of seeking individual and social transformation through words, as Paulo Freire forcefully theorized in his influential *Pedagogy of the Oppressed* (1970). According to Freire, the liberation of the excluded and the underrepresented requires as a necessary first step the recognition and subsequent replacement of the vocabulary of tyranny for one of respect and equality. In cases such as domestic abuse, racism, or sexism, the linguistic awareness of oppression may lead to the re-naming and performing of a new vocabulary of liberation that can trigger deep social transformation. From this point of view, the connection between Freire's theory and Cervantes' literary practice becomes explicit, for what is Don Quixote's quest if not an exercise in re-naming and performance? As revealed by the story of the humble hidalgo turned chivalric hero, the revolutionary act of renaming unleashes the protagonist's potential to rewrite the world via the creation and enactment of new social narratives.

At the core of his theory, Freire believes that our ability "to name the world, to change it" can help end oppression (69). However, the pedagogy of the oppressed does not merely propose a fundamentally linguistic revolution. For the creation of a new vocabulary of liberation to yield real change, the word has to be deployed within the realm of action. For Freire, "the true word—which is work, which is praxis—is to transform the world" (69). Freire's word thus achieves its full meaning only when put into action, for only through practice ("work") may it "transform the world." Freire's is a language that does things, and in this vein his proposal hinges on the same type of performative activism that drives the hidalgo Quijano to live out his chivalric fiction in the "real world."

In an academic reading reminiscent of Freire's prescription for social change, Charles Oriel looks to Don Quixote's performative prowess to explain the character's personal and literary success. Taking J. L. Austin's classic *How to Do Things with Words* (1962) as his main point of reference, Oriel explains how Don Quixote actually "does things with words" in Cervantes' revolutionary proposal. Building on previous theories on the functions of language, Austin's study of speech acts stresses the performative (and not solely the descriptive or constative) power of words, as when a bride or groom says, "I do," a judge sentences a defendant, or a country issues a declaration of war. According to Austin, language under these circumstances does not only describe reality; it also makes it happen—it defines it. As Oriel notes, the very creation of Don Quixote follows a similar pattern, whereby the self-proclaimed knight-errant turns "everything and everyone he sees into performing and performative participants—sometimes unwilling ones—of his own private (chivalric) language game" (81).

Extending Oriel's explanation beyond the book itself, my analysis reveals what I call the performative interpretation of *Don Quixote* that Brazilian activists have devised through practice, by putting Cervantes' creation into action.[2] The process by which words that do things transform both the individual and society constitutes the defining feature in *Don Quixote*'s journey through the Americas. In contrast to Eurocentric interpretations of Cervantes' classic, Brazilian activism places great importance on the subversive discursive strategies deployed by the obscure hidalgo Alonso Quijano to transform himself, frequently with calamitous effects for himself and others, into a chivalric (anti)hero. More than the outcome of the character's self-proclaimed heroism, what matters in the practice of living Quixote is the discursive and performative means by which individuals, particularly of underprivileged background, may rewrite and perform a new identity for themselves and others.

Quixote-inspired activism thus updates and tasks literature, art, and language in general with a social purpose of a revolutionary nature. Rather than government takeovers or armed rebellions, Quixote-inspired theater companies and nonprofits employ writing and performance to activate social change through conscious self-transformation. I call this form of cultural intervention performative activism, which differs from the popular and well-documented performances of Brazilianness analyzed, in particularly revealing ways, in *Performing Brazil*, edited by Severino J. Albuquerque and Kathryn Bishop-Sanchez. While the performance of Brazilianness concerns "cultural artifacts and representations of Brazil that are emotionally charged and that hark back to the nation both within and beyond its borders" (Bishop-Sanchez 17), performative activism is deployed at the community level and prioritizes social progress over feelings associated with the nation. As I will review more extensively in Part III of this book, the term *performative activism* has been employed in the past mostly to describe activist efforts that include public performances as a form of protest, as in Barbara Green's groundbreaking study on the suffrage movement (*Spectacular Confessions*, 1997). Instead of confining performative activism to only public protests, however, my definition zooms in on the revolutionary potential of performance as a means to rescript social roles, which the Brazilian Quixote-inspired initiatives have adopted as their main discursive tool for liberation. Due to its wide-ranging applications, the theory of performative activism reaches well beyond *Don Quixote*-based projects and the country of Brazil. While my object of analysis is primarily Brazilian artistic and activist movements, or what scholars such as Chela Sandoval and Wilson Valentín call "artivism," I tangentially probe a handful of relevant *Don Quixote* appropriations outside Brazil, specifically in Mexico, Colombia, and the United States.[3] In order to best contextualize and define my concept, in a few instances I also include examples of performative activism that do not directly concern *Don Quixote* but that propose a new performance of citizenship by those who feel excluded or ignored by the powers-that-be, particularly in Brazilian urban centers such as São Paulo and Rio de Janeiro. By examining other Quixote-inspired projects across the Americas as well as recent activist initiatives within Brazil, I aim to establish the broadest possible theoretical and cultural framework within which to analyze my very specific case studies.

Don Quixote in Brazil: Socio-Economic, Cultural, and Political Context

As I examine Cervantes' public influence in the Western Hemisphere, I provide concrete examples and a detailed account of the applied quixotism that I am trying to sketch here. Although this is a phenomenon that I pinpoint in numerous countries in the Americas, I focus mostly on Brazil for several reasons. First, the obvious linguistic and cultural barriers that separate Spanish-speaking nations from the former Portuguese colony attest to *Don Quixote*'s potential for effective transculturation not only across communities, but also across countries and languages. Secondly, for activists in cultural and theater-based organizations that to some extent adhere to the Freirean principle of transformation through words, *Don Quixote* provides a particularly fitting roadmap for social change, for the knight-errant comes into existence via the literary efforts of an hidalgo determined to rewrite his own identity in the likeness of chivalry. Lastly, Brazil is the largest country in Latin America in terms of both population and economic prowess, and it is a major world player in music, art, literature, and sports. Thus, for a variety of reasons, Brazil's cultural, economic, demographic, and geographical composition stands apart from that of its Spanish-language neighbors. Even so, the four-hundred-year-old Spanish-language novel *Don Quixote* has penetrated the Brazilian imaginary in deep and meaningful ways, as I document throughout this book. Examining the remarkable sway of *Don Quixote* in Brazilian public discourse thus provides a unique case study against which to test the endurance of all things Quixote in the whole of the Americas.

I study here cultural and activist initiatives that have been carried out primarily between 1998 and 2018, so a very brief overview of the state of the nation since the early aughts will help provide the necessary socioeconomic, cultural, and political context to my analysis. After all, these Quixote-inspired organizations work primarily with the most vulnerable populations (mainly at-risk children and youth), whose well-being remains directly tied to the national socio-economic and political climate. With approximately 206 million inhabitants, Brazil represented in 2017 the sixth-largest country in the world by population and ranked eighth among its most powerful economies. Despite the doom predicted by some on the right, the election of leftist union leader Luiz Inácio Lula da Silva in 2002 set off years of sustained economic expansion that culminated with a record 7.5 percent GDP growth in 2010, Lula's last year in office. With such financial bonanza, Lula's government pursued progressive social policies credited with lifting forty million citizens out of poverty. Due to high inflation and unsustainable government subsidies, these gains may turn out to be somewhat precarious, although a World Bank report suggests at least 43 percent of this upwardly mobile population appears thoroughly consolidated in the middle class. (Criteria to determine the stability of the middle class include long-term employment, access to social programs, and resources to weather a financial crisis.) Also according to the World Bank, the GINI index that measures inequality based on family income went down in Brazil from 58.6 in 2002 to 52.9 in 2013 (Costas). Between 2003 and 2014, the minimum monthly wage rose an astounding 72.31 percent (Garcia). Likely the most critical tool in the government's wealth-redistribution efforts, low-income families who send their children to school and undergo mandatory health checkups continue to receive modest monthly payments through the popular Bolsa Família (literally, family purse) federal program. In this favorable economic climate, cultural activities like the Quixote-inspired work received significant government support in the earlier part of the twenty-first century at local, state, and federal levels.

Part of the BRICS block, Brazil shares membership with Russia, India, China, and South Africa in the select club of leading emerging economies. For many countries, at least in the West, Brazil arguably embodied better than any of its BRICS counterparts the promise of a developing nation. By ostensibly adhering to democratic principles, neoliberal economic practices, and social fairness in equal parts, Brazil appeared in 2010 en route to achieve, as the motto inscribed in the national flag proclaims, both "Ordem e progresso" (Order and progress). During the prosperous first decade of the twenty-first century, Brazil re-wrote for itself a protagonist role in the global theater, most notably through its newfound position as international sports-event host. For decades, Brazil's global profile relied almost exclusively on its touristic allure and a wealth of legendary artists and sport figures. The organization of the 2013 Confederations Cup, the 2014 FIFA World Cup, and the 2016 Olympic Games were intended to prove that Brazil could not only win international sports events elsewhere; the country could now host them as well.

With the downturn in the global economy, however, a six-year period of steadfast expansion (2004–2010) turned into a contraction in 2011 and then a full-scale recession by 2014, while the impending celebration of the 2014 FIFA World Cup and the 2016 Olympic Games inched forward plagued by corruption and delays. The Brazilian financial boom had rested on the shoulders of another developing world titan, China, and its seemingly insatiable appetite for commodities, particularly natural resources. Toward the end of 2011, however, demand for commodities withered, and prices, including oil exports, plunged. With the global market imploding, Brazil was caught economically off guard, with a weak industrial output, a hesitant but exacting fiscal policy, and an exploding national debt. Despite the many years of economic expansion, Brazil's dismal education, health, and transportation systems never fully benefitted from tax revenues that reached an annual 36 percent of GDP, the highest in the developing world. Between 2014 and 2016, the worst recession in the country's history seriously damaged not only Brazil's economy, but also its evolving self-image (Garcia). Since then, the pressures on cultural organizations to find alternative sources of funding have been enormous; meanwhile, the challenging economic and political environment has pushed many vulnerable communities to the edge of social exclusion and poverty.

To make things worse, in political terms the country also fell into a downward spiral. Since at least 2012 President Dilma Rousseff, Lula's successor from his same *Partido dos Trabalhadores* (Worker's Party), had been facing strong political and economic headwinds. After winning a rather tumultuous and closer-than-expected reelection in 2014, Rousseff was impeached for administrative misconduct in 2016 by a Congress in which nearly half of its members also faced corruption charges. Engulfed in his own political scandals, her successor, former vice president Michel Temer, also teetered on the brink of impeachment throughout his two-year tenure. Dramatically, former president Lula himself, while leading the polls as presidential candidate for the upcoming 2018 election, was controversially sentenced in July 2017 to nearly ten years in prison for corruption and money laundering. Amid large protests and unrest, Lula was jailed in early 2018. In October of the same year, far-right candidate Jair Bolsonaro was elected to the presidency, promising a far-reaching reversal of social-minded policies and a law-and-order approach to crime. This succinct and necessarily incomplete overview is meant to frame the discussion of how the nation's complex socio-economic and political situation poses a challenging scenario for at-risk youth cultural entities in the immediate future, with little if any government support and millions of families in need due to ongoing economic strains.

During the first decade of the new century, a number of Quixote-inspired projects sprung up around the celebration of the novel's fourth centenary, particularly in the city of São Paulo, which proved a fertile ground for trailblazing cultural activism directly inspired by *Don Quixote*. Located in Southeastern Brazil, São Paulo constitutes the largest urban center in the country and the eleventh largest metropolitan area in the world with well over twenty-one million inhabitants. As the financial, gastronomic, and cultural engine of Brazil, the city's GDP is the highest of any Latin American urban center and would rank twenty-fourth globally if listed as a country. Racially, the city's population has a larger percentage of whites than the national average, which according to the 2010 Brazilian Institute of Geography and Statistics census stands at around 48 percent. In São Paulo, the same census found that over 60 percent of the population identified itself as white (mostly Italian, Portuguese, Spanish, and German descendants), 30 percent *pardo* (multiracial), and 2.2 percent Asian (São Paulo boasts the largest concentration of ethnic Japanese outside Japan, although Chinese and Koreans are also represented). The city is home to relatively large, vibrant Arab and Jewish communities. Due to significant domestic migration patterns dating back to the 1930s, 6.5 percent of the population identifies as black. Most Afro-Brazilians in São Paulo trace their roots to the country's Northeast, which includes the states of Bahia (Salvador), Ceará (Fortaleza), and Pernambuco (Recife) (*IBGE Cidades*).

Despite its phenomenal wealth and ethno-racial diversity, acute income inequality exists in São Paulo. According to the 2010 census, 2.2 million of its dwellers crowded into favela-like slums, approximately 12 percent of the total population (Adomaitis). Disproportionally, this lower-income population tends to be multiracial or Afro-Brazilian (Rizzini et al. 36). Although Brazil significantly reduced inequality under President Lula's government, by 2014 the country still ranked as the nineteenth most unequal nation in the World Bank's GINI index (*CIA World Factbook*). Ever since the 2014 economic crisis, which hasn't fully subsided, the existing data points to a worsening situation.

The coupling of a predominantly well-educated and relatively wealthy population with sizable underserved communities may be one of the reasons why *Don Quixote* has inspired the activist work of several theater companies and NGOs in São Paulo. Although Cervantes' 1605 classic remains widely known mostly because of the iconic qualities of the protagonist pair, the book's length, archaic language, and obscure historical and cultural references remain challenging for the most educated of readers. Nonetheless, besides popular, filmic, and children's adaptations of *Don Quixote*, the seventeenth-century masterpiece still reaches scores of youth as required reading in school curricula all over the Spanish- and Portuguese-speaking world, including Brazil. College-educated and well-traveled, the Quixote-inspired activists I encountered in my research (not all of them white and many of them female, as I discuss below) produced high-quality adaptations and sophisticated interpretations of Cervantes' work that will undoubtedly enrich academic discussions. Yet the Quixote-inspired activism scrutinized here centers on underserved communities with scarce access to quality education, much less to old foreign books such as *Don Quixote*. Through a seemingly effortless grouping of high culture and everyday practice, a seventeenth-century Spanish-language classic somehow did not feel to our activists too far-fetched a vehicle for promoting social transformation among the underprivileged today. At the street level, working particularly with at-risk youth, these individuals and entities not only keep *Don Quixote* alive but also "live" Cervantes' creation in their everyday praxis. As a consequence of this unique blend of cultural activism and neighborhood-based social work, a visitor may distinctly feel on occasion, as I personally experienced a few years back, the roaming presence of *Don Quixote* in the streets of São Paulo.

Don Quixote in the Streets of São Paulo

The anecdotal manner in which I stumbled upon Quixote-inspired activism in Brazil, and particularly in São Paulo, points to a substantial Cervantine footprint in the country's public imaginary, at least in urban centers. While I was initially researching the fourth-hundredth anniversary of *Don Quixote* on the Internet, the Projeto Quixote (Quixote Project), a São Paulo-based NGO founded in 1996 to provide educational, social, and clinical support to children and youth in high-risk social situations, came up on several of my online searches. Its premise, achievements, and the boldness of its quixotic discourse quickly caught my eye. The fact that they had already existed for over ten years attested to their commitment to *Don Quixote* well before and independent of the fourth centenary. As a side note to my research around the 2005 commemoration, in 2007 I decided to travel to Brazil, a country I knew little about, in order to acquaint myself with the Projeto's Quixote-related activities. Despite the geographical and historical continuities between Brazil and the rest of Latin America, as well as between Portugal and Spain, I did not speak Portuguese at the time and had never studied intercultural relations between Brazil and the Spanish-speaking world either at school or on my own. Yet, the Projeto Quixote already appeared to me far too developed, too sophisticated an initiative to stand alone in the Brazilian cultural and activist panorama. Intrigued by what I saw on the Projeto's website, I wondered whether *Don Quixote* had a life of its own in Brazilian activism.

I made an initial, very short visit to the Projeto in 2007. The Projeto staff welcomed me warmly, gave me a tour of their facilities, and introduced me to their methodology. However, before I could go any deeper into their operations, my time in Brazil drew to a close. I reluctantly departed with a clear sense that the Projeto constituted an extraordinarily sophisticated, vibrant appropriation of *Don Quixote* set in a unique location, both socially (an NGO that works with at-risk children and youth) and geographically (the urban heart of Brazil). During my years as a Cervantes literary scholar, nothing had prepared me for this kind of contemporary, activist, and Portuguese-language applied quixotism. In the context of a vast social enterprise, by 2007 the Projeto had already served thousands of children and youth through an elaborate appropriation of Quixote-inspired themes. Unfortunately, my scholarly training had never equipped me methodologically or otherwise to tackle the study of such a sophisticated organization (and I was soon to come into contact with several others), least of all because of language impediments. Nonetheless, as a literary scholar of the early modern period I felt compelled to study the Projeto's revival and update of *Don Quixote* for a marginalized and contemporary young audience. Formally trained to deal with centuries-old texts, I had a great deal of preparation in store to even begin tackling this project.

Previous commitments kept me from returning to São Paulo for a longer stay until two years later, in early June 2009. Upon arrival, I headed toward my hotel in the Avenida Paulista (Paulista Avenue), dropped my luggage, and took a walk to stretch my legs. Right next to my hotel, I fortuitously ran into an exhibition at the Instituto Cervantes (Cervantes Institute) of *Don Quixote* illustrations by Chilean Surrealist master Roberto Matta. About five minutes in the opposite direction, I encountered an enormous statue of Don Quixote (on horseback) and Sancho Panza presiding over the entrance hall of a condominium and shopping complex called the Conjunto Nacional. Made with recycled materials, the figures were the culmination of a project by a cooperative of artisans (called Cooperaacs) from vulnerable social situations (often former inmates or adults in street situations). On my way back to the hotel, across the street, I noticed Projeto Quixote stickers on wooden panels enclosing a construction site. And in São Paulo's weekly cultural calendar, which I picked up back at the hotel reception desk, three *Don Quixote*-related events (two stage adaptations and Matta's exhibition at the Cervantes Institute) were slated for that week alone.

In a city of some twenty-two million people, after just twenty minutes of improvised strolling around Avenida Paulista, I literally felt surrounded by *Don Quixote*. Exhausted from a long flight and a seemingly endless bus ride from the airport to the city center, I questioned whether my senses had betrayed me. Perhaps I was myself suffering from a strain of quixotic delusion. Is São Paulo a modern quixotic city and a dream come true for Cervantes enthusiasts, or was my own lack of sleep unleashing my literary fantasies upon the surrounding landscape in a most Cervantine way? Somewhat perplexed and positively energized, I headed back out to the Conjunto Nacional to study more closely the enormous statues of the fictional characters that, at least during my very first hour in the commercial and artistic heart of São Paulo, so uncannily proliferated around me. Unbeknown to me at the time, this book began to take shape that very morning. Within a few hundred yards of my hotel, the pieces of the quixotic puzzle scattered across São Paulo's main artery would only fall into place years later, after much additional research and several subsequent trips to the country. While the Conjunto Nacional figures now occupy a good deal of Chapter 1, Chapters 2 through 6 detail many other *Don Quixote* appropriations in the American hemisphere, but mainly in Brazil.

My six chapters are grouped into three parts. Part I, "Transatlantic Quixotes: Brazilian Transculturations of *Don Quixote*," provides the historical and cultural context to contemporary Brazilian appropriations of Cervantes' novel, including relevant examples from other countries in the Americas. In Chapter 1, I define the theoretical concept of transculturation in order to elucidate how a Spanish-language masterpiece of Western imperial connotations became a standard-bearer for progressive causes in contemporary Brazil. Through the analysis of the large Quixote and Sancho figures sculpted out of recycled waste by the São Paulo-based artisan organization Cooperaacs, I investigate Cervantes' bearing on Brazilian activism. Chapter 2 offers an overview of the afterlife of *Don Quixote* in the Americas at large, and specifically in Brazil. While in the early twentieth century Cervantes' classic was transculturated mainly in the context of nation-building projects, since the 1950s it has frequently been read through a social lens. A closer look at recent social justice appropriations of *Don Quixote* across the Americas, specifically in Mexico, the United States, and Colombia, provides a hemispheric framework for my subsequent analysis of Brazilian transculturations.

Part II, "Don Quixote of the Streets: The Performative Approach to *Don Quixote* in Brazil," focuses on Brazilian stage adaptations of Cervantes' classic with an activist slant, whose social justice message is reminiscent of the knight's own lofty goal of "righting all manner of wrongs" (I.1.21). These initiatives extricate the book from its original social and physical context, as well as from the implied elite audience to whom a literary classic seems bound, in order to appropriate it for, among other underprivileged populations, Brazilian at-risk children and youth. In Chapter 3, I examine how these artivist proposals give vulnerable communities a protagonist role through tactics such as representing their interests and concerns on stage; performing for underserved audiences; and casting marginalized individuals, such as inmates and street-connected youth, in the leading roles.[4] Influenced to varying degrees by Paulo Freire's critical pedagogy and Augusto Boal's theater of the oppressed, these plays propose to combat marginality with metatheater, a most Baroque as well as Cervantine of strategies. If the world's a stage, as the novel's protagonist, Alonso Quijano, implies by enacting his self-created knight-errant Don Quixote, the honing of literary and performative skills can enable vulnerable populations to rescript their public persona and thus change the prejudiced social narrative on, for instance, disadvantaged youth.

In Chapter 4, I analyze the creation of the knightly protagonist and his ultimate demise to elucidate the Brazilian (and more broadly, American) performative approach to *Don Quixote*. Rather than just a romanticized hero or a satirical emblem for the decline of the Spanish empire, as portrayed in traditional European readings, Cervantes' hero emerges in these social justice appropriations as an icon for the potential of performance to correct prejudices and inequalities. In order to limit the scope of my project, my work centers predominantly on the financial and cultural hub of the country, São Paulo, which, as I illustrated above, boasts a considerable appetite for all things *Don Quixote*. Among the numerous groups, schools, bloggers, and musicians who in the last two decades have appropriated Cervantes' story in São Paulo alone, and in the country at large, I only investigate theater companies with a proven track record for reaching large audiences, in the many thousands, through a stable presence in the community and an extended performance schedule. They are: Valéria di Pietro's *Num lugar de la Mancha* project with youth interns at the infamous juvenile detention center formerly known as FEBEM; Telma Dias's *Dom Quixote* with the Grupo Permanente de Pesquisa (Permanent Research Group); and Andreia de Almeida's *Quixotes* for the Circo Navegador (Itinerant Circus). Staged in Salvador de Bahia in 1998, Márcio Meirelles' *Um tal de Dom Quixote* project is also analyzed here because it advances a Brazilian activist and discursive interpretation of Cervantes that fundamentally anticipates and overlaps with the later São Paulo appropriations. In an effort to put their theatrical activism into practice, the companies discussed here quite literally take *Don Quixote* out into the streets of Brazil by updating its story for contemporary consumption, performing sometimes in public spaces, and engaging with underprivileged populations. As *Don Quixote* oscillates between the stage and the streets, the continuities between its theatrical versions and the modus operandi of Quixote-inspired nonprofits, which I study in my final two chapters, appear striking.

Part III, "Urban Quixotes: Performative Activism and Citizenship in Contemporary Brazil," probes the cultural strategies deployed by Quixote-inspired NGOs against the marginalization of children and youth in high-risk social situations. Chapter 5 reviews standard definitions of performative activism and its application to the two most consequential examples of contemporary street and social justice activism in the country's recent history: the 2013 Brazilian Autumn and the work of the arguably most emblematic cultural nonprofit in the nation, the Grupo Cultural AfroReggae (GCA) in Rio de Janeiro. Within a concept of citizenship that deploys its activism by rescripting and performing new social roles, particularly for the underserved, in my final chapter I concentrate on three nonprofits inspired by Cervantes' classic: the Projeto Quixote (Quixote Project), the Quixote Espaço Comunitário (Quixote Community Space), and the Instituto Religare (literally, Reconnect Institute, a reentry program), all based in São Paulo. These organizations employ discursive and performative strategies to transform urban spaces, increase the visibility of marginalized populations, and rescript their role in society. The Quixote-inspired activities and tactics undertaken by these organizations expose the merits and shortcomings of transculturating a classic in the context of Brazilian community activism. Besides perennial financial strains, these organizations contend with the vagueness of their mission, for defining clear outcomes and objectives to measure success in the context of rewriting social narratives remains an elusive task. Outside of the many specific testimonials and individual examples I cite throughout this book, assessing the personal and collective impact of Quixote-inspired activism (a key task to refine methods and achieve meaningful, long-lasting change) stands today as a near-impossible undertaking due to lack of data and personnel. Nonetheless, out of my close examination of their everyday operations emerges a new definition of the concept of performative activism that articulates the social work of Quixote-inspired NGOs and that could have significant implications for the performance of new forms of citizenship across Brazil and elsewhere.

In the conclusion, "Don Quixote Lives On: Performative Activism in the Americas," I summarize my revision of the concepts of both transculturation and performative activism from a community-engaged perspective, as well as the originally American and particularly Brazilian performative approach to *Don Quixote*. Additionally, I list some of the current limitations of Quixote-inspired initiatives and propose possible ways to overcome them. Lastly, a brief analysis of three recent examples of *Don Quixote* adaptations across three countries (the United States, Cape Verde, and again Brazil) illuminates the evolution of Quixote-inspired activism over the last few years as well as its potential future applications.

While I dabble in performance studies, ethnographic observations, social movements, and filmic analysis, this book remains a literary enterprise at heart that aims to elucidate how a seventeenth-century text is translated into contemporary community activism. The three parts of this book thus build on three theoretical concepts that are critical to the study of Quixote-inspired activism. Part I centers on the transculturation of *Don Quixote* in the Americas from nation-building projects to community-engaged activism. Mindful of both their historical and community-based roots, I examine contemporary *Don Quixote* appropriations in the Americas in the context of transatlantic, multilingual, and cross-historical relations.

In my reading of stage adaptations in Part II, a purely textual analysis cannot fully address the social implications of what I call here the performative interpretation of Cervantes' novel. Because Brazilian activists regard *Don Quixote* as an effective tool for individual and social transformation, I draw heavily from Critical Discourse Analysis (CDA), which probes the ways in which discourse determines and/or challenges social hierarchies. Since the 1970s, critics as influential as Michel Foucault and Stuart Hall have defined *discourse* as an amalgam of language and ideology that both reflects and influences our worldview. In this dual role, language never appears devoid of ideology, for as we label the world we inevitably imbue it with meaning. Through naming, we categorize and assess our identities and surroundings according to personal and societal values and prejudices. In this sense, the mission of Quixote-inspired activism precisely aligns with Teun A. van Dijk's definition of CDA as the study of "the role of discourse in the (re)production and challenge of dominance" (300).

The main tool that these cultural organizers and leaders adopt from *Don Quixote* and deploy at the community level is what I define in Part III as performative activism: the rescripting and performance of new social roles with the ultimate aim of changing individual and collective imaginaries. Certainly, Latin American performative activism goes well above and beyond *Don Quixote*'s influence in public discourse, but nonetheless it finds a most comprehensive and precise formulation in the Cervantes-based works discussed here. Beyond standard approaches to the *sobrevida* or afterlife of fictional or even historical figures (Che Guevara's global branding comes to mind), here I do not focus exclusively on illustrations, adaptations, or commercial applications of popular characters. In the case of Don Quixote in Brazilian artivism, the character becomes in his afterlife a model to be not merely consumed or reproduced but actually practiced, for he embodies an exercise in rewriting and performing a more egalitarian society.

Throughout this book, I elucidate how activists employ *Don Quixote* to challenge the impact of dominant discourses particularly where at-risk children and youth are concerned. By sharing the potential of language and art for social change, Quixote-inspired organizations and theater companies aim to replace a discourse of criminalization and exclusion with one that empowers at-risk youth to rescript their story in their own words. As the most creative and free manifestations of discourse, theater and creative expression in general open up spaces for experimenting with new ways to narrate "other" stories. Because fiction generally provides a safer environment for testing new stories than reality itself does, Quixote-inspired organizations believe that the "other" stories (the stories of and by the Other) can emanate from the margins of society via artistic expression. In the medium of art and performance, "uma outra história" or "another story" (the motto of the Projeto Quixote in São Paulo) prompts a new collective imagination that may gradually materialize into a more equal society. In this regard, Cervantes' *Don Quixote* stands for these organizations and activists as an essential handbook for social betterment.

The main objective of this study is thus twofold: one more specific to Cervantes enthusiasts and literary scholars in general, and the other, of much broader scope and appeal, at the intersection of cultural studies and community activism. First, I aim to add to academic and Eurocentric readings of *Don Quixote* a singularly American interpretation in the hemispheric sense, one that through a somewhat tangential partnership with cultural institutions unfolds mostly at the street level and brings the book to audiences that span all social classes, ages, and identities. Second, I recast the concepts of transculturation and performative activism, closely aligned with the development of grand Latin American national narratives and mass public protests respectively, within a community-activism context. In this regard, these appropriations for social justice purposes of a classic novel such as *Don Quixote* may challenge many preconceptions of the place and role of literature, and of the humanities in general, in the current social and political moment.

The noble efforts of Quixote-inspired activists and other cultural nonprofits I examine in this study illustrate the successes, contradictions, and challenges of performative activism. The good intentions summarized in the mission statements of these organizations cannot hide the many potential drawbacks inherent to the practice of social justice work, particularly of a cultural and performative persuasion. In characteristically sinuous ways, the idealistic goals of practitioners and participants in art-based activist projects and the broader socio-economic and political forces locally, nationally, and globally at times collide and create a hard-to-measure, highly unstable chain of transformative events. In Chapters 5 and 6, I discuss more in detail the material needs and the variety of factors that can quite abruptly derail lofty discursive goals such as changing the social narrative or giving the underrepresented a protagonist role in the public imaginary. The contributions, paradoxes, and sway of performative activism inevitably appear both real and to some extent inapprehensible, apparent at times and often ephemeral. Throughout this book, however, I provide documented evidence, even if individual and potentially temporary, of the deep transformation triggered by Quixote-inspired activism.

In that same spirit of reflection and self-assessment, I conclude this introduction with a consideration on the very role of academia, and particularly of humanists and literary scholars, in today's mass instant media and professionally oriented society. The fact that a four-hundred-year-old book such as *Don Quixote* can transcend linguistic, class, and cultural barriers in contemporary youth activism may invite serious reflection on how we as academics insert ourselves and our work into the analysis of remarkable instances of art- and discourse-based community activism. The implications of this deep adjustment in our goals and methodologies may prove far-reaching, for they might deeply affect how we study and teach classic literature today, including the addition of community-based methodologies to our scholarship and pedagogy. Throughout this study, in fact, the community-engaged, transnational, multilingual, and cross-historical nature of this project furthers the notion that books, even books published hundreds of years ago in a foreign language, can play a prominent cultural, political, and even socio-economic role in our communities today. Specifically, the premise that a four-hundred-year-old Spanish-language book can make an impact on the lives of at-risk children and youth in Brazil is an exhilarating proposition that anyone invested in the future of the humanities will no doubt find inspiring. From this perspective, *Living Quixote* will be most successful if it not only contributes to Cervantes scholarship but also raises awareness of these Brazilian appropriations, revealing the potential for individual and social change inherent in the practice of living Quixote.

PART I
Transatlantic Quixotes

Brazilian Transculturations
of *Don Quixote*

CHAPTER 1

"Transforming People through Art"

Transculturating *Don Quixote* in Brazil

With the four-hundredth anniversary of Miguel de Cervantes' *Don Quixote* in 2005 (part I) and 2015 (part II), countless original stage, visual, and written adaptations of the novel flooded theaters, bookstores, streets, and exhibition spaces around the world, and particularly in Spanish- and Portuguese-speaking countries. Given that *Don Quixote* epitomizes the Western European canon, the novel's transatlantic journey from the Iberian Peninsula into the former American colonies necessarily concerns issues of not only national identity, but also ethnic, racial, class, and gender relations. The concept of transculturation, first coined by Fernando Ortiz in 1940 to explain how Latin American nations developed an identity independent from their European colonizers, offers a theoretical framework to study the process by which the Spanish classic is appropriated in contemporary Brazil. While in the third centenary (1905) the bulk of *Quixote* appropriations served nationalistic and nation-building purposes (Riera; Britt Arredondo), this study documents how in the twenty-first century Cervantes' classic has been repurposed by social justice activism, especially in Brazil and the whole of the American hemisphere, as a cultural milestone in the struggle for equality and inclusion. Since Ortiz's concept remains the prevalent critical tool in the study of transatlantic cultural relations between Europe and the Americas, this chapter first interrogates how transculturation works in the current neocolonial context, whereby a Spanish classic thrives today in activist circles in the former Portuguese colony of Brazil. After my brief theoretical discussion, I then apply the concept of transculturation to one particularly representative example among *Don Quixote*'s contemporary Brazilian appropriations: the 2005 statues of Don Quixote and Sancho made out of recycled materials by a cooperative of artisans in São Paulo called Cooperaacs (Cooperativa de Arte Alternativa e Coleta Seletiva, or literally Cooperative of Alternative Art and Selective Collection). Because of its subject, the representation of classic literary figures, this artistic and activist project seemingly equaled itself to other statues of fictional and historical notables in public spaces that have historically been utilized as "a vehicle for conceptualising the nation-building process" (Johnson 52). In this case, however, the use of recycled materials and the very social composition of the artisans who sculpted the figures, including ex-convicts and homeless individuals, repurpose the use of statues in order to complicate the idea of national identity by exposing "how class, 'race' [sic], and gender differences are negotiated in public spaces" (Johnson 62). With its two imposing figures of Don Quixote and Sancho, how does Cooperaacs physically embody the activist transculturation of Cervantes' classic in the Americas? What does transculturation reveal about the way in which *Don Quixote* is appropriated in contemporary Brazil?

Cuban anthropologist Fernando Ortiz theorized the concept of transculturation to better understand the role of cultural interactions across the Atlantic in Latin American national and identity formation. As Latin American independence wars raged from the early 1800s on, transculturation became a critical battleground in the fight for independence from Spanish colonial rule. While conquest and colonization emphasized deculturation (loss of native culture under the weight of "modernizing" colonialist influences), the era of independence furthered conscious efforts to create a new hybrid identity—what Ortiz theorizes as neoculturation or the "creation of new cultural phenomena" (103). These efforts were spearheaded in the nineteenth century by American elites who, for the most part, were direct descendants of Spaniards, born in America but frequently educated in Europe. Although many of them had indigenous or African blood as well, they would often hide their non-European legacy, blatantly contradicting their own plea to create a truly hybrid American identity. In a most illustrative case, the *Libertador*, Simón Bolívar himself, the military hero and politician who contributed to the independence of at least five countries in the region, was a *criollo* or direct descendant of Spaniards and, in fact, may have had mixed blood.[1] Educated in elite schools in Spain, Bolívar regarded Americans as a "species" neither indigenous nor European but somewhere between the two. While emphasizing their distinctiveness, the fathers of independent Latin American countries relied on Eurocentric education and values to assert their patriarchal entitlement to rule the land over indigenous peoples, its "legitimate proprietors," as Bolívar himself nonetheless calls them (Bolívar 10). While praising the continent's original inhabitants against the Spanish invaders, American elites simultaneously deprived them of access to power and public discourse. Predictably, the negotiation for legitimacy at the core of transcultural projects reveals hierarchies based on race, gender, ethnicity, class, and national origin that generally perpetuate Eurocentric cultural and social norms, which in turn have historically privileged whiteness and maleness.

Since Fernando Ortiz first formulated the concept of transculturation, several influential critics have employed it to probe the creation of a differentiated Latin American identity from a cultural perspective. Critics such as Ortiz himself, and most famously Uruguayan Ángel Rama, celebrate the foundational role of transculturation in creating a Latin American cultural identity against colonial imposition. In his *Transculturación narrativa en América Latina* (*Narrative Transculturation in Latin America*, 1982), Rama traces a nation-building project spanning the independence wars through the 1940s that gradually constructs the singular character of Latin America versus its European colonizers. Nonetheless, the view of transculturation as a linear construction of a broadly uniform national identity proves inaccurate. Despite the elite's best efforts, cultural interactions do not occur sequentially or follow an ideological script but unfold over time in rather muddled and overlapping ways. As Ortiz himself recognizes, transculturation can never be fully controlled, for it triggers "extremely complex transmutations of culture" (98).

Recent scholars, in fact, questioned the notion that transculturation creates a well-balanced Latin American identity capable of transcending the violent history of its conquest and colonization. These scholars point out the strictly hierarchical relation between the many identities and positionalities (racialized, gendered, classed) that clash within the Latin American nation-building project. Anchored in a renewed attention to subaltern groups such as indigenous, racial, or ethnic minorities and women, Román de la Campa, to give but one example, critiques Rama's influential vision of the transcultural founding of Latin America as an implied celebration of the continent's entrance into a fundamentally Europeanizing modernity (56–65). In de la Campa's critical view of transculturation, Latin American elites produced a hybrid identity indeed, but one that remains essentially discriminatory against indigenous peoples, women, and Afro-descendants by its continued privileging of European ancestry, whiteness, and maleness.

Even when applied to the analysis of contemporary phenomena, transcultural scholars cannot seemingly escape a certain tendency to favor Eurocentric influences. For instance, Néstor García Canclini employs transculturation to dissect the "hybrid cultures" that emerged in Latin America in the 1980s through mass media such as television and print. Via a groundbreaking analysis of media and popular culture, García Canclini celebrates hybridism as the main marker of late twentieth-century everyday Latin American identity. However, as Abril Trigo points out, García Canclini's hybrid cultures still betray a "foundational grounding" that asserts the supremacy of Eurocentric modernity as conveyed by the white-dominated Latin American mainstream media of the time (93).

To some contemporary critics, thus, transculturation as a theoretical tool appears tainted by the inescapable inference that the lesser the female, indigenous, and Afro-descendant influence, the better for the Latin American hybrid mix. In this regard, hybridism does not resolve the contradictions and oppressions that still permeate Latin America today. At worst, critics such as John Beverley argue, transculturation hides them through the celebration of foreign modernizing forces capable of taming alternative identities, when not suppressing them outright. While cultures undoubtedly interact and produce new hybrids, Latin American elites crafted national narratives based on merely "a fantasy of class, gender, and racial reconciliation" that never displaced European values from their ideological core (Beverley 47). The "reconciliation" between indigenous, African, and European values (as well as between social classes, genders, and sexual orientations, I would add) simply did not materialize in the transcultural Latin American identity. As Eurídice Figueiredo ponders in the case of Brazil, transculturation may simply hide "a conciliatory and Eurocentric vision that wants to integrate subaltern peoples into the modernizing current represented by European colonialism" (56). Does transculturation, as Figueiredo and Beverley suspect, ultimately aim to embellish and elevate local cultures via European (or foreign) influence? Can a true fusion of cultural elements occur outside a colonial framework in which a Eurocentric vision of progress and civilization relegates indigenous and mestizo cultures to the margins? These questions appear particularly relevant in the case of *Don Quixote*, for the adaptation of a Western canonical novel in Brazil and the Americas in general inevitably reveals marked hierarchies in the mix of Europeanness and other influences that constitute the hybrid Brazilian identity. More directly stated, can *Don Quixote* embody genuinely American, or more specifically Brazilian, efforts toward nation-building and identity formation, particularly in the realm of social justice activism?

In an article on *Don Quixote*'s four-hundredth anniversary, Peruvian sociologist Aníbal Quijano identifies transculturation as the key process to understanding and overcoming Latin America's most enduring "ghost": its entrance into modernity (24). According to Quijano, the Eurocentric messianic vision that took upon itself the task of modernizing indigenous America rests on a stark dualism between what was seen as progress (linear, homogenous, Western) and what was considered the primitive, stagnant backwardness of indigenous cultures. As Quijano explains, Latin American elites simultaneously repudiated and fully embraced Eurocentrism as a superior, civilizing enterprise against so-called barbaric indigenous traditions. In exposing the ghost that still haunts Latin America, Aníbal Quijano also criticizes the often racist, classist, and sexist structures of Eurocentric transculturation. Somewhat surprisingly, then, Quijano identifies *Don Quixote*, an icon of European cultural supremacy, as a viable alternative to Eurocentric modernity on the basis of Cervantes' presumed rejection of imperialism and the very concept of linear, homogenous progress. According to Quijano, Cervantes' masterpiece mounts a sophisticated critique against Spanish despotism within its own borders. Historically, the Spanish monarchy's homogenizing impetus reached an apex early on in the national experiment with the decrees expelling Jews (1492) and Moriscos (1609–1614) from the peninsula. This drive toward a monolithic society also fueled efforts to suppress non-Castilian domestic nationalities and languages (the article cites Catalans, Basques, Valencians, and Galicians, among others). In contrast, Quijano argues, in his novel Cervantes favors heterogeneity and the co-presence of various forms of social existence as a tacit rejection of homogeneity, whether imposed within the peninsula or overseas (14). By opposing Cervantes' pluralistic vision of Spain against the Latin American elite's modernizing project, Quijano implies that, in its crudest formulation, transculturation may well have served as a conduit for European imperialistic values to take hold in Latin America even after independence. Yet, in a potentially contradictory move, Quijano identifies a European masterpiece as a proper alternative and desirable model for a more heterogenous, truly plural Latin American identity.[2]

In the case of Brazil, the publication of Oswald de Andrade's provocative "Manifesto Antropófago" ("Cannibalist Manifesto") in 1928 gave the transculturation of foreign and local traditions a singularly Brazilian and highly influential character, somewhat differentiated from the approaches taken by intellectuals in other Latin American countries. As the best-known poet and essayist of Brazilian modernism, de Andrade sought a distinct Brazilian cultural identity by "opposing the avant-garde notions of poetry as 'invention' and 'surprise' to the erudite, imitative art he associates with the colony and the Brazilian Empire (1822–1889)" (Bary 35). In his manifesto, de Andrade repudiates the mere copy of European cultural models by furthering a cannibalistic method that fundamentally destabilizes the central dichotomies in the construction of the Latin American identity, such as civilization versus barbarism and modern versus primitive. In his abrasive statement of purpose, de Andrade urges Brazilians to "eat up" European civilization, a reference to Tupi cannibalistic practices (Tupis are the original inhabitants of large areas in Amazonian and coastal Brazil). Such a "savage" approach aims to transculturate Western artistic and literary production into a genuinely nationalist enterprise. "Tupi or not Tupi: that is the question"; he cannibalizes Hamlet's existential angst into a uniquely Brazilian conundrum (de Andrade 38). In his manifesto, written in Portuguese, de Andrade does include a short Tupi poem, but he also resorts to quotes in English and French, alongside many references to European authors, historical figures relevant to Brazil's past, and a handful of Tupi deities. Provocative and fecund, the "Manifesto" is a visceral avowal of the aesthetic and political value of the ugly, the discarded, the primitive, and the violent in Brazilian cultural production.

In de Andrade's proclamation, thus, a distinct Brazilian culture can only emerge out of chaos and cannibalism. This foundational statement carries two important consequences for our analysis. First, while traditionally Eurocentric Brazilian and Latin American elites ignored and actively eradicated indigenous peoples, de Andrade situates the "legitimate proprietors" of the land, in Bolívar's expression, at the core of the Brazilian cultural enterprise. Second, rather than a sanitized sense of beauty and aesthetics, de Andrade positions the crudeness of cannibalism, digestion, and excretion at the core of Brazilian culture. In principle, then, any product, material, topic, or behavior, no matter how ugly or marginal, can be utilized or recycled into an artistic object. The more unconventional, irreverent, and fringe the artistic practice, the better (Bary).

De Andrade's powerful combination of the lowly and the marginal, for it is cannibals who become the drivers of artistic production and transcultural identity, coalesces again in two critical moments in recent Brazilian cultural history. First, de Andrade's urge for uninhibited hybridity fueled the popular Tropicália movement after the military junta took power via the 1964 coup d'état. In the countercultural period that ensued, artists such as Gilberto Gil and Caetano Veloso boldly combined high and low cultural genres as well as indigenous and foreign influences in music, art, and theater. Through tropicalism, for instance, previously undervalued genres from popular culture such as samba and bossa nova blended with rock and roll and avant-garde electronic music, gaining domestic and international recognition in the process. In parallel, in the 1960s Cinema Novo (New Cinema) produced films centered on marginal characters who tackled social-equality issues head-on. Influenced by Italian Neorrealism and the French Nouvelle Vague, its bare, "realistic" aesthetics evolved, as the movement progressed into the 1970s, into what filmmaker Rogério Sganzerla called an "aesthetics of garbage." In several movies associated with this subset of Cinema Novo, Sganzerla and a handful of other directors turn their cameras to "those living on the fringe trying to 'recycle from the garbage'" (Didaco). After all, as Robert Stam states in a revealing study on the connections between the "Cannibalist Manifesto," Tropicália, and Cinema Novo, "Garbage, like death and excrement, is a great social leveler" (89). The counterintuitive relation between trash and art thus proves particularly fertile in Brazilian contemporary cultural history, especially in relation to marginalized communities. Several decades later, this same artivist strategy articulates Cooperaacs' adaptation of *Don Quixote*.

The recycling of trash into art indeed plays a central role in Cooperaacs' transculturation of *Don Quixote* into contemporary Brazilian activism. Artisan Sandro Rodrigues founded Cooperaacs in 2004 as a nonprofit co-operative of "talentos anônimos, muitos deles excluídos da sociedade" (anonymous talents, many of them excluded from society) dedicated to recycling waste into artistic objects (Cooperaacs). As Rodrigues told me in personal communications, the idea for creating Cooperaacs grew out of his work at a homeless shelter. Radically inclusive, the cooperative embraced individuals of all backgrounds, including ex-convicts, the mentally ill, and people discriminated against on the basis of their gender identity or sexual orientation. In parallel to the refashioning of waste into art, thus, Cooperaac's "talents ... excluded from society" partook of the possiblity of social recycling, of a second chance to escape marginalization via their artistic and personal talents. For each project commissioned to Cooperaacs, the participants received professional training, a modest stipend, and were duly credited for their work. Between July and October 2005, Cooperaacs artists fashioned their large Don Quixote and Sancho figures out of discarded objects, including one hundred fifty kilograms of plastic, thirty kilograms of paper, two thousand soda cans, and four thousand beer tops. The two impressive statues do not conform to stereotypical notions of how monuments should solemnly commemorate cultural classics. Instead, trash constitutes the core of this project not only in material terms, but also in its activist dimension, for even the artists themselves were excluded, metaphorically discarded, by mainstream society. How does Cooperaacs' conversion of a literary classic into a recycled art object illustrate the process of its adaptation into Brazilian artivism? And how can it more broadly help us reformulate the concept of transculturation in community-based contexts?

In the hands of Cooperaacs artists, *Don Quixote* becomes a transcultured object that symbolizes the power of art to transform both material waste and the individuals whom society excludes as irredeemable. Since the early 2000s, "the artistic treatment of garbage and the tactical utilization of recycling or cleaning" that the "Manifesto Antropófago" inspired has made a powerful comeback in Brazil as an equalizing tool in the artivist struggle to better society (Morrison 187). Most famously, and thanks in part to the film *Waste Land* (dir. Lucy Walker, 2010), São Paulo-born artist Vik Muniz gained international recognition for his *Pictures of Garbage* photographic project with *catadores* (trash pickers) in the Jardim Gramacho landfill in Rio de Janeiro (Ibarra). Behind Muniz's project there lies the familiar transcultural paradox with which Cooperaacs also contends, for Muniz photographs *catadores* in poses and settings that for the most part reproduce classic European paintings. Then Muniz "paints" these images with trashed items or everyday products such as peanut butter and jam, before taking a photograph of the resulting composition (C. Schmidt). Within this renewed attention to the symbiosis between trash, art, and marginalization, Muniz, artists, and collectives such as Alexandre Orion or Projeto Imargem (Morrison), and Quixote-inspired Cooperaacs powerfully embody the notion that by recycling waste into artistic objects we can also achieve the transformation of the collective imaginary, particularly in relation to the marginalized and the underprivileged, and by extension of society as a whole. In the specific case of Cooperaacs, by employing socially excluded artisans to change material rejects into public exhibitions, the organization metaphorically and in practice promotes the social inclusion of its members.

The Don Quixote and Sancho project was commissioned and fully financed by the Conjunto Nacional condominium complex in central São Paulo, which houses private residences, businesses, and a shopping mall. While the Conjunto Nacional enjoys a privileged spot in one of the city's best-known streets, the Avenida Paulista, it offers a relatively unpretentious experience to the over forty-five thousand shoppers, customers, and residents who wander through it on an average day. Unlike exclusive shopping centers, this particular mall sits at street level with no security guards at the entrance and houses businesses of all sorts, including the country's largest bookstore, Livraria Cultural. All Cooperaacs project participants were registered as co-authors of the project (Silvio Galvão led construction of the Quixote and Sancho figures and Sandro Rodrigues of the horse, Rocinante), and all were paid a modest stipend by the Conjunto Nacional.

In the Cooperaacs version, Don Quixote appears on horseback while Sancho holds the reins on a shiny Rocinante. As explained in a freestanding sign adjacent to the bulky sculpture, the *aventura quixotesca* (quixotic adventure) behind this project sought the *transformação* (transformation) of "lixo em arte" (trash into art) and, in turn, of "pessõas através da arte" (people through art). Proof of *Don Quixote*'s penetration into the Brazilian collective imaginary, Cooperaacs claims to employ solely "motivos da cultura brasileira" (Brazilian cultural motifs) to demonstrate how artistic transformation can infuse waste with social value. According to the anonymous artists, Don Quixote and Sancho typify, as a presumedly Brazilian cultural motif, the kind of *coragem* (courage) that Cooperaacs promotes,

FIGURE 1.1. Don Quixote and Sancho sculptures by Cooperaacs at the Conjunto Nacional in São Paulo. Photo courtesy of the Conjunto Nacional

for in a most quixotic manner social change will occur when "tudo e todos se transformam com ousadia e confiança" (everything and everyone transform themselves with audacity and confidence).[3]

A testament to the complexity of transcultural relations, the case of *Don Quixote* provides a particularly rich mosaic of the many factors at play in the adaptation of foreign cultural influences. By building their projects on Cervantes' literary prestige, Brazilian Quixote-inspired organizations such as Cooperaacs seemingly embrace the preeminence of Eurocentric cultural canons. However, the progressive Brazilian interpretation of *Don Quixote*, embodied in Cooperaacs' recycled statues, tackles the issue of authorship and nationhood from a point of view that substantially differs from that of cultural elites on either shore of the Atlantic. By virtue of its production and exhibition methods, the Cooperaacs recycling proposal effectively cancels out grand nationalist and Eurocentric narratives. The mundane nature of the materials employed and the everyday location where the statues are exhibited call the viewer's attention to art's potential to occupy and transform quotidian spaces. Quite literally, Cooperaacs triggers a cycle of consumption and creation: Its artists recycle what common people discard, while viewers shop for new products that may eventually become once again the stuff of art. In this whirlwind of usage and re-interpretation of products, the Cooperaacs project incarnates what John Storey considers the very task of cultural critics: the study of how "people use the texts and practices they consume to make culture" (xii; see also 160–61). Simultaneously cultural critics, consumers, and producers of art, the Cooperaacs artisans insert an icon of *Don Quixote*'s global stature into São Paulo's cycle of everyday consumption and production. Devoid of totalizing narratives of modernity and national origins, Spain's literary treasure escapes national and academic control. *Don Quixote* leaves traditional spaces of knowledge, such as libraries and universities, to become, in Fernando Coronil's apt description of how canonic works are transcultured, "products of a common history, the achievement of popular collectivities" (xlvii).

Although the adjacent sign mentions *Don Quixote*'s author and its Spanish provenance, the artists do not differentiate the Spanish novel from, in their own words, the "motifs of Brazilian culture" behind all Cooperaacs projects. In blurring national origins, this artistic and activist venture extricates *Don Quixote* from its Spanish-language, elitist environment to adapt it into a genuinely Brazilian symbol of the transformative power of art. A cultural treasure taken out into the streets of São Paulo both at the moment of production (participants identify as socially excluded) and exhibition (a public commercial space), the recycled figures of Don Quixote and Sancho sit at the entrance hall of a popular shopping mall for free-of-charge mass consumption. In this regard, Cooperaacs' appropriation of *Don Quixote* produces a transcultural mix seemingly outside nation-building that is neither Spanish nor Brazilian, high nor low culture, elitist nor popular, but simultaneously both. While many regard transculturation as a critical effort to consolidate a differentiated identity ("Brazilian" rather than indigenous, African, or European, for instance), I pose that Cooperaacs' Don Quixote illustrates the complexities of what it means to be Brazilian.

Cooperaacs produces its adaptation of *Don Quixote* as an open-ended process with no definitive and straight path to overcoming dichotomies such as "us" versus "them" or "high" versus "low." Their exercise in transculturation proves highly revealing of the unstable nature of cultural hybridity. As Mark Millington explains, any sense of resolution from the combination of diverse elements into a hybrid cultural identity stems only from "the purposes of the person providing the answer" (258). In other words, transculturation operates as a highly subjective process within ever-shifting political and identity paradigms.[4] In the Cooperaacs project, transculturation occurs in its purest form. For its creators, Cervantes' universal characters embody a message of social transformation that develops in everyday spaces and that aims to change everyone, regardless of their social status. An a-partisan though deeply political effort, the Cooperaacs project reveals itself as a bewildering act of transformation with a concrete point of departure (recycled waste, Cervantes' characters, the urge to change society, the physical location at a mall entrance) and a thoroughly uncertain destination. The instability of transculturation is physically embodied in the recycled figures themselves: How can we possibly ensure the preservation of statues made of such low materials? In public spaces, who can ever assess who observes these statues and how they are interpreted? How can we determine just how and when the transcultural process achieves the transformation of its disparate elements (Don Quixote, waste, a shopping mall) into a genuinely hybrid product? In stark contrast to foundational and nation-building grand narratives, which aim to fix the meaning and purpose of national culture, Cooperaacs offers a product that unapologetically shines the spotlight on the unstable and open-ended nature of art, and consequently of activism as well. They implicitly answer the somewhat abstract questions about the consumption, nature, and meaning of art by denying the viewer conclusive answers, for transformation remains a fundamentally subjective process. Unlike the certainty sought by nation-building schemes, built on oppositions of the us-versus-them nature, social justice activism exposes the ambiguity and contradictions of cultural contacts without any urge or even will to provide a conclusive response to the questions they raise.

The broadly understood social justice mission that underwrites the Conjunto Nacional figures offers crucial insights into the Brazilian efforts to transculturate *Don Quixote* into artivist praxis. If even waste holds the potential to elicit an aesthetic experience, as the project creators explain, art itself operates as a transformative tool with the potential to change both individuals and society at large. A prime example of the elevating qualities of art, the character of Don Quixote shows, according to Cooperaacs, the *couragem* (courage) to change his life and the world around him by literary means. His compulsive consumption of chivalric texts prompts and enables his personal transformation from marginal old hidalgo, or low nobleman lacking in resources, into protagonist of his own story. Significantly, Cervantes anticipates the potential social impact of the protagonist's self-transformation within the novel itself. Because the hidalgo/actor Quijano literally embodies his fictional creation, many characters who encounter him along his travels are forced to take part, mostly unwillingly at first, in his new social performance. Caught in Don Quixote's creative thrust, they enter deeply into his game, often against their will but at times also intentionally. Some of them, from the priest and barber in part I to Sansón Carrasco and the duke and duchess in part II, will even disguise themselves to play extreme knightly or courtly roles in the hidalgo's fantasy. These characters all become part of a society of what Silvia Spitta calls transcultured subjects, "consciously or unconsciously situated between at least two worlds, two cultures, two languages, and two definitions of subjectivity, and who constantly mediate between them all" (24). In *Don Quixote*, the two worlds and languages in constant collision are those of literary chivalry (bucolic, epic, and other traditional genres temporarily replace chivalry as literary points of reference) and Spain's harsh social reality at the peak of its imperial expansion. In a contemporary and neocolonial environment, Cooperaacs artisans adopt a similar stance when they take binary oppositions such as Spanish and Brazilian, exclusion and acceptance, high and low culture, or waste and art and create out of their clash a product of unexpected beauty and renewed social value. They speak from a transcultured location where extremes converge and collide in a perfect creative storm, both transformative and utterly unstable.

From that transcultured space, the Conjunto Nacional figures proclaim the transformational power of art in a self-referential manner that mirrors the artistic, literary, and theatrical self-awareness of many of Cervantes' characters, including the obsessive reader Alonso Quijano. Standing adjacent to the statues of Don Quixote and Sancho, a rather large sign details the intricacies of the artistic process that produced the imposing figures, including construction methods and the specific quantities of waste materials used in the project. Most importantly, the sign spells out Cooperaacs' social purpose and activist message, much like the hidalgo Quijano states his own purpose upon converting himself into Don Quixote (in his case, "[to win] eternal renown and everlasting fame"; I.1.21). Via Cooperaacs' statement of intent (to transform trash into art and people through art), the project reveals explicitly, almost brazenly, its ethical backbone, the message that justifies its very activism. If art can transform waste into beauty, the sign affirms, then it can also change individuals and even society. By explicitly formulating its raison d'être, Cooperaacs favors advocacy over ambiguity and takes an activist approach to the production and consumption of its art. This is how the audience ought to react to the Quixote statue, the sign preemptively explains, and not in any other way. Despite the ideological directive to employ art as a means for change, however, Cooperaacs' recipe for personal and social transformation remains fundamentally open-ended. The artists prescribe *transformação* to correct social ills, but they don't provide a formula for what, who, when, and how this process ought to occur. It is up to each one of us to find our own way to transform society and ourselves.

Cooperaacs' open-ended activism fully embeds *Don Quixote* into de Andrade's cannibalistic tradition by turning the Spanish classic into a Brazilian motif, as well as the ugly (recycled waste) into an artistic object. Messy, playful, and explicitly activist at once, Cooperaacs' transculturation of *Don Quixote* pivots on the very interaction between art and trash. On the one hand, the artisans toy with the idea of devaluing foreign influence through an arguably irreverent appropriation. With figures made out of waste, does Cooperaacs "trash" Cervantes' masterpiece in public view? Does this project imply that *Don Quixote*, the first European modern novel, constitutes a pile of rubbish in itself? Rather than employing noble materials for an effigy displayed in a central square or at the entrance of a prestigious institution, as is the case in cities across Spain and Latin America, Cooperaacs commemorates Cervantes' characters (a Brazilian cultural motif in their reading) with recycled waste. Fittingly, then, they exhibit their work amid the ordinary frenzy of commercial shopping and consumerism.

On the other hand, however, the viewer could reasonably take the opposite view and consider the statues as an implicit recognition of the superior character of European culture. Does Cooperaacs suggest that only Western high culture can dignify the wastefulness of a society whose inferior (colonized, racialized, gendered, and classed) nature requires a beautifying coat of proper Europeanness? Does Latin American "progress" hinge on the modernizing qualities of a Western cultural icon? Is the injection of European prestige into Brazilian cultural motifs the only way to elevate waste to an art form? Although the answer to these questions ultimately lies in the eye of the beholder, the Cooperaacs statues undeniably succeed at turning Conjunto Nacional's entrance hall into a "contact zone" in Mary Louise Pratt's widely accepted, expansive formulation: as a social space "where disparate cultures meet . . . often in highly asymmetrical relations of domination and subordination" (7). Moreover, they transform the shopping mall into a space where art questions its own boundaries, purpose, and relation to its producers and consumers. Like Don Quixote in Cervantes' story, Cooperaacs' artists turn the world into a stage or an exhibit space wherein art becomes the main object of discussion and admiration. Art turns the conversation upon itself, catches all the attention, and fuels the debate around its very essence and purpose. It provides no definitive answers for its consumers, but it certainly raises important questions about the role of art in activism and society.

Cooperaacs' artivist proposal blurs the line between high and low art, for it uses recycled materials, foments collective authorship by artists of marginal provenance, and situates the artistic object in an everyday location. The project's point of departure remains unequivocally hierarchical in that it contrasts waste, located at the bottom of the aesthetic and consumeristic ladder, with art, situated at the top. At the end of the artistic process, however, the Don Quixote and Sancho figures fuse together waste and beauty into an indistinguishable aesthetic and social experience that fundamentally questions the judgmental, moralistic approach inherent in traditional cultural imposition. There is no good or bad here, no high or low, authentic or false, original or plagiarized. Trash and art blend together into a powerful mix for the free consumption of common people going about their daily lives. The artists don't only preach a message of transformation; they practice it as well. They enact open-ended hybridity through the self-reflective practice of artivism. While the Cooperaacs project seemingly aims to harmonize some of the tensions inherent in asymmetrical processes of cultural interaction, it does not conceal them. Quite the opposite—in a blatantly self-referential way, it exposes them. Its contradictions (Don Quixote as a Brazilian cultural motif), ambiguity (their play with the concepts of trash and art), and indetermination (the urge for transformation without a concrete roadmap or destination) all point to a latent conflict between clashing forces that remains firmly anchored in the current neocolonial context. The product of a complex history of conquest, violence, and colonization, Latin America remains embarked on the construction of its hybrid identity.

Against the backdrop of the elite-driven projects that undergird the founding of independent Latin American identities, transcultural efforts in the context of community activism reveal a more nuanced, multidirectional process in identity formation and cross-cultural fertilization. A case in point, Cooperaacs' Don Quixote and Sancho figures do not offer a transcultured product that opens up Homi Bhabha's famous "third space," one in which hybrid cultures may "elude the politics of polarity" (114). Instead, Cooperaacs confronts polarity and transformation head-on by openly revealing the oppositional binaries that underlie their proposal. Their coupling of trash and art, anonymity and authority, or Spanishness and Brazilianness, does not resolve ambiguity or avoid contradiction, but rather triggers the messy process of transformation that de Andrade celebrated as genuinely Brazilian. If transculturation opens up a third space, in this case it is certainly not a neutrally hybrid space devoid of hierarchies. The location and composition of the Conjunto Nacional figures reveal the contradictions of coloniality and nation-building as they compel the public to continue to change and recycle at the neighborhood and everyday levels. In Cooperaacs' view, the coupling of disparate cultural elements aims to trigger the urge for recycling and open-ended transformation. In this regard, transculturation ceases to be an end in itself—most notably, the consolidation of a fixed national identity—and serves instead as a conduit for ongoing personal and social change.

Caught between an unfulfilled desire for Eurocentric modernity and the urge to overcome colonial oppression, the ghost that, according to Aníbal Quijano, haunts Latin America continues to fight its never-ending battle in the transcultural field. To this effect, the Cooperaacs statue transculturates *Don Quixote* in a context that proves simultaneously activist, for it combats social exclusion at the street level, as well as largely indifferent to the theoretical debate over Latin American (post)modernity. As documented by the large sign adjacent to the figures, the Quixote and Sancho figures do not prescribe the foundation of a predetermined societal and national model, whether Eurocentric or not. Devoid of a foundational narrative, initiatives such as Cooperaacs' do not partake of the modernizing project that privileges European over African and indigenous values (or male over female, heteronormative over queer, and so on). In other words, activist organizations do not engage with the broader nation-building and modernizing efforts of the founding fathers in their creation of a unified Latin American identity. On the contrary, transculturation at the community level destabilizes rigid cultural, national, and legal identities in its call for never-ending change toward greater equality. Given the particularities of transcultural projects such as Cooperaacs' and the several other *Don Quixote* appropriations examined throughout this book, Latin American activism demands new critical tools to investigate its appropriation of Western cultures. From this perspective, the concept of transculturation can remain useful if further revised to account for contemporary cultural activism.

In recent decades, the study of transculturation has certainly evolved into a variety of approaches with abundant terminology. While some critics developed variations on Ortiz's basic concept (Spitta's transcultural subjects, Pratt's contact zones, and the like), others turned their attention to highly specific transcultural phenomena. For instance, the "mythic idea of *latinidad* based on Anglo . . . projections of fear," labeled by Frances Aparicio and Susana Chávez-Silverman as hegemonic tropicalization, refers specifically to how Latino cultures are represented ("tropicalized") by Anglo-America (8). Concepts such as *mestizaje*, creolization, and hybridity remain closely interchangeable, although some scholars warn against their biological and genetic connotations (Millington 260).[5] As the academic vocabulary to tackle the contact zone continues to grow, Mark Millington cautions against both its decontextualization and its overuse, for not every contact between two or more cultures counts as transcultural phenomena. Heeding Millington's warning, I opt to avoid neologisms and radically new definitions of old terms. My analysis of Brazilian appropriations of *Don Quixote* adopts instead an eminently practical stance in two fundamental ways: It derives from my examination of a very specific example, that of recent Brazilian Quixote-inspired initiatives, and it studies not only the production and reception of new hybrid cultural products but also their expediency to community activism. Consequently, in this study I emphasize how historical, gendered, ethnic, and class factors take part in the process of transculturation.

Transculturating *Don Quixote* in the streets of urban Brazil does not provide definitive answers to issues of cultural identity, and it will certainly never solve endemic poverty or child abuse. However, transculturation provides community activism with a cultural roadmap to social betterment, a theoretical framework that I use throughout this book for the analysis of Quixote-inspired activism. First and foremost, a transcultural project such as Cooperaacs' hones the self-awareness, self-esteem, and self-reflection of its participants, for it explicitly addresses the process of its own creation. Because transformation can occur through art and performance, society at large, and particularly underserved populations, are encouraged to become aware and intentionally sharpen their performative and creative skills. Furthermore, the process of transculturation exposes power relations among producers, mediators, and consumers of culture. Who possesses cultural capital, who sets and enforces the rules of art production and consumption, and who defines the meaning and value of high and low art affect how a cultural product travels across nations and languages, as well as within communities. While transculturating a classic such as *Don Quixote* does not necessarily free the subaltern and underprivileged from cultural hierarchies, it certainly reveals those hierarchies in ways that foster awareness and invite reflection. By promoting self-consciousness and self-transformation, community activists expose the instability of identity and the malleability of one's role in the social narrative. If we can adapt and change a classic of *Don Quixote*'s stature, then we may also be able to alter the narrative that determines our place and function within the social storyline. For the subaltern in particular, this can be a profoundly transformative experience, for rather than accepting a pre-conceived narrative, we can be free to imagine, rescript, and perform our own identity and surrounding environment as they should be, not necessarily as we have been told they are. In this endeavor, the hidalgo Quijano and not the knight-errant Don Quixote emerges as a hero of metamorphosis, for it is he who fuels his self-transformation with his knowledge of literature, name-changing abilities, and courage to consciously challenge the status quo with his remarkable performative powers.

Equipped with literary and theatrical knowledge, Cervantes' hero models a process of self-transformation that mirrors the transculturation of the novel itself. Unbounded by academic readings or official commemorations, *Don Quixote* the book is adapted into Brazilian activism by a highly educated group of artists, pedagogues, and healthcare professionals who seek to equip young vulnerable populations with the discursive and professional tools to turn themselves into actors, rather than spectators, of their own story. In this regard, Quixote-inspired activists lean on the controversial notion that agency, or the ability to speak (act, write) for oneself, is intrinsically liberatory for the subaltern. The case studies that I examine here thus beg the question: Do children in vulnerable situations improve their prospects for a better future for themselves if they cultivate and practice agency through a *Don Quixote*-inspired model? While this conundrum proves critical to the nonprofits examined here, it has much broader theoretical and practical implications. Would Brazilian underprivileged youth obtain a more equitable outcome if their activism were not mediated by a Western cultural icon? Can they find a voice that is devoid of any traces of colonialist influence? Is *Don Quixote*, the canonical Spanish-language masterpiece, a facilitator or an impediment to their liberation from marginality?

Community-engaged transculturation among vulnerable populations cannot be dissociated from the debate over cultural agency; its implications for our *Don Quixote* adaptations cannot be overstated. At a theoretical level the question of whether the subaltern (in its broadest definition: the oppressed, the ignored, the outcast) can even speak has concerned a number of critics, including one of the first and most influential voices in Subaltern Studies, Indian scholar Gayatri Spivak. In a lecture first delivered in 1983 and later published in 1988, she famously denied the possibility of creating a discursive space outside the colonizer's (the oppressor's) framework from which the subaltern can effectively speak (Spivak). For Quixote-inspired activism, this warning rings particularly true, for it is a group of educated professionals who propose the transformation of underprivileged youth's social narratives through Cervantes' four-hundred-year-old masterpiece, a towering example of Western cultural power. However, this argument seems to presuppose two premises that in my view are inaccurate. First, it is implied that there can exist separate and uncontaminated discursive spaces for oppressors and oppressed. In the case of the Americas, for instance, Western colonialism brutally imposed itself upon indigenous communities after the arrival of Europeans to American shores. Nonetheless, pre-Columbian times were not free of oppression and cultural imposition either. It has been amply documented that conquest, colonialism, slavery, and other forms of inequality and oppression permeated the Americas even before Columbus' arrival (the Inca and Aztec empires in fact dominated large areas of the continent). In the broadest terms possible, I do not think that there exists a pure space devoid of oppression from which the subaltern can speak or that the space of the colonizer or oppressor may not also be plagued by many other forms of aggression from within, including for instance gender or sexual orientation discrimination. Secondly, because of its essentialism, Spivak's argument may not sufficiently explore the intricacies and potential of the "cannibalistic" (again citing de Andrade) actions of the subaltern. If the underprivileged can "talk back" to the oppressor, in Edward Said's intriguing proposition from his *Culture and Imperialism* (1993), then Quixote-inspired activism may effectively have a chance at transforming mainstream narratives about underprivileged youth. Even in the elitist, less consequential realm of literary criticism, Quixote-inspired activist appropriations may potentially contribute to or even modify prevalent academic interpretations of *Don Quixote*, as I submit in this book. In our exploration of Quixote-inspired activism, evidence indicates that the possibility of mutual, reciprocal influence between dominant and subaltern discourses does exist.

While cultural agency thus remains a central tenet of the Quixote-inspired enterprise, the ways in which cultural activism can achieve meaningful change must be discussed in some detail. Among other critics, John Storey (159) and Arturo Ortiz (x) recognize that cultural agency does not automatically enable the subaltern to empower themselves. Rather, true empowerment comes from the complex negotiation among various cultural influences and interests. In order words, simply rejecting dominant discourses in order to employ only subaltern voices, in its most simplistic and essentialist definition, does not guarantee a more just outcome for the underprivileged. In fact, many subaltern movements rely on the discourse of the oppressor to further their cause, despite Audre Lorde's famous warning that the master's tools will never dismantle the master's house. For instance, the indigenous Zapatista rebels in Chiapas, Southern Mexico, fully embraced Christian rhetoric and Western cultural icons such as *Don Quixote* to connect with the rest of the country and the world through their main spokesperson, the mestizo from Northern Mexico and university-educated Subcomandante Marcos. On January 1, 1994, the day NAFTA (the North American Free Trade Agreement) went into effect, the Zapatistas took up arms against the Mexican government. Described as the "first postmodern guerrilla hero" by the *New York Times* (Golden), Marcos took it upon himself to garner international support for the indigenous rebels' unwinnable war against the powerful Mexican army. Marcos' deployment of Western cultural codes, which most prominently featured Cervantes' *Don Quixote* (Marcos, *Conversations with Durito*; Iffland; Vanden Berghe), obeyed to the need to "speak about themselves to others" in ways intelligible to their target audience (Gollnick 178). In cases such as our Quixote-inspired guerilla spokesperson, according to Brian Gollnick, the key question would not be whether the subaltern can speak outside of the language of the (colonialist) oppressor, but rather whether and how the underprivileged can "amplify their voices" in order to increase their ability to effectively represent their own interests (182).

From this perspective, the discursive, individual, and social transformation prompted by transculturation depends more on its process and effects than on who initiates it. Critics such as Roberto Rivera suggest otherwise by distinguishing between transculturation promoted from the top, in reference to the elites, versus from below, the subaltern (143). In my own view, however, origin alone should not be the only factor to consider in transcultural phenomena. In our case study, the transculturation of *Don Quixote* into Brazilian community activism undeniably originates from an educated elite of well-traveled and well-read artists and professionals—or, as Rivera would say, from the top. Nonetheless, the deployment and consequences of a transcultured *Don Quixote* may feed into a circulation of ideas and praxis that could potentially not only transform subaltern identities but also change hegemonic perceptions in the broader society. As a case in point, this book investigates new ways to interpret and put *Don Quixote* into practice through community-engaged projects. This alone constitutes a radical departure from the notion that classics stay confined mostly to elitist and academic circles or that their primary function rests with nation-building projects.

This utilitarian view of cultural agency is further complicated by scholars of globalization who regard subaltern positions as an amalgam of, in Arturo Ortiz's expression, "polyvalent identities" that include factors such as nationality, race, religion, gender, sexual orientation, and ethnicity, which often may compete with each other (x). Along similar lines, Abril Trigo defines transculturation as a cultural-production process that concerns "antagonistic social agents [who] negotiate new, inherently unstable politico-cultural formations" (106–7). In this complex web of social and cultural relations, transculturation may unfold less as a unidirectional imposition from the oppressor onto the oppressed than as a "circulation" of cultural influences that, while still subjected to hierarchies and unequal relations, may effectively destabilize hegemonic cultures. Through the Brazilian adaptation of Cervantes' classic, for instance, the rescripting of roles via a revolutionary reading of *Don Quixote* overlaps with what Diana Taylor describes as the most critical goal of contemporary Latin American theater: To encourage and enable audiences "to change their role in an oppressive society" ("Transculturating Transculturation" 101). Social justice outcomes can be pursued even through the adaptation of classics traditionally safeguarded by academia and cultural elites.

Obviously, transculturation is no panacea for inequality or any other social ill (Millington 267), but it does add a layer of complexity to the issue of cultural agency. Agency must be redefined outside Spivak's implied essentialism in order to best capture the potential for re-imagining new individual and social roles through resistance tactics such as the transculturation of classics. If we agree with Richard A. Rogers that culture is not bounded by identity but rather operates as "radically relational" (499), then agency becomes a process of negotiation among individuals and groups with competing and overlapping interests. To return to our case study, Quixote-inspired project participants, whether staff, youth, or their families, interact with each other across different socio-economic and cultural levels as they immerse themselves in the very circularity of transculturation. At different stages and in different capacities, they all contribute to the adaptation of *Don Quixote* into community activism. Rather than eradicating hegemonic oppression, which I would submit is a utopian and essentialist goal, transculturation may "decenter" it by "a sharing rather than crossing of borders" (Taylor, "Transculturating Transculturation" 102). In a constant circular motion of mutual influences, transculturation facilitates "long term reciprocities" (103) through which dominant cultures modify but are also modified by the subaltern.

In a community-based activist context, thus, transculturation of an icon such as Cervantes' classic may still come from an educated elite but suggests a process that may effectively be participatory as well as open-ended. Although often with government support, corporate sponsorships, and academic ties, social justice community organizations engage both subaltern and mainstream populations in projects that have broad goals (rescripting one's role in society, for instance) and no prescribed outcome (they do not dictate what these new roles should be). Instead of a guided interpretation, community-based readings of foreign cultural influences seek to increase the self-reflectiveness and self-awareness of project participants. Conscious of the circularity of transculturation through which the foreign and the local, as well as the elite and the subaltern, inevitably engage with each other, community-based activist initiatives emphasize the importance of developing a process rather than achieving a predetermined end product.

In conclusion, transculturation must be re-conceptualized as it applies not only to nation-building but also to community-based projects that focus on the underserved and the underprivileged around issues of race, ethnicity, gender, nationality, sexual orientation, religion, and/or class. In the context of social justice work at the street and neighborhood levels, transculturation does not unfold in a linear and straightforward manner, for changing people and social structures takes time. In my reading of Brazilian adaptations of *Don Quixote* into community activism, I thus concur with Diana Taylor that transculturation "describes a process . . . [that] rather than being oppositional or strictly dialectical . . . *circulates*" ("Transculturating Transculturation" 101). At the service of deep individual and collective transformation, cultural adaptation furthers community activism in idealistic as well as concrete ways. A painstaking process fraught with constant challenges and setbacks, the pursuit of a more just society undoubtedly exhibits a certain quixotic flair, for Cervantes' protagonist embraces like no other character perseverance as a way of life. In the everyday, the activist aspiration to change both individual and social stories requires a level of tenacity that only those with broad imagination and lofty ideals can sustain. But for Quixote-inspired organizations, idealism is only one side of the coin; the everyday, harsh reality of marginalization serves as a stark reminder of the material needs of the dispossessed and the excluded. While the nonprofits I study here seek to activate the imagination through art and performance, they also take to the streets in an effort to look "real life" in the eye. Quixote-inspired activism may erect windmills, but it certainly tilts at giants.

When deployed at the community level for activist purposes, rather than as a nation-building tool, transculturation thus hinges on four fundamental traits. First, it engages in constant negotiations of multiple cultural influences, identities, and interests that unfold in a variety of social contexts. At the street level, transculturation seeks to potentially engage all races, social classes, genders, and other identity markers. In contrast to historical Latin American national projects, at the community level negotiations are inclusive and aim to diversify, not limit, the points of view with which social relations are conceived and implemented. Second, due to its radical inclusiveness, transculturation sets broad social justice goals for itself but prescribes no specific outcome or end result. It does not apply a single political ideology or aim to produce a pre-determined social model. Third, because it does not envision a fixed role for individuals or impose a preconceived image of society, transculturation functions as intrinsically self-reflexive and self-aware. It emphasizes the process and method of transformation rather than its end. For this reason, theater, art, literature, and even social work practice meta-critical approaches and continual self-reflection as they adapt and apply a classic such as *Don Quixote* to a social justice cause. Last, transculturation promotes a concept of agency that does not automatically empower the subaltern but that rather questions who speaks, whether they can even do so, and most importantly *how* they speak, to whom, through which media, and in which socio-economic, gendered, and ethno-racial contexts. Ultimately, transcultural agency at the community level must assess its impact on individuals, the community, and the larger society. Who initiates the transculturation of, in particular, foreign influences (in our case studies, a highly educated group of artivists) cannot be the only question, or even the main one, that we ask ourselves about the effectiveness of transcultural projects such as Quixote-inspired activism. Whether in nation-building or community contexts, the study of transculturation must focus not only on national identity but also on its potential to transform individuals and communities, particularly the underprivileged and the excluded. Based on my contemporary case studies, *Don Quixote* seems in this regard as much at ease in the company of the elites as among the vulnerable.

CHAPTER 2

American Quixotes

The Afterlife of *Don Quixote* in the Americas

Cervantes' *Don Quixote* has played an important cultural role in the Americas from the earliest efforts to consolidate an American identity independent from European empires through today. Founding fathers of nations across the hemisphere, from South to North America and the Caribbean, found inspiration in the revolutionary transformation that turned the hidalgo Quijano into the knight-errant Don Quixote. Since the end of the twentieth century, *Don Quixote* has also become an icon, particularly in Brazil, for social justice organizations that regard rescripting and performance as a critical tool to achieving a more equal social narrative. In order to contextualize my contemporary case studies, I review the afterlife of *Don Quixote* in Brazil and the Americas at large in the context of transculturation, as a Spanish-language novel from the early 1600s travels to the American shores. How and why has Cervantes' universal classic enjoyed such a rich afterlife in the Americas and specifically in Brazil? And how is a four-hundred-year-old Spanish-language classic adapted today by educated activists in the Americas, and specifically in Brazil, for underprivileged audiences? To answer these questions, I first discuss the unique nature of Don Quixote's afterlife. Despite its length and complexity, Cervantes' novel has become one of the most universally translated and appropriated cultural works in theater, music, art, literature, film, and even commerce. Then, I reconstruct the evolution of the role of *Don Quixote* in public discourse in the Americas, with particular attention to its two defining moments: nation-building projects in the first half of the twentieth century and social justice efforts from the latter part of the twentieth century through today. I conclude this chapter with a brief analysis of three examples from as many countries (Mexico, the United States, and Colombia) that also took place around the fourth centenary of Cervantes' masterpiece in 2005. These multi-national samples will provide a rich hemispheric framework for my later and more detailed examination, in Part II, of my Brazilian case studies.

Because Don Quixote is arguably the most influential fictional character of all time, his afterlife appears unique in at least two ways. First, Cervantes himself cultivated his protagonist's legacy in part II (1615) of his two-volume story, in which most of its leading characters have actually read and prove eager to discuss the novel's part I (1605). Published ten years earlier, the first volume serves as a point of reference for myriad conversations between many characters and the protagonist pair in part II, including discussions on the veracity of the published story versus the pair's own "lived" experiences. In fact, many of the sophisticated and often cruel jokes that other characters inflict upon Don Quixote and Sancho in part II (the court of the duke and duchess being a case in point) spring from their intimate knowledge of part I. Moreover, while Cervantes was giving the final touches to his continuation, an anonymous author, signing as Alonso Fernández de Avellaneda, published a "false" *Don Quixote* sequel in 1614. Despite the fact that Cervantes dismisses it as inferior, he cites the false continuation in part II as proof of his literary success. In a stroke of genius, toward the end of the book Cervantes has Don Quixote and Sancho run into a character from Avellaneda's sequel, Don Álvaro Tarfe. After a brief encounter with the "real" pair, Tarfe readily denounces Avellaneda's lies and solemnly declares before a public notary the authenticity of Cervantes' protagonists (II.72). Rather than subjecting its protagonist to other false sequels, Cervantes' part II concludes with Quijano's death. In a characteristically ironic style, Cervantes establishes authorship of the story already in his prologue in order to ensure that no other writers take credit for the trials and tribulations of his iconic knight-errant: "I give you a somewhat expanded Don Quixote who is, at the end, dead and buried, so that no one will dare tell more tales about him" (II.458).

In a Russian doll effect, Cervantes deploys Don Quixote's *sobrevida*, or "àquelas práticas em que reconhecemos a personagem como entidade refigurada" (those practices in which we recognize a character as a refigured entity; Reis, "Para uma teoria" 129), from within. The characters themselves, the fictional narrator of the story, and the prologue's "author" comment throughout part II on the refigurations of Don Quixote and Sancho through lengthy ruminations on how the 1605 volume was received by the reading public: its inaccuracies, the false Avellaneda sequel, and even the protagonists' growing fame. Burst open, the book's fictional world in part II builds itself on the material reality of a book (part I) that by then had already amassed an extensive and devoted readership. From then on *Don Quixote* only grew in popularity, imitations, continuations, adaptations, and all kinds of appropriations for literary, commercial, visual, political, and other purposes. Traveling across space, time, and genres, the hidalgo/knight-errant populates from early on and through today what David A. Brewer describes as "the virtual communities of imaginative expansion" that secure the afterlife of fictional characters as they "migrate from text to text" (22).

Despite its unparalleled popularity around the world, *Don Quixote*, an expansive novel published in Spanish four centuries ago, presents at least two seemingly insurmountable challenges to its appropriation in public discourse: one, its length and complexity; and two, its very prestige as a universal literary masterpiece. However popular, *Don Quixote* remains a novel of epic proportions whose myriad characters and complex plots resist staging and defy theatrical logic. Yet, countless adaptations of Cervantes' story have been brought to life, particularly on stages and screens around the world, since as early as 1605. Shortly after the publication of part I, famed Valencian playwright Guillén de Castro composed two plays based on different episodes of *Don Quixote*, *El curioso impertinente* (*The Man Who Was Recklessly Curious*) and *Don Quijote de la Mancha*, both dated around 1606 (Ardila 239). In 1614, the prologue to the apocryphal *Quixote* describes part I of its original model as a "comedia en prosa," or comedy in prose. The visual qualities of many of the knight's adventures, such as the windmills episode or Maese Pedro's puppet show, underscore the powerful iconic force of the character himself, easily recognizable around the globe through images as popular as Pablo Picasso's drawing of Don Quixote and Sancho on horseback (Riley). Cervantes' story has been translated and adapted into dozens of languages, as well as illustrated, drawn, and painted on countless occasions, from Gustave Doré's classic 1863 engravings to Santi Moix's 2008 twelve-print series. Since Guillén de Castro's early plays, *Don Quixote* has inspired a myriad of other performance works including ballets, operas, symphonic pieces, zarzuelas, and musicals, as well as dozens of animated and live-action films and television shows (Canavaggio). Such is their visual appeal that Don Quixote and Sancho might end up leaving planet Earth for outer space in the near future. For the last decade or so, the European Space Agency has been planning an asteroid-deflecting mission to be carried out by two spacecrafts. The first one, *Sancho*, would orbit an asteroid on a possible collision course with the Earth to gather data. With *Sancho*'s information, a second rocket, called *Hidalgo*, would crash into the asteroid to deflect its trajectory. An idealistic enterprise worthy of Cervantes' imagination and the subject of the 1998 Hollywood blockbuster *Armageddon*, the project remains under development (Gálvez and Carnelli).

What explains, then, the widespread and unabated appetite for staging Cervantes' story since its publication? What in Cervantes' text continues to speak so forcefully to theater professionals and audiences alike? As Dale Wasserman, the author of arguably *Don Quixote*'s most popular stage adaptation (*Man of La Mancha*, 1965) asserts, "the novel is inherently theatrical" (128). Certainly, the plot brims with theatrical episodes of a various nature. Episodes such as the debate between the canon and the priest on the state of theater in seventeenth-century Spain (I.47–48), the knight's encounter with the theatrical cart of "the assembly of death" scene (II.11), the wedding of Camacho (II.19–21), and the pervasive theatricality at the court of the duke and duchess in part II, thoroughly embed performance and play into the novel (Maestro; Checa; Reed 72). The relevance of dialogue and the frequency of role-play throughout the book foreground the Baroque persuasion that the world is a stage. As a compositional strategy, the weaving of theater into prose affirms "la esencia de esta novela: la experiencia de un ilusionismo que nunca pierde su relación crítica con la realidad" (the essence of this novel: the experience of an illusionism that maintains a critical stance toward reality; Maestro 42–43). Whether in his narrative or plays, Cervantes elaborates a nuanced reflection on the relationship between life and acting, as he ponders the theatricality of the world as well as the worldly applications of performance (Reed 82).

Not only is theater prevalent in numerous episodes throughout the book, but also, for many critics, the dual protagonist Quijano/Quixote conducts himself as a skilled performer. As early as 1958, Mark Van Doren suggested that Don Quixote's "profession" was really that of an actor, not a knight-errant (Van Doren; see also Predmore). For Gonzalo Torrente Ballester, the life of Don Quixote as performed by Quijano constitutes above all a game in which the hidalgo consciously performs a role (Torrente

Ballester). If we accept that the character's apparent madness does not preclude the possibility of his acting, then we must conclude with Javier Blasco that "la verdad del protagonista cervantino no está ni en don Quijote . . . ni en Alonso Quijano, sino en la pugna de Alonso Quijano por ser don Quijote" (the character's true nature resides not in Don Quixote . . . nor in Alonso Quijano, but in Alonso Quijano's struggle to become Don Quixote; 157). From this point of view, Quijano and Quixote are not separate entities, as Howard Mancing and many other critics tend to categorize Cervantes' "dual" protagonist (Friedman, "Executing the Will" 106), but a rather complex character that comprises both the hidalgo and the evolving product of his performance, Don Quixote.

The intrinsic theatricality of the novel does not explain, in any event, why *Don Quixote*, a four-hundred-year-old work written in Spanish, so forcefully resonates in Brazil today and, in particular, in progressive cultural-activist circles. This is a question that I have actually posed to a number of Brazilian activists, mostly in São Paulo and Salvador de Bahia, of diverse educational, gender, class, and racial backgrounds. Although purely anecdotal, the answers I collected prove for the most part vague and based on a personal, non-academic relationship with the text. In essence, the activists and artists I interviewed had all read the book in their youth and were inspired by Don Quixote's unrelenting drive to better society, a goal that all of them obviously share. In our informal conversations, no senior staff person in any of these organizations demonstrated any particular knowledge of the Brazilian trajectory of Cervantes' book, although all of them had read it several times and consulted historical as well as scholarly sources at one point or another. Their Quixote-inspired projects had developed independently; they only came to know of each other through my research. Fortunately, though, *Don Quixote*'s pervasive presence in Brazil enjoys a long and rich history dotted with precedents germane to the contemporary social justice appropriations at the core of this study. Let us then briefly review *Don Quixote*'s travels in Brazil's literary history, a journey that inextricably runs along Cervantes' fortunes in the broader Latin American context.

Cervantes' story arrived in the Americas shortly after its publication. Over three hundred copies of *Don Quixote* were shipped off to the new world in 1605 (Leonard, ch. 18–19; Velásquez Martínez 6). The book's two main characters quickly became enormously popular in both print and theatrical adaptations, including formal plays and street festivals such as carnivals and parades. Early testimonies of the Don Quixote and Sancho characters appearing at costume parties and street festivities all over the Spanish territories abound, with the pair's popularity increasing exponentially over time (Uribe-Echevarría 17–30). But how and when did *Don Quixote* reach Brazil? We simply do not know. The first edition published in Brazil, along with a separate abridged translation by K. D'Avellar, materialized only in 1898. The first Portuguese translation, however, came out in 1794 on the Iberian Peninsula and likely also reached the Brazilian market. Already in 1733, although once again in Portugal, Brazilian-born António José da Silva (1705–1739), better known as António José O Judeu (the Jew), staged a puppet play in Lisbon entitled *Vida do Grande Dom Quixote de la Mancha e do Gordo Sancho Pança* (*The Life of the Great Don Quixote and Fat Sancho Panza*) (Pérez Rodríguez 3–4). The abundant bibliography on O Judeu does not reference any performances of this play, also labeled an opera for its musical interludes, in Brazil (see, among others, Chartier; Costigan). In fact, the Documentos para a História do Teatro em Portugal (Documents for a history of theater in Portugal) project, out of the University of Lisbon, registers a 1942 performance as the first recorded occasion in which the *Vida* was staged after its premiere in 1733 ("Ficha de texto"). However, the governor of Goiás, Dom Luiz de Cunha Menezes, wrote to King Peter III in 1778 that in 1774, in the village of Pilar, he "saw an opera inspired by Miguel de Cervantes' novel" (qtd. in Amado 4). While there is no written record as to whether this opera was O Judeu's, the point about Cervantes' popularity at the time can be soundly argued. Since Goiás remained a historically and geographically isolated state until the federal capital of Brasília was built there in the late 1950s, it is reasonable to conclude that this or other musical and stage adaptations of *Don Quixote* may have been rather popular around the country. Furthermore, O Judeu's adaptation predates the first Portuguese translation of *Don Quixote* (1794), which suggests that the Spanish-language original already circulated widely in the neighboring kingdom of Portugal and in its largest American colony, as well. Don Quixote's presence in Brazil, however, goes beyond the perpetuation of a character by authors other than its original creator, as Bernard A. Drew narrowly defines literary afterlife. Cervantes' protagonist not only remains a famous, popular character in the Brazilian imaginary, but his influence also reaches deep into the country's national identity.

As in the rest of Latin America, *Don Quixote*'s significance in Brazilian literary and political circles intensified and coalesced around the birth of the modern state. Throughout the nineteenth and early twentieth centuries, most Latin American nations sought to consolidate a fully modern narrative for their recently formed national self. Frequently, the nascent American countries resorted to the transculturation of European culture as a pillar of their new hybrid identities, as discussed in Chapter 1. In at times blatantly contradictory ways, many noted American intellectuals in fact turned to Don Quixote as the embodiment of the national values to which they aspired. In doing so, they inserted Cervantes' character, the paramount accomplishment of Spanish literature, into the foundational narrative of countries that had only recently broken free from Spain's imperial rule. For the sake of brevity, I offer only a small but representative sampling of prominent nationalist intellectuals who employed *Don Quixote* to define the new Latin American idiosyncracy.[1] This brief overview will sketch the ideological background against which Brazilian nationalists also utilized Cervantes' protagonist in their efforts to define Brazilianness.

Colombian historian and fervent pro-democracy activist Germán Arciniegas (1900–1999) hails Don Quixote as "the great democrat." In Arciniegas' view, the knight-errant treats Sancho as an equal and, in the squire's stint as governor of Barataria, defends Sancho's right to rule on the premise that good government is based on personal merit and not mere lineage (*El Quijote visto desde América* 224–27). In this regard, Arciniegas seems to forestall a social justice-oriented reading of Cervantes' masterpiece. At the same time, however, he deems Christopher Columbus the original American Quixote, for following in the hidalgo's footsteps, he invests himself with the honorific title "Don" that his social class did not afford him by birthright. Furthermore, in ways akin to Cervantes' character, the Genoese also fuels his rather improbable dream with sheer idealism (219). While some of these comparisons may ring true, Arciniegas' argument ultimately proves flawed. If Don Quixote stands for freedom and a merit-based system of government and Columbus incarnates the original American Quixote, then Columbus should be regarded as a great democrat himself. Needless to say, this assertion contradicts all historical evidence about the Almirante, which fundamentally invalidates Arciniegas' interpretation of the hidalgo/knight-errant.

Another prominent intellectual voice in the consolidation of Latin American identity, Uruguayan essayist José Enrique Rodó (1871–1917), also sees Don Quixote as the embodiment of the indomitably idealistic spirit that conquered America. A fierce critic of North American utilitarianism, Rodó celebrates Cervantes' knight as the spiritual as well as Eurocentric alternative to US political and ideological dominance. In Rodó's somewhat extravagant proposal, Latin Americans ought to muster and deploy the very quixotic forces that colonized them in order to defeat, in the new hemispheric scenario, US materialism (*El Quijote visto desde América* 95–97). In the end, in the ongoing battle between two empires Rodó simply favors Spanish idealism, embodied by Don Quixote, over US pragmatism.

Lastly, Guatemalan Miguel Ángel Asturias (1899–1974) considers Fray Bartolomé de Las Casas, and not Columbus, as the most fitting historical incarnation of Don Quixote (*El Quijote visto desde América* 197–99). First bishop of Chiapas, Mexico, Las Casas fiercely denounced the immorality and illegality of the conquistadors' mass extermination and enslavement of indigenous populations by affirming their wholesome humanity. In contrast to previous identifications with Columbus and the spirit of conquest, Asturias' interpretation of Las Casas as the genuine American Quixote better fits a progressive reading of the novel. After all, the bishop of Chiapas stands out in the history of colonization for his tireless fight against the conquistadors' greed and brutality. Still a major player in the imperial project, however, Las Casas favored the forced conversion of indigenous people to Christianity. Endowed with a soul, natives had to be conquered spiritually. While this American Quixote rejects the mass murder and enslavement of indigenous peoples (not a minor feat at the time, indeed), he still fully operates under European religious, socio-economic, and cultural coloniality.

All in all, the transculturation of *Don Quixote* by early to mid twentieth-century Latin American intellectuals sought the continent's entrance into a modernizing project firmly anchored in Eurocentric values. Public figures involved in nation-building initially depicted the knight as either champion of the European conquest of the Americas or, in its most benevolent version, savior of indigenous peoples in need of Catholic conversion and European civilization. Although somewhat divergent, most if not all of these interpretations fall squarely within the ideological parameters of the European imperial project. Throughout the first half of the twentieth century, preeminent Latin American intellectuals locate *Don Quixote* in a contact zone that, as Mary Louise Pratt warns, is not purely European any longer, yet continues to pursue a Europeanizing nation-building project. While liberal creole and mestizo intellectuals celebrate an "original" Americanness clearly distinct from European identity, they simultaneously embrace "old world" political and cultural values in detriment of indigenous and African paradigms (172–73). In the end, whether Don Quixote represents Columbus or Las Casas, and even if these foundational appropriations appear "originally" American, their cultural compass continues to point solely toward Europe.[2]

Don Quixote's appeal to nation-building movements in the Americas proves somewhat surprising. Not only does Cervantes' book appear at the peak of the Spanish imperial expansion, but its old hidalgo protagonist is regarded as mentally unstable by most fellow characters and readers. Beaten up and mocked throughout the book, Cervantes' hero embodies in his fragile physique and delusional mind the impending decadence of the Spanish empire. Even so, Don Quixote's iconic prowess in American nation-building projects transcended not only borders, but also languages.

Brazilian nationalist intellectuals and public figures appropriated the knight-errant's epic character in ways strikingly similar to those of Spanish-speaking Latin American nations. During the early to mid-twentieth century, Cervantes' masterpiece took on a prominent role in Brazilian literary manifestations of nationalist sentiment. Cervantes' influence is extensive in works by Brazil's most revered author and founder of the Brazilian Academy of Letters, Joaquim Maria Machado de Assis (1839–1908), whose sway in Brazilian culture to this day cannot be overstated. According to a variety of scholars, defining features of Machado de Assis' art, including his love of self-conscious fiction (Fuentes, "Machado de La Mancha"), the layers of authorship in his narrative (Maura), the use of humor, and the blending of different genres (Vieira, "El *Quijote* en la prosa"), can all be traced back to Cervantes. In his selective personal library, Machado cherished two of the Spanish author's books: *Don Quixote* and the *Exemplary Novels*. Nonetheless, while extensive, Cervantes' presence in the works of Brazil's greatest writer manifests itself mainly through Machado's use of Cervantine literary techniques, not via clearly identifiable plots or characters. In the works of several openly nationalist writers of the early to mid-twentieth century, however, *Don Quixote*'s influence reveals itself as both direct and explicit.

In 1911 Alfonso Henriques Lima Barreto (1881–1922) published in serial form the novel *Triste Fim de Policarpo Quaresma*, tellingly titled *The Patriot* in Robert Scott-Buccleuch's 1978 English translation. An ultra-nationalist government employee, Quaresma speaks several languages but reads only Brazilian authors and books on Brazil. His outlandish behavior creates comical situations that, as the story progresses, become more somber. In a truly *triste fim* (tragic ending), Policarpo is executed under orders from his previously admired President Floriano Peixoto, a historical figure who served as Brazil's second president between 1891 and 1894. In yet another example of transcultural paradox, the book satirizes Brazil's infatuation with foreign cultures while it models its own protagonist after none other than Cervantes' Don Quixote (Vieira, "Tipología quijotesca"). Among other petitions addressed to the Brazilian government, Policarpo proposes in exuberantly nationalistic terms to replace Portuguese, deemed an instrument of colonization, with Tupi, one of Brazil's indigenous languages. Despite its Spanish literary ancestry and parodic characterization, Policarpo Quaresma's anticolonial scheme resonated with a number of nationalist public figures and intellectuals of the time. In fact, during the 1930s a cohort of Brazilian intellectuals learned to write in Tupi in a deliberate effort to put into practice Policarpo's call to arms against Brazil's colonial language (Olinto viii). Following in Policarpo's footsteps, these nationalists attempted to recover their indigenous cultural and linguistic "souls" in order to fight the very Iberian colonizing force that, by means of Cervantes, paradoxically inspired Lima Barreto's novel. *Triste Fim de Policarpo Quaresma* simultaneously models itself after *Don Quixote* and undermines its influence with anticolonial fervor, thus anticipating by almost twenty years de Andrade's call for Tupi-like cannibalism of European sources.³

Another key figure in Brazil's literary and nationalist circles, José Bento Monteiro Lobato (1882–1948), published *Dom Quixote das crianças* (*Don Quixote for Children*) in 1936. An outspoken critic of Getúlio Vargas's dictatorship (1930–1945), Monteiro Lobato developed a nationalist stance throughout his work, anchored, once again, in latent but provocative contradictions. Instrumental in the development of the Brazilian publishing industry, his own company, the Companhia Editora Nacional, edited as many as half the books printed in Brazil during the 1920s. Up to the early 1900s, the former colony imported most of its books from Portuguese and French presses. Because, in his own words, "a nation is made by men and books," Monteiro Lobato encouraged Brazilian writers to find inspiration not in foreign stories but in their own culture and language (qtd. in Milton 213). Yet, he adapted a number of foreign works and published numerous translations of English, German, and French authors. Fittingly, Monteiro Lobato achieved his greatest literary success with an adaptation of Cervantes' masterpiece for children, which has been reprinted almost every year since 1936 (Cobelo 112). The success of *Dom Quixote das crianças* can hardly be explained by the scarcity of such versions of Cervantes' story on the market. Although around 2013 nineteen prose adaptations of *Don Quixote* for children (plus seven comic-book versions and three in *cordel*, or popular poetry) crowded Brazilian libraries, Monteiro Lobato's version still commanded the biggest sales and the highest levels of popularity (Cobelo 112).

Monteiro Lobato's famous children's books are all set in the Sítio do Picapau Amarelo (Yellow Woodpecker Ranch), where Dona Benta lives with her two grandchildren and fantastical characters such as Emília, a ragdoll. In *Dom Quixote das crianças*, it is Emília who finds the two thick volumes of *Don Quixote* in Dona Benta's library. Unable to understand the antiquated style of the original, Emília asks Dona Benta to translate the adventures of the knight-errant of La Mancha into plain Portuguese. Although the ranch's owner edits out a number of episodes, including Don Quixote's death (Emília can't bear the thought of her hero's passing), for the most part Dona Benta limits herself to paraphrasing Cervantes' original episodes, and the intricate process of updating the knight's adventures to Brazil's contemporary realities does not yet fully materialize in Monteiro Lobato's adaptation.[4]

During the second half of the twentieth century and especially around the four-hundredth anniversary in 2005, *Don Quixote*'s afterlife in Brazil progressively anchored itself in socially minded discourse. As the country's national identity consolidated under the authoritarian presidency of Getúlio Vargas, *Don Quixote* started to function as a symbol for progressive strivings and leftist politics. Brazil's historical conditions in the second part of the twentieth century favored a more socially conscious interpretation of Cervantes' story, particularly with the advent of the military dictatorship that ruled the country with an iron fist between 1964 and 1985. Early signs of the incremental change from nation-building to community activism came from a most unexpected source: The 1950s Formoso peasant revolt (*revolta de Formoso*) in the interior province of Goiás provides both a historical precedent to *Don Quixote*'s socially minded interpretation as well as a remarkable example of the knight-errant's penetration into Brazil. From the late 1970s to the mid 1980s historian Janaína Amado conducted research in the municipality of Uruaçu on the famous peasant uprising against landowners. In 1979, she interviewed a local informant, identified by the pseudonym Fernandes, whose description of the revolt's leader, José Porfírio de Souza, included many Quixote-like features. De Souza, Fernandes initially claimed, rode a horse named Rocinante, and a Sancho-like figure accompanied him throughout the revolt. These assertions soon proved blatantly false, leaving the historian intrigued as to the peculiar nature of her informant's fantasies. Upon close examination, Amado realized that her informant had incorporated passages and even direct quotes from Cervantes' *Don Quixote* into his narrative. Puzzled by the quixotic twist in Fernandes' testimony, Janaína Amado returned to Uruaçu to further investigate the issue. As she soon discovered, not only Fernandes but also all of the elderly villagers demonstrated a remarkable familiarity with Cervantes' story. According to collective memory, they had come in contact with Don Quixote when Europeans first settled in the region sometime in the second half of the eighteenth century. Transmitted through collective readings and oral culture, the knight-errant's adventures helped Fernandes endow the revolt's hero with a legendary status. By inserting Don Quixote's story into de Souza's heroic narrative, the informant favored a symbolic and mythical portrayal of the revolt's leader over a rigorous account of historical facts (Amado 1–4).

Around the mid twentieth century, the shift toward revolutionary politics and social justice concerns surfaced again in the Southern city of Porto Alegre. Between 1947 and 1961 the Grupo Quixote (Quixote Collective), composed of local poets and intellectuals, undertook numerous initiatives to democratize access to poetry and modernize the literary scene in their home state of Rio Grande do Sul. Rejecting conservative aesthetics and political attitudes, the group published a literary magazine and organized poetry festivals that sought to establish renewed ties with their more liberal Spanish-speaking neighbors to the south, Uruguay and Argentina. By expanding the reach of poetic creation across class, linguistic, and even national as well as linguistic barriers, the leftist group turned *Don Quixote* into a symbol for cross-cultural and progressive cultural intervention (Vieira, "El *Quijote* y las huellas cervantinas" 95–98). The rebellious and egalitarian nature of Grupo Quixote consolidated a new kind of Quixote-inspired, art-based activism that provided the broad ideological foundation upon which Brazilian contemporary appropriations rest.[5]

At the turn of the twenty-first century, and particularly around the fourth centenary of Cervantes' classic, Don Quixote's presence in community activism in the American hemisphere, and specifically in Brazilian urban initiatives, took on a fundamentally applied, lived nature. Rather than seeking nation-building or promoting a romanticized notion of idealism, recent appropriations of *Don Quixote* by socially minded cultural organizations in a variety of American countries encourage their spectators and participants, particularly children and youth in vulnerable social situations, to imitate the hidalgo's rebellious act of rewriting his own role in society. In this sense, the book's afterlife has become embedded in the very mission and methodology of the nonprofits and theater companies that appropriate it for their social justice-oriented work. Before I delve into my Brazilian case studies, thus, it is critical to establish the broader parameters within which social justice appropriations of *Don Quixote* occur across the Americas. Notably, my Brazilian examples fit into a hemispheric pattern of transculturation that centers on the most marginal members of society yet has proven successful in terms of audience and critical reception. Across Latin America, numerous plays link the artistically transformative nature of the quixotic enterprise to their social justice message, particularly focused on the underprivileged. Rather than generating a catalogue of Latin American versions of *Don Quixote*, however, I want to briefly comment on adaptations outside Brazil that prove relevant to our examination of the liberatory potential of Quixote-inspired activism. As with any selection, I will certainly fail to acknowledge many worthy versions, but here I present only those that, on the one hand, explicitly address social marginality through their theatrical practice and, on the other, do so with high impact in terms of audience outreach and artistic quality. These works are all relatively accessible through published scripts and/or video recordings. Given space and time constraints, I limit my analysis to three particularly bold and successful proposals: Arturo Morell's *Don Quijote, un grito de libertad* (*Don Quixote: A Cry for Freedom*, 2012) in Mexico; Bill George's *Don Quixote of Bethlehem* (2005) for Touchstone Theater in Bethlehem, Pennsylvania; and Santiago García's *El Quijote* (1999) for La Candelaria company in Bogotá, Colombia, which was in turn adapted in the United States, Mexico, and Brazil in ways that are relevant to my later discussion of Brazilian appropriations. The examination of these examples documents how the shift from nation-building to community activism expands the social reach and purpose of *Don Quixote*'s transculturation in the Americas.

Between 2004 and 2007, Arturo Morell staged a Spanish-language version of Dale Wasserman's *Man of La Mancha* with more than five hundred male and female interns at penitentiaries in Morelos, Tlaxcala, Querétaro, and Mexico City. From an initial meeting with the interns to a post-performance conversation, Morell captured the Morelos production on camera for his thrilling 2012 *Don Quijote, un grito de libertad* documentary. Although not an original adaptation of *Don Quixote*, this project blended the seemingly disparate worlds of prison life, theater, and literary criticism in a novel way, for the staging of *Man of La Mancha* was complemented with spontaneous discussions of the text itself as well as with the concurrent recording of rehearsals and performances for the documentary. Morell explained to me in personal communications that he holds several *Don Quixote* editions annotated by inmates from five different penitentiaries. During rehearsals for the show, inmates would circulate copies of the book from cell to cell, reading and marking passages at will. I have not been able to read these annotations myself, but Morell tells me that they are "auténticas joyas" (real treasures) and that he would frequently exchange letters and notes with inmates on the meanings and human dimension of the book.

At the film's onset, Morell describes his project as an "artistic intervention" that aims to reveal the transformative power of art and performance to participants and audience alike, a goal shared by the Brazilian organizations I later examine. Toward the end of the film, in a post-performance conversation, actors as well as audience members zoom in on how Morell's artistic intervention triggers transformation. First, several interns claim that their participation in the show stimulates their imagination and sense of freedom. As one of the inmates claims in a voiceover, performing enhances their ability to dream despite and beyond the prison bars: "Ya no importa que te cierren la reja... porque ahora sí sueñas, soñamos, sentimos... somos libres" (It doesn't matter that our doors are locked... because now one dreams, we dream, we feel... we are free; 59:36–59:48). Furthermore, as a weeping mother in the audience dramatically states, during the performance she saw in her son "lo que jamás imaginé: que es un gran ser humano" (what I never imagined: that he is a great human being; 56:17–56:23). Overwhelmed with complex emotions, this mother recognizes for the first time her son's greatness, as he proves his worth on stage by incarnating a character from Wasserman's musical. The dual transformation that sets inmates free and reaffirms their human worth through acting also undergirds the Coooperaacs project discussed earlier and the Brazilian plays examined in subsequent chapters. By situating marginality and performance at the core of their activism, these proposals cast Don Quixote as a performative hero who can transform himself and society through art and theater.

Notably, Pennsylvania-based Touchstone Theater's motto is "Theater That Transforms," which squarely locates its artistic and activist practice within the social justice and community-engaged paradigm of *Don Quixote*'s transculturations prevalent in the Americas over the last twenty years. With the goal to promote transformation through performance, the company was formally founded in 1981 by improvisational bilingual street-theater practitioners who had been active since the mid 1970s at Lehigh University and in its surrounding, mostly Puerto Rican and Caucasian, neighborhoods. Since turning professional, Touchstone has performed original ensemble pieces and free adaptations of classics and Greek myths in theaters and in the streets, sometimes through what they call a "theatricade," or a combination of performance and parade. Written by Bill George and directed by Jennie Gilrain, the *Don Quixote of Bethlehem* traveling performance paraded from the Lehigh University campus through the diverse South Side neighborhood "inspired by the desire to bridge the gap between the Anglo and Latino cultures" ("The Don Quixote Project"). Joining the troupe's own professional actors, the performance involved over one hundred participants from the community, as well as the public library, school district, neighborhood churches, senior center, and other local entities. In a documentary entitled *The Making of Don Quixote of Bethlehem*, directed by Anisa George and Petra Costa, the activist dimensions of the project become fully apparent. Throughout the preparations for the theatricade, residents and troupe members discussed issues that to this day deeply affect and at times divide the city of Bethlehem along ethnic lines, such as migration (though Puerto Ricans are US citizens, some Anglo residents still regard them as foreigners); integration versus the preservation of non-Anglo, Puerto Rican cultural legacies; and the status of Puerto Rico itself as an unincorporated territory of the United States. In a representative scene from the actual play, Sancho's stint as governor (II.32–53 in the original) includes here a dispute mediated by Sancho between white police officers and two Puerto Rican residents, one speaking in Spanish and the other in English. In *Don Quixote of Bethlehem*, everyday concerns of the local communities, from issues of law and order to ethnic relations, unfold in the very streets where these interactions take place on a daily basis. Inserted into the quotidian reality of the South Side, a cast of residents and professional actors experienced through an adaptation of *Don Quixote* the transformative power of performance, for during the play many community members appeared as both actors and spectators of their own play. Testing solutions to everyday problems on stage, a diverse cast and audience coalesced around the aesthetic and ethical value of a theatricade that inserted a centuries-old Spanish story into the South Side neighborhood.

The question "Who is Don Quixote?," which serves as the heading for a section of the aforementioned documentary, underscores both the equalizing character of theater and the cultural differences underlying the neighborhood. In fact, the responses varied significantly between the two main ethno-cultural communities in Bethlehem. For several Anglo residents and troupe members, Don Quixote simply went mad, and his enterprise revolved mainly around either his love for Dulcinea or the chaos instigated by the knight-errant himself, an "arrogant idiot with a noble cause," in

FIGURE 2.1. *Don Quixote* performance by Touchstone Theater in the streets of Bethlehem, Pennsylvania. Photograph by Hub Willson

director Jennie Gilrain's (rather accurate, I would add) description. As Gilrain herself admits, however, the Latinx community understood best who Don Quixote was: "They get it immediately," she muses; they are "right there before we (non Latinxs) are," even if they have never read the book. Two female Latina community residents, one in Spanish and the other in English, answer the question "Who is Don Quixote?" by stating that Cervantes' character, in contrast to what Anglo-American residents stated, was not crazy. "Had Sancho thought that his master was merely a madman, would he have followed him?" one resident asks herself in English. But if not madness, what then caused Quijano to transform himself into a knight-errant and embark on his high-risk adventures? As the Spanish-speaking female resident claims, Don Quixote (Quijano) was just trying to add some fun to his life, some *entretenimiento* (entertainment). With their short but insightful answers, these two Latina community residents emphasized the self-conscious, intentionally theatrical mission of an hidalgo whose performance turns his unremarkable life into the heroic story of a traveling entertainer. In the context of a theatricade of over one hundred participants, this project implicitly affirms that we can all be Quixotes, spectators and readers turned actors and creators of our own social narratives. It is significant in this regard that Ricardo Viera, former director and chief curator of the Lehigh University art galleries, conceived in 1978 a *Don Quixote* street performance on the premise that "Todos somos Quijotes" (We're all Quixotes). When this theatricade, which served as a precursor and inspiration for the 2005 project, was staged in the streets of Bethlehem and the Lehigh campus, printed t-shirts worn by performers and audience members alike proudly proclaimed in Spanish: "Yo soy Quijote" (I am Quixote). For the Latinxs involved in the project, Don Quixote was not simply a madman but an actor whose performative activism is contagious and thus potentially revolutionary.

In 1999 Santiago García, one of the most influential figures in Latin American theater over the last four decades, wrote *El Quijote* for the legendary La Candelaria company, which he co-founded in 1966. Based in Bogotá, Colombia, La Candelaria responds to "la necesidad de construir 'arte propio'... para expresar la realidad desde Latinoamérica" (the need to practice our "own art"... to convey reality [as seen] from Latin America). In its stated goal, La Candelaria partakes of the transcultural founding project that throughout the hemisphere and over a period of two centuries longed to create a genuinely Latin American point of view. While explicitly vowing to combat "el colonialismo cultural" (cultural colonialism), the company creates an "espacio 'dialéctico'" ("dialectical" space) that combines European, indigenous, and Afro-Colombian motifs. By embracing canonical and community-oriented traditions, La Candelaria deploys "un 'nuevo' mundo posible" (a "new" world of possibilities) that fuses its various heritages into a true Latin American theater (Florián Navas and Pecha Quimbay 157).

Although it does not adhere to any one theoretical school, La Candelaria's trajectory overlaps with the Brazilian as well as the larger Latin American tradition of community and social justice theater in more than one way. Intentionally, the company adopts the name of the downtown neighborhood in Bogotá, La Candelaria, where it has been housed since its inception. Out of its very specific geographical location, a popular neighborhood fraught in the late 1960s with urban decay and poverty, La Candelaria company pinpoints its precise social location. (Over the last two decades many of La Candelaria's streets and most emblematic buildings have been restored). Around the time of its founding, the company unambiguously stated its ideological underpinnings and identified its ideal audience: "Queremos un teatro transformador y por consiguiente ponernos al lado de la clase social determinada por la historia para hacer esa transformación" (We practice a transformative theater and thus take the side of the social class determined by history to carry out that transformation; qtd.

in Florián Navas and Pecha Quimbay 161). Beneath the Marxist rhetoric of determinism and class relations, the transformative power of theater undergirds La Candelaria's proposal as it did Morell's project in Mexican prisons and the *Don Quixote of Bethlehem* theatricade. In the specific case of *El Quijote*, one of the long-term actresses at La Candelaria, Patricia Ariza, explicitly identifies, like most of the Brazilian appropriations, "los jóvenes y los excluidos" (the young and the excluded) as its ideal audience (17). Yet, La Candelaria's dialectical worldview does not escape contradictions similar to the ones affecting other Quixote-inspired transcultural projects such as the Cooperaacs figures. First, the company's repertoire is rife with Western classics such as *Don Quixote* and is delivered in the Spanish language with minimal presence of indigenous cultures and languages. And second, their experimental nature and texts of high literary caliber, including their adaptation of *El Quijote*, may render their performances somewhat inaccessible to the popular audience they mean to engage.

In García's version, art and specifically theater seek to ignite individual as well as broader social advancement. In order to foreground the liberating practice of performance, García turns his play inside out by exposing the protagonist's intrinsic theatricality and name-changing prowess. Right from the start, the play condenses in just a few pages of dialogue the three moments, scattered throughout the one thousand-page book in the original, in which the hidalgo Alonso Quijano crafts his Don Quixote identity solely by changing names. These three episodes, spread apart between volumes I and II in the original text, here appear in close succession: first, Quijano's transformation into Don Quixote (I.1 in the original text); then his renaming by Sancho as the Knight of the Sad Countenance (I.19); and finally Don Quixote's self-proclamation as Knight of the Lions after his encounter with a lion (II.17) (García 19–25; see also Abril Sánchez 229–31). Central as well to my Brazilian case studies, the act of (re)naming is here emphatically highlighted as a key tool for personal transformation. Furthermore, metatheatrical discussions on the subject of performing pervade the play. Unlike most other adaptations of the book, García employs *Don Quixote* part II as the basis for his play. Unusually, he dispenses with the most famous and visually recognizable adventures from part I, such as the charge against the windmills, in favor of metatheatrical episodes like the encounter with the enchanted Dulcinea, the court of the duke and duchess, and Sancho's governorship. In part I, an exuberantly mad Don Quixote charges against everyone and everything, which often results in scenes dominated by physical humor (bloody battles and falls) and a fast-paced theatricality more easily transferable to the stage, while, in a self-referential turn, in part II Don Quixote encounters numerous readers of the first volume of his life story and even of the apocryphal second part by Avellaneda. Heavy on dialogue and slower in pace, many adventures in part II turn out to be elaborate jokes at Don Quixote's expense carefully staged by characters who have read the story of the crazed knight-errant published in volume I. With several key characters increasingly taking control of the protagonist's performance, *Don Quixote* part II and, consequently, García's version consist of a succession of plays within the protagonist's larger play. Inserted into Quijano's revolutionary performance, a variety of characters take a stab themselves at the art of performing fictional stories outside existing social orders. Brimming with theatricality, part II readers of *Don Quixote* part I become main actors and directors in the extended, revolutionary performance of Quijano/Quixote. The hidalgo's fearless creativity has now infected secondary, perhaps less well-intentioned characters. In some profound ways, the hidalgo has seemingly fulfilled his theatrical mission, for a cohort of fellow readers and spectators now take up discursive arms to perform and even direct scenes that escape the control of government, norms, literary genres, and even the church. As the hero surrenders command over his story, however, secondary characters often deride and humiliate Don Quixote for their own personal entertainment or benefit. Over time, Don Quixote's theatrical success paradoxically causes his own personal demise.[6]

El Quijote's metatheatrical, performative message around *Don Quixote*'s applicability to contemporary times rests on two key premises that also articulate the Brazilian adaptations, as we will see over the next two chapters: the hidalgo Quijano is not crazy; and Quijano does not die at the end. In a September 9, 2000, interview, García himself explains how he interpreted Quijano as "no loco, es decir, el que se hace el loco [. . .] La locura como una manera de ver" (not crazy, [but] someone who acts [like he is] crazy. [. . .] Madness as a way of looking at reality; García, "El Quijote" 14:44–15:02). Instead of a character that simply loses his mind, in this version Don Quixote becomes the product of intentional madness, the result of an unconventional way of looking at the world. In the play, Don Quixote lucidly explains his performative madness to Sancho: "no se aprende de la vida sino de la fantasía y de cómo logramos nuestras imaginaciones" (one doesn't learn from real life but from fantasy, and from how we accomplish our dreams; 62). Far from the romanticized idealism that fuels nation-building interpretations of *Don Quixote*, fantasy and theater act in this adaptation as a safe, staged rehearsal for the actual process of transformation required to achieve true liberation in the real world. Change is practiced performatively by spectators-turned-actors, who will then enact their rehearsed revolution on the social stage.

Since performance brings about and sustains change, Don Quixote cannot die, for he exists as the ongoing act of Quijano's groundbreaking role-playing. His mission is endless, a perpetual cycle of acting and discursive rehearsal toward liberation. Caught in the constant practice of performance, consciously acting out his madness, Don Quixote can only start all over again at the end of each performance to keep his revolutionary pursuit alive. Although García's version adapts adventures primarily from part II of the book, the end of his play circles back to the very beginning of part I. At the end of the first volume in the original novel, the priest and the barber devise a plan to literally capture Don Quixote, placing him in a cage in order to forcibly return him to his village (I.46–47). García chooses this scene to bring his play to a shocking conclusion. Once captive, Don Quixote in La Candelaria's version vows to a group of weeping ladies that he will be back soon, stronger and more committed than ever ("No lloréis, señoras, os prometo regresar con más entereza y ánimos que nunca"; 92). Instead of the last scene in the original, which portrays a repentant Alonso Quijano on his deathbed, García delivers a (meta)theatrically enticing final scene. One of the weeping ladies solemnly takes center stage and, as the curtain falls, recites the famous first line of the book: "En un lugar de la Mancha, de cuyo nombre . . ." (92). Shunning the protagonist's death, *El Quijote* ends by returning full circle to the narrator's first words: "Somewhere in La Mancha, in a place whose name . . ." (I.1.19). From then on, we can only guess, the story starts all over, and with it Quijano's continual performance of his own personal hero, Don Quixote.

As *Don Quixote's* afterlife greatly intensified around the 2005 commemoration, its transculturation into the American hemisphere took a decisive turn away from nation-building and toward social justice discourse, particularly in its stage and activist adaptations. The pervasiveness of Cervantes' story in the Americas, and its frequent appropriation in cultural activism against social marginalization as the fourth centenary neared, prompted bewildering intersections and overlaps. A case in point, Santiago García's *El Quijote* was staged in two seemingly disparate locations, Chiapas and São Paulo, that have critically bolstered *Don Quixote*'s presence on the Latin American, and specifically the Brazilian, social justice-oriented cultural map. In 2001, as part of its thirty-fifth anniversary celebration, La Candelaria company traveled around the world with *El Quijote*. Besides stops in Bolivia, Cuba, Portugal, and other countries, the troupe spent several weeks in Chiapas, México. Since 1994, the Zapatista anti-neoliberal, pro-indigenous movement in Chiapas had been linked to *Don Quixote* through its best-known spokesperson, the legendary Subcomandante Marcos. For this icon of the global revolutionary left, Cervantes' work remains the best book of political theory ever written (Marcos, "The Punch Card"). Although La Candelaria never came into direct contact with Subcomandante Marcos, they performed before Zapatista audiences, including at times non-Spanish speaking residents who could thus not follow the text itself (Badillo Pérez, "Las andanzas" A10). Whether Marcos' passion for Cervantes had any influence on the play's enthusiastic reception by local audiences is unknown to me and perhaps even unlikely. Nonetheless, the connection between García's version and the Zapatista discourse must have been evident to the promoters of this initiative and even to local audiences themselves. This overlap of theater and activism under the auspices of the Zapatista movement would point to a common thread underlying all of the social justice-oriented adaptations of *Don Quixote*: the combination of marginality and metatheater as a critical tool for achieving more egalitarian social roles, particularly for the underserved and the excluded.

More pointedly, in October 2009 *El Quijote* was staged in a marginal neighborhood of São Paulo, Cidade Tiradentes, as part of a Latin American community-theater initiative. This project in many ways summarizes the character, strengths, and challenges of the Brazilian Quixotes featured in this study. Funded by the Brazilian government, fifteen companies from ten countries developed, using García's version as a point of departure, their very own *Quijote Latinoamericano*. Due to his failing health, Santiago García was replaced at the helm of the project by César Badillo, cast in the protagonist role since the play premiered in 1999. The project grew out of the second Conference on Ibero-American Culture, whose unifying theme in 2009 was "Culture and Social Transformation." As it developed, this initiative prompted the creation of a Red Latinoamericana de Teatro en Comunidad (Latin American Network of Community Theater), which shares the values embodied by the *Quijote Latinoamericano* project. As Badillo himself explains, fifteen companies staged with their own actors and in their own languages, both European and indigenous, the twelve scenes from García's play. Given the necessarily convoluted nature of a project carried out by a multinational, multilingual ensemble of companies and casts, furnishing the *Quijote Latinoamericano* with a common aesthetic and ethical thread quickly became a priority. According to Badillo, the same principles identified by García for the original staging of his play held true for this project.

Out of the chaotic mesh of nationalities and languages, this project adopted as its guiding principle a second key tool for personal and collective transformation, name-changing being the first one: The ever-shifting, malleable nature of identity. In a groundbreaking and conscious authorial decision, *Don Quixote* recounts the story of a dual protagonist in constant toil to mutate his birth-given identity as hidalgo into that of a literary knight-errant. In a remarkable parallel, Badillo compares the multiplicity of languages, national identities, and theatrical practices that the *Quijote Latinoamericano* polyphonic performance engenders with the malleability of personal and social identity that Quijano demonstrates in his becoming Don Quixote. When Badillo recognizes that, in this project, "la identidad no podía ser rígida e intocable; tenía que flexibilizarse" (identity could not be rigid and fixed; it had to become flexible; "El *Quijote latinoamericano*"), he is equating the flexible nature of the play itself (its multinational and multilingual character) with the elastic core of the dual protagonist. After all, the hidalgo bends his social identity to the breaking point in order to discursively rescript it via literary codes (chivalric, bucolic, and others) and a risky, all-out performance as a medieval knight-errant in the early 1600s. Inspired by chivalric literature, his command of the art of renaming and acting enables him to effectively transform himself as well as the world around him. Never military or strictly ideological, his prowess can only be described as literary, performative, and discursive.

In conclusion, the afterlife of *Don Quixote* in the Americas, and particularly in Brazil, has evolved from nation-building projects in the first part of the twentieth century to an activist approach around the four-hundredth anniversary that takes Cervantes' hero out of academic spaces and into the margins of society. Its revolutionary message remains essentially performative, for it rehearses on stage the rescripting and enacting of more egalitarian roles, which can then be transferred to the practice of the everyday. In the examples examined so far, Cervantes' hero strides along the streets of Latin America with self-conscious theatricality and a keen focus on marginality. In the case of contemporary Brazilian appropriations, the subject of the remainder of this book (stage versions in Part II and community activism in Part III), the afterlife of *Don Quixote* presents some unique features that further reinforce an activist and transformative transculturation of the Spanish classic in community contexts. The next four chapters investigate how a four-hundred-year-old classic translates into Brazilian community activism, particularly in urban centers and, more specifically, in the financial and cultural powerhouse of São Paulo.

PART II
Don Quixote of the Streets

The Performative Approach to *Don Quixote* in Brazil

"Theater can be a weapon for liberation. . . . Change is imperative."
AUGUSTO BOAL

CHAPTER 3

Don Quixote of the Streets

Marginality and Metatheater in Brazilian
Don Quixote Stage Adaptations

Don Quixote and Sancho continue to roam the streets of Latin America in the twenty-first century. Even in Brazil, a Portuguese-speaking country, original stage adaptations of remarkable success have advanced an activist interpretation of the Spanish classic in recent years. Through these plays and other artivist initiatives such as the aforementioned Cooperaacs statues, Brazilian appropriations offer sophisticated proposals to transculturate Cervantes' masterpiece into community engagement. How do these plays adapt a classic into a contemporary icon that serves as a model for, in particular, disadvantaged children and youth? How do they convey the notion that the theatricality of social relations can help the excluded rescript and perform a new role for themselves within a more equal society? Before detailing in Chapter 4 the deeply original interpretation of *Don Quixote* rendered by recent Brazilian stage adaptations, in this chapter I address the theoretical framework within which these appropriations occur. After briefly presenting the four plays analyzed here, I first ponder on whether and how theatricality and social betterment also intertwine in Cervantes' novel itself. Then I discuss the potential tensions and contradictions derived from the transculturation of a four-hundred-year-old, canonical Spanish-language novel in the context of urban-youth community activism in Brazil. Third, I identify Paulo Freire's pedagogy of the oppressed and Augusto Boal's theater of the oppressed as my theoretical framework for the analysis of contemporary Brazilian stage adaptations of *Don Quixote* across the Americas. And last, a handful of representative examples from two of the four plays serve to illustrate how (meta)theater and marginality further their activist agenda in *Don Quixote*'s Brazilian transculturations.

I focus on only four theatrical versions of *Don Quixote* that adapt Cervantes' classic to the Brazilian contemporary context and, along the lines of the Cooperaacs project, explicitly aim to engage and in some cases cast underserved populations. I chose these four plays not only because of their intrinsic theatrical quality, but also because, unlike many short-lived artistic projects, these performances reached significantly large audiences, in the many thousands, over a period of, in most cases, several years. They are: Márcio Meirelles' *Um tal de Dom Quixote* (Salvador de Bahia, 1998); Valéria di Pietro's *Num lugar de la Mancha* (São Paulo, 2000); Telma Dias and Robson Vellado's *Don Quixote* (São Paulo, 2005); and Andreia de Almeida's *Quixotes* (São Paulo, 2005). Significantly, none of these artistic and social initiatives coordinated their efforts or even knew of each other until I contacted them for this research project. Remarkably, however, despite a total lack of communication, their activist proposals developed in strikingly cohesive ways within just a handful of years. The theater companies I examine here concern themselves mainly with at-risk youth and make every attempt to reach them where they are: in the streets, at school, in community centers, and in shelters. Consequently, community organizers and artists implement their Quixote-inspired interventions not only in institutions and theaters, but also in public spaces such as streets, squares, and parks.

The stage adaptations across the American hemisphere that were discussed in the previous chapter and these Brazilian versions share the notion that performance can change the individual and society, as illustrated by Alonso Quijano's own transformation into Don Quixote. So central is Quijano's transformative prowess to its Brazilian transculturation into community activism that we must first ponder whether and how Cervantes discusses the potential of art and performance for social betterment in his own masterpiece. Is *Don Quixote* itself concerned with these issues, does it even consider theater as a weapon for liberation from oppressive social structures? Despite the worthy efforts of a handful of scholars (Helen H. Reed and James Iffland come to mind), most academic and popular readings of *Don Quixote* have failed to thoroughly address Cervantes' sharp focus on the discursive nature of human relations and, more specifically, on social performance as a vehicle for transformation.[1] The very quixotic conflation of theatricality with social betterment through self-writing and performance fits into a broader historical pattern that Stephen Greenblatt first outlined in his *Renaissance Self-Fashioning* (1980). Greenblatt's notion applies specifically to English Renaissance writers who, through their mastery of the word, practice "the fashioning of human identity as a manipulable, artful process" (2). Shakespeare, More, Spenser, Marlowe, as well as some of their peers and fictional characters, blur the boundaries between literary and worldly life by employing art to climb the social ladder. They all were "talented middle-class men [who] moved out of a narrowly circumscribed social sphere and into a realm that brought them in close contact with the powerful and the great" (7). In contrast to Greenblatt's English middle-class writers, however, Cervantes homes in on the outlaws (swindlers), disenfranchised (gypsies), and the politically irrelevant (rural hidalgos), a choice that could potentially explain *Don Quixote*'s popularity in Brazilian social justice circles.[2] Not only may writing and performance enable upward social mobility, but literature and theatricality might also provide the underprivileged a path out of extreme marginality.

In Cervantes' story, personal transformation represents a blunt challenge to socio-political and religious orders, for Don Quixote lives outside not only the rules of society but those of nature and God as well. Chapter 1 presents us with a rural hidalgo (a nobleman of modest means and negligible political influence) whose family name and town of origin go conveniently unrecalled. In a matter of only a few pages the nameless hidalgo, an obsessive reader, seemingly loses his mind to the point of re-fashioning himself into the ridiculously named "Don Quixote of La Mancha," as if parodying his own invention. Humor and madness, whether self-conscious or not (Canavaggio, *Don Quijote* 31), enable Cervantes to diffuse the radically subversive nature of his protagonist, who breaks at least three tenets of his time. First, Don Quixote's genesis parodies God's making of the world by the power of the divine Word (*Genesis* 1:3 ff; *Saint John* 1:1–3; *Psalm* 33:6; *Judith* 16:14). In Cervantes' book, the unremarkable Quijano supplants God in the discursive creation of life and a new (chivalric) world (Oriel). Don Quixote's sudden genesis rests on words that contradict reality and provoke laughter. In a matter of a few days, a squalid nag becomes Rocinante, a peasant woman embodies the noble Dulcinea, and an old hidalgo from La Mancha (Spain's dry central plateau) reinvents himself as a chivalric hero. Through this godly, creative whirlwind of linguistic performativity, our unlikely hero attempts "by seizing the opportunity and placing himself in danger . . . [to win] eternal renown and everlasting fame" (I.1.21). The new human god that creates new worlds through his literary Word ultimately seeks everlasting fame, a social position and a kind of eternal life that have little to do with a religious sense of the beyond or with the concrete gains of military conquest. Second, the new (anti)hero is born old from an unnatural, non-biological birth mediated by the antiquated literary genre of chivalry. Don Quixote has no biological parents, for his disjointed, Frankenstein-like identity is lifted from many dated books full of knights and evil enchanters (Dudley, ch. 3). And last, Cervantes' protagonist challenges social mores by adopting the honorific title Don, historically denied to hidalgos. In an absolutist regime built on strict class boundaries, Quijano breaks a time-honored rule in such a blatant way that throughout the book various characters comment upon his social recklessness (Miñana, *Monstruos que hablan* 145–56). In sum, Quijano's performance of Don Quixote frees the hidalgo from biological, social, and religious constraints in a most subversive way. He gives birth to a hybrid character who, with no biological parents, lives outside the strictures of birth-given rights. He seeks to enact the deeds of literary heroes in a grand theatrical performance lacking stage boundaries and intermissions. Exercising the God-like quality of discursive creation, Quijano turns Don Quixote into living proof that the world, should we be crazy enough to accept it, is a stage. In his creative submission to knight errantry, however, Don Quixote eradicates the Quijano self and thus sets the stage for his own defeat. The urge to undermine the social persona afforded by birthright forces Quijano to gravely subvert the social order. The more extreme the self-fashioning, as is the case here, the more certain the hero's demise.

The paradoxical nature of the hero/fool Don Quixote nonetheless facilitates a more positive reading of Quijano's revolutionary, potentially dangerous transformation. Arguably, his chivalric impersonation garners him not only the admiration of some of his fellow characters but also, most importantly, the devotion of generations of readers and cultural consumers across four centuries. The hidalgo's ultimate source of power emanates from his artistry and theatricality, for he is esteemed not for his meager and often misguided military impetus but for his courage to act (or perform) heroically. If the world is a stage, then artistic and performative skills are invaluable tools for social advancement, particularly for individuals in high-risk social situations who can benefit the most from a heightened awareness of theatrical tactics and their impact on their social standing. In Cervantes' works, many characters who turn themselves into deliberate actors, profoundly self-conscious of their art, start as hidalgos (*Don Quixote*), swindlers (among other examples, *Pedro de Urdemalas* or *Pedro, the Great Pretender*), or ruffians (*El rufián dichoso* or *The Fortunate Ruffian*) but aspire to climb the social ladder into knights errant, royal confidants, and even saints, respectively. In contemporary Brazil and in the larger context of Latin America, it is at-risk youth, former and current inmates, and other vulnerable populations who take on Quixote-inspired artistic and metatheatrical roles to improve their chances at a better life.

Despite the decades-long evolution of American *Don Quixote* appropriations into socially conscious readings, however, the likelihood for Quixote-inspired activism to unwillingly devolve into yet another Europeanizing intervention remains high. Is a European cultural powerhouse such as *Don Quixote* the best model for at-risk youth to get ahead in contemporary Brazil? As Coco Fusco warns, transcultural analysis must contend with "the power dynamics that shape specific intercultural relations at both the 'centers' and the 'margins' of global culture" (4–5). At the center of global culture, a canonical masterpiece once again enacts a protagonist role before a subaltern audience (São Paulo's at-risk youth in this case) populating the country's geographical, social, and cultural urban margins. Via a top-down approach, a culturally privileged population of mostly university-educated, well-traveled artists and activists with progressive leanings chose *Don Quixote* to symbolize the struggles of marginalized youth who have likely not read and may never read the book. The most classic of European texts travels to America to speak yet another colonizing language (Portuguese) in order to help Brazilian at-risk adolescents free themselves from oppression.

Despite these potential implications, Brazilian Quixote-inspired organizations do not feel particularly troubled by the threat of Eurocentrism in the daily running of their activist operations, which tackle arguably far more pressing issues at both individual and systemic levels. In the eyes of these nonprofits' leaders, they are simply appropriating a Western literary work of universal and timeless resonance in a singularly Brazilian way and doing so for a lofty and worthy goal, willfully brushing aside the potentially (neo)colonialist dynamics at play. Quixote-inspired organizations choose to regard Cervantes' character as a progressive icon to a large degree unencumbered by national borders, language, or historical context. Self-admittedly, Brazilian Quixote-themed projects aim to equip at-risk youth with tools (mostly artistic, as well as therapeutic and occupational) to free themselves from oppression. In mission statements, scripts, and performances, as well as from what I have been able to gather through personal communications with senior staff, these theater companies and NGOs all express the belief that *Don Quixote* puts forward a discursive, actionable notion of personal and social change. They harbor no doubts as to whether a European canonical work can serve Brazilian at-risk children and youth whose relationship to Cervantes might be described as negligible at best. After all, the chances that youth choose to read and interpret the novel on their own are slim. Given the potentially paradoxical nature of this work, the productive but ever-present tensions embedded in the act of selecting a Western literary icon to pursue greater social equality characterize the efforts of Quixote-inspired Brazilian activism.

This new phase in the transculturation of *Don Quixote*, from unexpected nation-building icon in the Americas to a progressive icon for personal and collective transformation, finds in Paulo Freire's *Pedagogy of the Oppressed* (1970) its ethical backbone, as well as abundant methodological possibilities. Paulo Freire, a most influential figure in Brazilian and international progressive circles, offers in his well-known work a rather reductionist theory of transculturation. While he rejects the idea of "cultural invasion" (the imposition of a superior foreign standard after which the "invaded" ought to model themselves), he favors a rather nebulous concept of cultural synthesis that offers "no imposed models." Such a process reconciles "the contradiction between the world view [sic] of the leaders and that of the people, to the enrichment of both" (162). In essence, cultural synthesis does not privilege any singular reading of a creation such as, to return to our case study, *Don Quixote*. Instead, readers and audiences ought to develop their own interpretation. If properly implemented, then, the synthesis of Cervantes' story attempted by Brazilian social justice activists ought to enrich audiences across class, gender, and racial divides outside of cultural imposition. What Freire fails to clarify, however, is how any cultural product, much less a literary character of Don Quixote's stature and history, can be appropriated in an ideological vacuum devoid of imposed models, and thus how a true synthesis can take place without some level of cultural invasion.

In Brazilian social justice appropriations of *Don Quixote*, no other tenet proved more influential than Freire's articulation of discourse as the primary weapon for liberation. Liberation or critical pedagogy, as Freire's theory is known, identifies the act of naming as the defining characteristic of humanity, and the stepping-stone toward radical change. "To exist, humanly, is to name the world, to change it," proclaimed Freire, for "the true word—which is work, which is praxis—is to transform the world" (69). Counter to the elite's self-given right to name the world, and thus define its power structures, the oppressed must produce, through critical reflection and action, a "true" language of liberation with the ultimate goal of uncovering and combating oppression. Freirean social justice activists in Brazil and around the world share the belief that fiction in general and theater in particular provide a safe space for revolutionary renaming. As names change, the theory goes, the very meaning of things and the hierarchies that rule social interactions also evolve. In a fictional environment, actors and writers can safely experiment with language. Thus, plays and fiction in general constitute a critical stage in which deep transformations are rehearsed and perfected through words before they are implemented on the social stage.[3]

Significantly for this analysis, the Freirean belief in the liberatory potential of naming and performance takes on an equally seminal role in Cervantes' *Don Quixote* and, subsequently, in its Brazilian adaptations. The book's opening chapter homes in on precisely the transformational power of (re)naming. Regardless of whether we explain the hidalgo Quijano's conversion into Don Quixote as an act of madness or self-conscious theatricality, or any combination of the two, the fact remains that Cervantes' protagonist transforms himself and the world around him through words. The first few pages of the book introduce a nameless hidalgo in a village that the narrator does "not care to remember" (I.1.19). In social and geographical isolation, the hidalgo reads so compulsively that one night he decides to insert himself into the fantastic world of chivalry. It will take him at least twelve days to rename himself, his horse, and his lady into chivalric characters (I.1.22–24). Although condensed into only a few paragraphs, this could well represent Don Quixote's hardest and longest-fought adventure in the entire book. With great effort, the hidalgo's linguistic performativity opens up a liberatory space where the forlorn villager can exercise agency. Saturated with literary references, the old hidalgo metamorphoses into an outlandish fictional entity, a hilarious palimpsest of texts and courtly heroes. Underneath layers of humor and parody, Don Quixote's very existence rests on Quijano's off-stage, revolutionary performance against the "real" (socially sanctioned) names of things and people. He attacks the existing order by renaming people, animals, and objects, thus fundamentally altering their individual and social identity. And as such, Don Quixote's enduring adventures inscribe themselves in the hidalgo's attempt to combat oppressive structures through naming, as Freire prescribes almost four hundred years later.

One of the book's most hilarious adventures best illustrates the revolutionary potential of naming. In chapter 21 of part I, Don Quixote attacks a barber because he confuses his basin with the famous helmet of Mambrino. In chapter 44 of part I, the same barber happens upon Sancho and Don Quixote at an inn and reclaims his basin. A chaotic scene ensues, in which the barber and Don Quixote argue over the name and, at a deeper level, the nature of the object (Spitzer). As someone who has one foot in Don Quixote's fantasy and another in reality, Sancho brilliantly captures the playfulness but also the violence of Don Quixote's extreme project. According to the quick-learning squire, the object has now become something else, the hybrid "basin-helmet" (I.44.390). This *baciyelmo* in the original Spanish, a made-up compound of *bacía* (basin) and *yelmo* (helmet), describes a new object whose hybridity can hardly contain the semantic as well as physical violence that erupts around it. Of course, the compromise does not satisfy anybody, and a physical altercation between Don Quixote and friends versus the barber and his allies quickly ensues. Bursting at the seams, Sancho's neologism underscores the very real dangers of re-naming that characterize the quixotic as well as the Freirean enterprises.

Re-naming people and things transforms society when the resulting entities (in our examples above, Don Quixote and the baciyelmo) are acted out both individually and collectively. Fixed entities then become malleable, unstable, as they acquire meaning only within the context of their performance. On this ideological and theatrical foundation, Augusto Boal, arguably Brazil's best-known stage director and theorist of the last half a century, adapts Freire's liberation principles into his *Theater of the Oppressed* (1973). In the American hemisphere, Freire as well as Boal insert themselves within social justice movements that deploy alternative forms of discursive activism to "unsettle dominant cultural meanings" (Álvarez, Dagnino, and Escobar 7). In the milieu of Latin American progressive theater specifically, as Diana Taylor explains, playwrights in general and Boal in particular aim to encourage their audiences to change societal roles, thus destabilizing identities as well as the collective imaginary ("Transculturating Transculturation" 101). The conflation of social justice movements and theater in Latin America around the rescripting and performance of social roles is remarkable, yet to a great extent logical. Because institutional and canonical forms of knowledge ordinarily enforce structures of oppression, the Freirean school of thought argues, challenges to top-down social systems must develop from non-formal, popular applications of educational and cultural practices (Williamson 210).

The late Augusto Boal dedicated the better part of his life's work to nurturing the connection between theater and social transformation through rescripting and performance. In Boal's formulation, which tacitly shares much with the hidalgo Quijano's radical proposal, theater functions as a "weapon for liberation" and social advancement that can unlock people's potential to free themselves from oppression (*Theater of the Oppressed* ix). According to Boal, true liberation rests on the premise that "s/he who transforms reality [through art] is transformed by the very action of transforming" ("Aesthetic Education"). In his view, theater affects social change most aptly when ordinary citizens replace the elites in the collective staging of economic and political injustices (*Theater of the Oppressed* 155). Boal's political and activist theater urges spectators to hone their skills in fictional plays as actors or "spect-actors" who can then improve their social performance. If the masses seize control of their performative roles first on and then offstage, Boal argues in his *Legislative Theater*, ordinary people will play a more active role in their own governance. From this point of view, Boal may well have, if unconsciously, theorized the essence of quixotism—or at least of quijanismo. At its core, Cervantes' book recounts the story of the hidalgo Quijano, who surrenders his passive role as a mere spectator/reader of chivalry to create and perform the role of the knight-errant Don Quixote. Bookended by the dull presence of Quijano in the first and last few pages, the two-volume story of Don Quixote personifies Boal's ideal of the spect-actor, a sort of theatrical vigilante who self-consciously employs performative tactics to alter the social status quo. We can only speculate, but the fact that the hidalgo/knight-errant incarnates Boal's most combative spect-actor, even four hundred years avant la lettre, helps explain the rich repertoire of *Don Quixote* adaptations in contemporary Brazilian social justice theater.

Classics are no strangers to Brazilian community and liberatory theater. In fact, Augusto Boal himself staged classic plays (including early-modern Spanish *comedias*) throughout his career, although his approach was as deliberate as controversial. In response to prevalent bourgeois interpretations of canonical works, Boal insists that the ideological message of classic theater be rendered unequivocally "progressive" and tailored to a working-class audience (*Técnicas latinoamericanas* 30). In a clear example of the politically charged nature of his adaptations, Boal staged Lope de Vega's *El mejor alcalde, el Rey*, or *The Best Mayor, the King* (1620–1623), "as if [it] had no theatrical or national tradition behind [it]" (*Theater of the Oppressed* 164). Instead, his adaptation interwove Lope's text with contemporary Brazilian struggles over land ownership and labor conditions in rural areas. So effective was his strategy that in post-performance conversations some audience members identified Lope's characters with the names of fellow real-life landowners and peasants (*Legislative Theater* 218).[4]

Within the broad theoretical framework of liberation pedagogy and theater as a tool to achieve greater social justice, the Brazilian adaptations of *Don Quixote* each develop in distinct and highly sophisticated ways. Despite some commonalities with Boal's approach, none of the four Brazilian plays adheres exclusively to any one model or school.[5] Instead, they all draw from the rich, eclectic tradition of Brazilian community and liberatory theater. Outside the regular channels of for-profit, theatrical production and consumption, plays produced for and/or by vulnerable communities constitute an ideal platform for social justice activism (Marín 218). They flex their activist muscles by transforming a literary classic written at the peak of Spain's imperial rule into a weapon for social change in the contemporary Brazilian context. In contrast to standard popular theater, which in Steven E. Noble's narrow definition depicts only "immediate, concrete, lived realities" performed and created by and for "the people" (47), these Quixote-inspired plays further their social justice mission by adapting a literary classic. Resisting the likely futile attempt to fix the meaning of as complex a book as *Don Quixote*, the four Brazilian companies I discuss here challenge their audiences to discover the meaning of Cervantes' story for themselves. By directly engaging spectators through post-show dialogues or at unannounced street performances, these adaptations urge audiences to freely produce their own meaning, a principle of popular education and popular theater in the purest Freirean tradition (Noble 49). Rather than feeding a progressive interpretation of the classics to an allegedly passive audience, as Boal favored (*Legislative Theater* 220), these plays foster an open-ended approach to *Don Quixote* that endows spectators with the characteristically elitist prerogative to interpret the cultural canon. In fact, Cervantes himself asked nothing less of his reader in the prologue to part I: "you have a soul in your body and a will as free as anyone's . . . [so] you can say anything you desire about this history" (3–4). Dedicated to the meticulous deconstruction of authority, Cervantes' book as a whole replaces, as Robert Bayliss has pointed out, "a clear, stable and ethically consistent narrative voice [with] a dizzying narrative hall of mirrors" (389; see also Gerli). Through multi-layered, often contradictory sources, Cervantes' narrative undermines the very source of unquestionable, divine authority that sustains absolutist societies. Instead, he offers an explicit call for readers to think freely, to consume and produce meaning independently. Exposing the inherent contradiction in Boal's limiting approach to the classics, *Don Quixote* and its Brazilian adaptations encourage every reader and spectator to experience for themselves the liberating effects of free interpretation.

This general call for freely rescripting and re-enacting individual and collective roles anchors itself, nonetheless, in clearly defined social and artistic parameters. Certainly, liberation does not happen in a vacuum, and neither does the appropriation of a classic for community activism. How do these companies, then, articulate a social message relevant to twenty-first-century Brazilian audiences around a four-hundred-year-old classic written in Spanish? As their creators explained to me, the Brazilian stage adaptations of *Don Quixote* discussed here amplify theater's potential for social betterment by focusing on two conspicuous themes that equally concern other appropriations of Cervantes across the Americas, as discussed in the previous chapter: marginality and metatheater. In these metatheatrical plays, underprivileged characters take center stage in order to expose the fictional, conventional nature of societal roles. Through dramatic strategies such as a play within a play, breaking the fourth wall between actors and spectators, and onstage references to the theatrical nature of the world, metatheater destabilizes both the practice of theater and the rigidity of social categories (Abel). Through these self-reflexive tactics, metatheater reveals how theater can impact social relations, a notion that sociologist Erving Goffman popularized in his 1956 book *The Presentation of Self in Everyday Life*. Key to the construction and delivery of one's public persona, performance produces social roles through "the enactment of rights and duties attached to a given status" (16). In their theory of the oppressed, Freire and Boal submit that when the excluded becomes aware and masters the performance of social relations, roles assigned to the oppressed by the oppressors may be modified. If the renaming and re-enacting of individual and social identities can ignite the liberation of the oppressed, then artivist projects such as the Quixote-inspired statues of Cooperaacs or its youth-oriented stage adaptations require a constant revision of their discursive and linguistic strategies. The language of liberation thus emerges as a discourse that continuously reflects upon itself, for it can only be effective when its practitioners remain conscious of its power to subjugate as well as emancipate. Returning to the example that concerns us here, liberation occurs for Alonso Quijano when he takes up literary and performative arms to rename himself and the world around him. From the margins of society, under the mantle of madness, the avid reader Quijano deploys his literary and theatrical mastery in order to perform a new role for himself and others. Inscribed within the text itself, this powerful mix of marginality and metatheater unlocks the activist potential of *Don Quixote* in Brazilian social justice-oriented adaptations.[6]

In São Paulo alone, numerous stage adaptations and Quixote-based initiatives materialize on a regular basis and with no apparent coordination among them. Over the last five years or so, examples include a yearlong reading and discussion of a children's version of *Don Quixote* at the Miguel de Cervantes school; a Portuguese-language revival of *Man of La Mancha*, directed by Miguel Falabella, of unprecedented success; a *Don Quixote* presentation for the 2016 carnival by the Imperador do Ipiranga samba school, located in one of the most underserved sections of the city; and exhibits, performances, and concerts of various sorts. However, here I do not intend to produce an exhaustive catalog of all Quixote-related activities taking place in São Paulo, or much less in the whole of Brazil. Rather, I choose organizations that over a long period of time have deployed a sophisticated and original reading of Cervantes' text for large audiences. Out of the eight projects I focus on in this and the next chapter (four plays and four nonprofits), I pay particular attention to whether these initiatives all share a distinctly socially conscious interpretation of *Don Quixote*. An in-depth overview of eight activist appropriations of Cervantes' masterpiece in fact provides meaningful insights into a uniquely Brazilian way of reading and practicing *Don Quixote*.

Although the Salvador de Bahia as well as the São Paulo stage versions featured marginal characters drawn from the Brazilian contemporary moment, these plays proved anything but marginal in their ability to locate themselves centrally in their respective theatrical and activist scenes. Undoubtedly, positioning these theatrical enterprises in the cultural landscape of their respective cities can help us gauge their actual ability to implement an artistic and activist agenda. Let us briefly discuss each case in chronological order. Márcio Meirelles' *Um tal de Dom Quixote* was written specifically to celebrate the re-opening of the legendary Vila Velha theater in downtown Salvador. A cultural center with a distinguished history of activism against the Brazilian dictatorship (1964–1985), the renovated Vila Velha features a permanent tile mosaic of Don Quixote and Sancho just outside its main entrance. Because of its physical space (the Don Quixote mosaic) and the Cervantes-inspired play commissioned for its re-inauguration, Bahia's best-known theater will permanently remain associated with *Don Quixote*. Moreover, two of Brazil's most celebrated actors, the late Carlos Petrovich and the award-winning Lázaro Ramos, played the leading roles. Despite its central position in Salvador's theatrical scene, Márcio Meirelles and Cleise Mendes' *Um tal de Dom Quixote* had a somewhat shorter run than its São Paulo counterparts, likely because of its specific purpose to mark the opening of the remodeled Vila Velha. It premiered on April 8, 1998, and the building was officially inaugurated on May 5. After a very successful run, the play closed in August but was revived again in 2014 for a transnational project involving three Portuguese-speaking countries: Brazil, Portugal, and Cabo Verde. Representing Brazil, Meirelles took his *Don Quixote* project to host-country Cabo Verde, where a group of young Cape-Verdians under his direction collectively wrote and staged *Em defesa das causas perdidas—Uma carta para Dom Quixote* (*In Defense of Lost Causes: A Letter for Don Quixote*), which I briefly discuss in the conclusion to this book.

Within São Paulo's extraordinarily vibrant cultural scene, the three local adaptations of *Don Quixote* I discuss here enjoyed large audiences and a long performance schedule. As part of a pilot project with interns at the Fundação Estadual para o Bem-Estar do Menor (State Foundation For The Well-Being of Minors) or FEBEM, São Paulo's infamous juvenile penitentiary,[7] Valéria di Pietro adapted and staged Mário García-Guillén's *Num lugar de la Mancha* (*Somewhere in La Mancha*, 1995) between 2000 and 2006. As she shared with me in personal conversations, di Pietro's original intention was to stage the Brazilian version of Dale Wasserman's *Man of La Mancha* (1965), premiered in São Paulo with extraordinary success in the 1972–1973 season. Unable to afford the high copyright permission fees for the famous musical, di Pietro then opted to adapt García-Guillén's text herself. Several dozen performances took place both on prison grounds and throughout the city. Staged in the street on a handful of occasions, as well as in sites as prestigious as Oscar Niemeyer's Memorial da América Latina (three performances), Centro Cultural São Paulo (three), Teatro São Pedro (one), Tuca Arena (two), and the Miguel de Cervantes school (one), *Num Lugar* reached a total audience of between five and six thousand people, in the director's calculation. In 2002, di Pietro also founded the Instituto Religare in the Barra Funda district of São Paulo, which formalized and expanded her groundbreaking work with FEBEM interns and at-risk youth through performance- and art-based reentry programs. Dedicated to theatrical training and art production, on its homepage and brochures the Instituto vows to employ art and culture to help youth in high-risk social situations "pensar melhor sobre o mundo que o cerca" (better reflect on the world that surrounds them). Telma Dias and Robson Vellado's Grupo Permanente de Pesquisa has offered nearly a hundred performances of Dias' *Dom Quixote* in numerous schools and theaters around the city, including the Ewa Vilma, Ruth Escobar, and Paulo Eiró theaters, as well as their own Teatro Resurreição in the popular *bairro* (district) Jabacquara. In a June 2010 e-mail, Telma Dias told me *com certeza* (for sure) that the show has been seen by more than ten thousand people between its premiere in October 2005 and the end of 2007. Lastly, Andreia de Almeida and Luciano Draetta's Circo Navegador has since 2005 presented de Almeida's *Quixotes* in a variety of venues (streets, public squares, schools, and theaters) throughout the city of São Paulo and in other parts of the state. With a street-theater feel and minimalist staging, as of October 2011, *Quixotes* had reached approximately 10,200 spectators through its over ninety performances in open spaces and theaters. As the centerpiece of Andréia de Almeida's Quixote-inspired initiatives, in 2010 *Quixotes* received a federal grant to be performed weekly between January and March 2011 at the legendary Teatro de Arena in São Paulo, where Augusto Boal first experimented with his theater of the oppressed. *Quixotes* continues to be performed occasionally; I myself attended a live performance in July 2015.

The kind of change endorsed by such activist appropriations of *Don Quixote* remains as deeply personal as it is firmly anchored in the local. Frequently, performances take place in underserved neighborhoods and involve vulnerable communities through a variety of strategies, as I document throughout this book. Although different in style, casting choices, and target audiences, the four plays (the first one in Bahia and the three in São Paulo) adopt in this regard a strikingly similar approach to their adaptation of *Don Quixote*. In personal exchanges I had in preparation for this book between 2009 and 2017 with Márcio Meirelles, Valéria di Pietro, Andreia de Almeida, and Telma Dias, they all underscored their explicit commitment to adapting the book as comprehensively as they possibly could within their technical and financial means. In the process of staging *Don Quixote*, they all studied it closely, conducted extensive research, and weighed many different episodes and characters as potential stage material. Besides some of the book's most recognizable adventures, such as the wonderfully theatrical charge against the windmills, these plays also explore a variety of relatively lesser-known episodes, as discussed in detail below. However, the deference that these versions show toward the original text did not preclude them from speaking directly to the socio-cultural realities of contemporary Brazil and, more specifically, to the challenges faced by at-risk children and youth and other marginalized populations, including Afro-Brazilians and women. These adaptations of *Don Quixote* all rest on a pointed socio-political call to fight social injustice through the rewriting in the Brazilian imaginary of the role of the excluded. Imbued with a community-oriented sense of purpose, these plays celebrate the universality of Cervantes' icon by highlighting its applicability to the local context. The script, production, and casting choices reflect concerted efforts to adapt Cervantes' fictional world to a local audience. All four plays add musical interludes based on Brazilian rhythms and dances (ciranda, xote, capoeira, and maculelê, among others) and feature issues that disproportionally affect the disadvantaged, such as homelessness, police brutality, and the need for *mudança*, or change. Consequently, the authors liberally rework and relocate various scenes and characters into highly localized and often marginalized contexts. To give but one example, the scene in which Don Quixote "frees" young Andrés from his master Juan de Haldudo in I.4 appears in most social justice-oriented stage adaptations as a commentary on police violence against street-connected children.

In previous paragraphs I established the theoretical framework for my analysis (liberation pedagogy and social justice theater) and introduced the four works I analyze here. Before I reconstruct their adaptation of *Don Quixote* in the next chapter, I want to conclude this one by probing in depth the ways in which metatheater and marginality interact in order to turn not just Cervantes' classic but also theater in general into powerful weapons for liberation. Out of the four plays in question, two situate themselves in spaces of particularly acute marginality: Márcio Meirelles' *Um tal de Dom Quixote* celebrates the re-opening of a theater in a highly marginalized neighborhood in Salvador de Bahia, and Valéria di Pietro's *Num lugar de la Mancha* originates at the FEBEM and casts its interns on stage. While *Num lugar* illustrates how theater can transform underprivileged youth, *Um tal de Dom Quixote* exposes how activism can transform theater by situating marginality at the very core of its practice. Beyond the mere inclusion of storylines about the excluded, these theatrical projects feature disadvantaged actors and/or perform for underserved audiences (the other two plays, Dias' *Don Quixote* and de Almeida's *Quixotes*, cast professional actors and are performed on various stages and for diverse audiences). By contending not only with stories of marginality but also with the lived experience of marginality, these two plays truly take *Don Quixote* into the streets of Brazil. In this process, furthermore, theater self-consciously reflects on its potential (and its limits) to change society for the better.

Di Pietro's FEBEM project most pointedly illustrates the potential of performance to transform the lives of marginalized youth, particularly of those who performed in the play. In a 2007 blog entry, Peterson Xavier, the intern who played the protagonist role in *Num lugar de la Mancha*, explains how he escaped life imprisonment or sure death as a young career criminal by becoming a self-described *Dom Quixote das ruas*, or Don Quixote of the streets (Xavier, "Dom Quixote das ruas"). He first came in contact with Cervantes' character between January and November 2000 as an intern at the FEBEM. Despite Xavier's initially unruly behavior, Valéria di Pietro cast him in the title role. In "Viver para representar!" (Living to perform!), Xavier explains that he overcame his reticence to commit to this project because "eu via no Dom Quixote muito dos meninos da Febem" (I saw much of the FEBEM kids in Don Quixote; 69). Marginalized, ignored by society, FEBEM interns were eager to embrace Don Quixote's creative mission to rewrite his role in society through words and performance. Intrigued by the prospect of transformation, Xavier accepted di Pietro's invitation to perform the leading role.

With a crew of some 150 *FEBEM* interns, *Num Lugar de la Mancha* premiered on October 11, 2000, at Oscar Niemeyer's Memorial da América Latina, a colossal cultural complex inaugurated in 1989 in São Paulo. The performance posed a number of challenges at a variety of levels, not only artistically but also in terms of security. With dozens of interns freely moving about the stage and hundreds of relatives and friends in the nearly full sixteen-hundred-seat Simón Bolívar Auditorium, security forces were as on edge as the performers themselves. A police helicopter hovered over the venue as numerous vehicles and agents secured the building's perimeter. Both a security threat and an amateur acting crew, FEBEM interns performed superimposing and rather diverging roles even before they took the stage.

Unfazed by the logistical and artistic challenges, Valéria di Pietro appropriated *Don Quixote*, a towering work of Western literature, for the most marginalized of social stages, a youth prison, and presented it on the most monumental of theatrical stages, the Memorial da América Latina. At a variety of levels, di Pietro's project illuminates the nuanced and somewhat contradictory role that Western classic literature may play in social justice activism. On the one hand, the adaptation of a four-centuries-old Spanish masterpiece into the Portuguese language and a contemporary Brazilian context updates Cervantes' text for twenty-first-century consumption. Performed by an amateur acting crew, *Num lugar* targets a broad audience unburdened by prohibitive ticket prices and traditional theater etiquette. Furthermore, Valéria di Pietro infuses a classic such as *Don Quixote* with a sense of social justice urgency. Imprisoned youth stage Cervantes' masterpiece as both a redeeming act of contrition for past crimes and an affirmation of their worth as cultural producers. On the other hand, however, it could be argued that di Pietro's egalitarian message rests on a canonical work published at the peak of the Spanish imperial enterprise. Potentially alienating *Don Quixote*'s elite readership for its activist slant, di Pietro's version could equally disaffect a progressive audience by employing a Western cultural powerhouse to address Brazilian social and economic inequities.

The premiere was a resounding success. In a rare turn of events, not only relatives and friends, but also audience members and even security officers enthusiastically praised the young amateur crew for their intellectual and artistic abilities. Amid thunderous applause, the dramatic value of the play and the cast's personal qualities fused into one emotional spectacle. As Neil Cameron observes with regards to his production of *The Elephant Man* with at-risk youth in Melbourne, "the reality of the actors' situation [became] the emotional power of the piece" (131). Similarly, di Pietro's project conflated with the stories of those performing it, for the hidalgo Quijano's efforts to become more socially visible paralleled the cast's struggle to transcend their criminalized personae. After the performance, Xavier's initial hunch proved right: Many of the FEBEM interns had indeed become Don Quixote. Despite the heavy security detail, the acting crew quickly dispersed and mingled with the audience, receiving *parabéns* (congratulations) from family, friends, and agents alike. Through the power of *Don Quixote*'s story, the young actors were endowed that evening with a renewed sense of pride and dignity. For once, their (on-stage) performance was appreciated rather than repudiated. They were closely watched in admiration rather than with fear or aversion. For project participants, as in Diane Conrad's experiences with incarcerated youth in Alberta, Canada, acting helped awake "the potential for making positive change in our lives and [contributing] to a greater social transformation" (Conrad 139). By performing Cervantes' self-transforming characters, the actors experienced self-transformation themselves. At least for one evening, the location and appeal of their public persona shifted in the eyes of both the general audience and the security officers, dramatically altering the rigid societal structure of prison. That evening the fourth wall between the stage and the audience, which in this particular setting separated interns from both freedom and recognition, was shattered in true Brechtian style, if at least temporarily, by the power of Don Quixote's story.

Performing Cervantes' hero indeed transformed Peterson Xavier forever. In November 2000, the day after his release on parole, Xavier recalls everyone's surprise when he returned to the FEBEM to continue peforming Don Quixote. "Ninguém entendia por que eu voltava para aquele lugar" (Nobody understood why I would go back to that place), he confesses ("Viver" 69). Initially, di Pietro procured him a temporary position at the FEBEM as her assistant, and over time Xavier became a professional actor and community activist who remained committed to working with at-risk youth at the Instituto Religare in the Barra Funda district of São Paulo and beyond (70). The father of two, Xavier undertook a journey of self-transformation that turned him into a new, hybrid being, as he explains in his personal blog. Renouncing all forms of violence, he embraced the power of education and theater to such extent that he renamed himself the Don Quixote of the streets: "eu o dom Quixote das ruas . . . eu o dom Quixote educador com espada e escudo derrotando gigantes, eu Peterson Xavier Quixote de la Mancha" (I, the Don Quixote of the streets . . . I, Don Quixote the educator with a sword and a shield defeating giants, I, Peterson Xavier Quixote of La Mancha; "Dom Quixote das ruas"). This self-appointed Don Quixote of the streets took up theatrical arms to educate his audience and defeat social evils through acting. For him, change is imperative and can be achieved through a Quixote-inspired, performance-based process of transformation.

In a commentary on Xavier's experience, Brazilian rapper, author, and activist MV Bill explains the perverse process by which social invisibility fuels the dehumanization of at-risk children, which in turn results in further marginalization and even crime. As a *Dom Quixote do cotidiano* (Don Quixote of the everyday), in contrast, Xavier deploys theater and art to reverse this cycle of invisibility. By literally providing a stage for at-risk youth to be seen, understood, and appreciated, theatrical performance enables the rescripting of individual and collective narratives. Through art, Peterson Xavier transformed his marginalized role from criminal to activist, from subaltern character in sordid stories to protagonist of an educational mission that extends its reach with each new play and each new workshop. As MV Bill recognizes, "Não existe a mudança coletiva . . . se ela não começar no homem" (There can't be collective change . . . if it doesn't begin with each individual; 72). Peterson Xavier had to change himself in order to incite others to also reimagine a different future. This deep transformation first took place for Xavier on stage, for playing Don Quixote made him feel that, despite his internment, "eu era livre" (I was free; "Dom Quixote das ruas"). In 2007, already as a professional actor and community activist, he premiered a piece titled *Mutatis* (Latin for *change*) that follows the story of a group of youth from the "tempos sombrios," or "dark times," of their imprisonment to the "tempos da transformação a partir da arte," or "times of transformation through art." In this not-too-veiled autobiographical and allegorical play, which combines Greek tragedy-like features with rap and spoken word, the actors on stage free themselves from oppression and strive for a better society through music, art, and theater-based activism.

As the Brazilian adaptations seek to inspire youth in high-risk social situations to transform themselves through art and theater, these plays turn their plots into a profoundly self-reflective study on the very act of performing. In this regard, the story of *Don Quixote* becomes the perfect vessel for a far-reaching metacriticism of the revolutionary potential and the very real limitations of performance as a tool for liberation. Bahian playwright and director Márcio Meirelles' *Um tal de Dom Quixote* project offers a particularly complex example of the transculturation of Cervantes' universal icon into a character of local resonance that fuses marginality and metatheater as an effective recipe for social advancement. In 1990 Meirelles and Chica Carelli, two non-Afro-Brazilian directors, co-founded the internationally recognized Afro-Brazilian theater company Bando de Teatro Olodum.[8] Since its inception, Meirelles and Carelli's company has staged both original plays and adaptations of classics with a keen focus on racial relations and inequality. Written by Meirelles and Cleise Mendes, *Um tal de Dom Quixote* premiered in 1998 to mark the grand re-opening of Salvador's Teatro Vila Velha (Old Town Theater) in the then-deteriorated and predominantly Afro-Brazilian downtown Maciel-Pelourinho district. Originally established in 1969 to house the Companhia Teatro dos Novos, Salvador's first professional acting company, the Teatro Vila Velha currently serves as permanent home for the Bando, the Companhia dos Novos, and three other companies.

According to journalist Marcos Uzel, the company had to contend with racial prejudice from its founding. The third largest city in Brazil, according to the official 2010 census, Salvador de Bahia could be said to be the unofficial cultural capital of the Northeast, which boasts the largest population of Afro-Brazilians in the country. Roughly half of Salvador's population self-identified in the census as *pardo* (multiracial), 28 percent as black, and 19 percent as white. Boasting a vibrant musical and artistic scene, the city also suffered the highest murder rate in the country as recently as 2014; violence and poverty remain a significant challenge to this day. The company grew out of a workshop directed by Meirelles that aimed to engage local children and youth in theater and the arts. But when this activist project developed into a professional troupe, misperceptions about its composition and even its repertoire abounded. In some national press outlets, the Bando's Afro-Brazilian actors were portrayed as "prostitutes and street children" rescued by the middle-class, educated Meirelles for the stage. As Lázaro Ramos, one of Brazil's best-known actors denounces, the Bando was initially hailed for giving Afro-Brazilians the opportunity to share their alleged personal stories on stage. In reality, however, the company performed both original and adapted plays that often had little, if any, autobiographical content (Uzel 219). Thanks to the breadth of their repertoire, Bando actors played a wide variety of roles beyond the ones traditionally assigned to black performers at the time. Whether staging original plays or adaptations of works by foreign authors, from Cervantes to Bertold Brecht and William Shakespeare, the group nonetheless built their theatrical proposals around issues that felt relevant at the community level. Through sophisticated performances that underlined their self-conscious and socially engaged theatrical competence, Bando performers contested mainstream perceptions of an all-black cast's marginality while combating exclusion at the street level in the Maciel-Peulorinho district that houses the company.

Significantly, the play chosen to inaugurate the remodeled Vila Velha was an adaptation of *Don Quixote* performed jointly by the Bando (Lázaro Ramos played Sancho) and Companhia dos Novos (then-seventy-year-old Carlos Petrovich took on the main role).[9] As Meirelles explained in a personal interview, they chose *Don Quixote* to celebrate a Bahian cultural milestone such as the Vila Velha because Afro-Brazilians, much like the hidalgo Quijano, strive to gain visibility in a society that deprives them of a protagonist role. Both the Bando and the knight-errant employ theatricality to create a grand spectacle at the center of which they can no longer be ignored. As proof of the company's commitment to their activist reading of *Don Quixote*, their metatheatrical efforts to combat marginalization were inscribed in the building itself. From an architectural point of view, the Vila Velha physically welcomes its patrons with *Don Quixote* imagery at the street level in an area of the city that at the time showed evident signs of decay. Spectators reach the Vila Velha's underground entrance through a curved ramp whose sidewall features a mosaic of Don Quixote, with Sancho at his side, charging at a monstrous dragon with windmill sails at the end of its tail. Fashioned of white tiles set into the cement wall, the knight's figure on horseback permanently greets theatergoers to the renovated performance hall. This mosaic takes the *Don Quixote* adaptation that marked the Vila Velha's reopening quite literally off stage and into the street. Furthermore, the inside of the building features a physical structure that facilitates the mingling of actors and audience, with an open stage surrounded by balconies that can accommodate both spectators and actors. In fact, almost all of the theater's indoor spaces can be used as performance and/or seating areas. At the Vila Velha the stage merges with the house and spills into the outdoors to create a unifying space of Quixote-themed theatrical and worldly performance. Since 1998, the Maciel-Pelourinho neighborhood boasts a remodeled center of theatrical activism at whose main entrance Don Quixote charges on.

In an explicit effort to break down barriers across genres as well as social strata, Meirelles' *Um tal de Dom Quixote* situates Cervantes' text within both the Western and Afro-Brazilian traditions. A Greek tragedy-like female chorus voices politically charged arguments and moves the plot forward, while allegorical characters such as Death appear in key scenes. Combining classical elements with local cultural practices, secondary characters, dancers, and at times Sancho Panza sing and dance samba and xote (a traditional Northeastern dance influenced by European polka), among other Brazilian musical rhythms. Significantly, in most of his adventures Don Quixote confronts the economic, political, and racial inequities familiar to contemporary Brazilian audiences. *Um tal de Dom Quixote* remains to the best of my knowledge the first stage adaptation to specifically include at-risk youth and street children in its plot. In one of his first adventures (chapter 4 in the original text), Don Quixote encounters farmer Juan Haldudo whipping his young servant Andrés for lack of diligence in guarding his sheep. The knight-errant forces Haldudo to release Andrés and pay him back wages, but he leaves the scene on the peasant's word that he will later compensate the servant. As soon as Don Quixote rides on, of course, Juan Haldudo ties Andrés up again and whips him even more cruelly (I.4.36–38). Meirelles and Mendes' version situates this episode in the context of Brazil's military dictatorship (1964–1985). A character from another of Olodum's plays, Soldado Leão (soldier Leão)

FIGURE 3.1. Don Quixote, a Soldier, and a Child (*Um tal de Dom Quixote*)

beats a *menino* (a child) merely on the suspicion that he has been caught "wanting" or "attempting" to steal something ("querendo roubar"; 8–9). Once again, marginality (a street child) and a metatheatrical reference (the Soldado Leão borrowed from another Olodum play) fuse into a powerful denunciation of military abuses against the most vulnerable population —a *menino* in this case. Needless to say, Don Quixote's intervention here achieves the same meager results as in the original; he exits the scene upon the soldier's promise to free the child, who later suffers the consequences at the hands of his abuser.

The play's characters inhabit a contemporary Brazil plagued by inequities and immersed in a struggle to achieve fairer conditions for all. Dressed in overalls reminiscent of a blue-collar worker, Don Quixote encounters situations and individuals that embody some of the country's most entrenched current social conflicts. Don Quixote's unfortunate encounter with the Yanguesans and their mares (I, 15) becomes in Meirelles' version a protest by the *trabalhadores sem terra*, or landless workers (I, 7), Brazil's dispossessed farmers who demand fair access to land ownership. The examination of Quixano's library and burning of his books (I, 6) references the 1968 student uprising against the military government, which culminated on June 28 with the One Hundred Thousand March in Rio de Janeiro after the killings of several students and the arrest of hundreds more during the previous weeks (*Um tal de Dom Quixote* I, 9). Lastly, the galley slaves that Don Quixote frees (I, 22), all of them guilty of some crime, end up viciously attacking their liberator in the original. In Meirelles' project, the prisoners freed by Don Quixote prove truly innocent citizens caught in unfortunate circumstances for which they became mere scapegoats (II, 7). Their freedom here is well justified, and thus Don Quixote emerges as a deliverer of justice who stands against the corruption that plagues the Brazilian judicial system.

As with Soldado Leão's inclusion in the Andrés episode, however, the most elaborate condemnations of local injustices rest on one form or another of metatheatrical intervention. The transculturation of Cervantes into theatrical activism does not only relocate Spain's seventeenth-century social landscape into contemporary Brazil; it also distils *Don Quixote*'s self-conscious, metaliterary foundation into a powerful mix of marginality and the potential of performance to combat inequality. One particularly relevant example will for now suffice to illustrate this point. In Cervantes' original, beautiful and wealthy orphan Marcela chooses to live a pastoral existence without the company of men. With Don Quixote's support, she rejects the accusation that her "disdainful" attitude caused the death of one of her suitors, Grisóstomo. In the 1605 text, however, her apology of a woman's right to pursue the lifestyle of her choice cautiously remains within the patriarchal parameters of the time. While she manages to stave off marriage, she promises to live virtuously in the woods (I.14.98–100). In *Um tal de Dom Quixote*, Meirelles stresses both Marcela's feminist qualities as well as the crude nature of patriarchy. The free-spirited peasant is played by not one but nine women who refute the viciously misogynous comments made by several of the ten male actors who participate in the scene. According to various men, "Mulher é só para abrir a perna" and "é um ser desprovido de intelecto [e] não passam de uma vagina" ("women are good only to open their legs," and "they lack intellect [and] are nothing but a vagina"). The brutality of such statements intensifies the contrast between the men's beastly disposition and the uncompromising defense of women's dignity articulated by the nine Marcelas. While Cervantes sets the scene in a pastoral background populated by shepherds fully competent in highbrow conversation, here the language employed reproduces late twentieth-century commonplaces of the most abusive and vulgar sexist character. By having nine actresses from diverse racial backgrounds play Marcela, the play offers a polyphonic pushback against a misogynous society that regards women of all races as brainless objects of male desire.

This representation of a collective feminist voice fighting off multiple sexist insults dramatically exposes the scene's (meta)theatrical nature. One character, Marcela, fragments herself into nine actresses, as her voice leaps from one end of the stage to the other and bounces from one body to another. The trick turns a feminist statement into a simultaneously feminist and theatrical proposal. Before the spectators' eyes, the theatrical illusion of an actor's embodiment of her character is shattered. The conflation between character and actor simply cannot occur as we, the audience, witness a collective response (the nine Marcela actresses) to gender discrimination and violence against women. This scene underscores that the fight for social equality demands a brave, shared, and public performance of dissent, and that such action requires self-awareness, rehearsal, and intentionality. In a dazzling parallel with the story of the hidalgo who transforms himself into knight-errant, the proliferation of Marcelas echoes the need for a performative solution to societal challenges. In this scene, collective performance combats the objectification of women by finding alternative sources of authority (the nine Marcelas) and altering the vocabulary of gender. Marginalization can thus be alleviated through performance, for theater can serve as a weapon for liberation.

Meirelles' theatrical project pays explicit attention to the dimensions of class, gender, and race typically absent from the traditional Romantic approach to *Don Quixote*, which mainly celebrates the protagonist's essentialized idealism. While maintaining a certain aura of heroism, Meirelles' Don Quixote is humanized by his personal circumstances. Played by then-seventy-year-old Carlos Petrovich, Don Quixote appears rather fragile and disoriented throughout the play. His on-stage peers see him not merely as a hero or a fool, however, but as an individual inscribed within a clearly defined social paradigm. In scene 12, the housekeeper Siomara criticizes "Seu Quixana" (*señor* Quixana) for taking all his money with him, leaving his employees in economic despair without "crédito na venda" (credit at the store; 12). The play's racial, class, and gender politics inform Don Quixote's depiction as a "bom macho branco adulto cristão intelectual" (good white adult Christian-educated *macho*) who, in order to pursue his lofty goals, needs "mulheres cuidando da casa, e de um negro para lhe carregar as bagagens" (female homemakers and a black man carrying his luggage;

FIGURE 3.2. Don Quixote and Sancho (*Um tal de Dom Quixote*).

I.10.11). Meirelles' adaptation squarely locates Don Quixote within a privileged social space with all the attributes of the oppressor, not the liberator. His racial, gender, class, and religious identities (he is white, male, educated, middle-class, and Christian) enable him to aim for a higher purpose only because women and blacks tend to his everyday needs. Casting *Bando*'s Lázaro Ramos as Sancho Panza no doubt adds a racial dimension to the plot, for the contrast between the knight's whiteness and Ramos' blackness visually mirrors the multi-layered inequality upon which their relationship rests. While Don Quixote encounters typically Brazilian problems (the sem terra, street kids, the twenty years of dictatorship), he fights injustice from a highly localized social site, one that is itself fundamentally plagued with inequalities. The white, adult, Christian, educated, and heterosexual justice fighter leaves three servants behind (there is only one housekeeper and a niece in the original) to take care of his house, and a black Sancho carries his belongings.

A sophisticated, intersectional discussion of race, informed by concurrent issues of class, colonialism, and gender, underlies many scenes in *Um tal de Dom Quixote*. Influential white male characters in Cervantes' book play a diminished and often negative role in this play. Notably, the priest, the barber, and Sansón Carrasco, who involve themselves heavily in Don Quixote's adventures and orchestrate his utter defeat, are stripped of any positive qualities. Unlike in Cervantes' original, these characters cite financial gain as the underlying motive for intervening in their neighbor's escapades. When one of the housekeepers, Adélia, pleads for her master's return home, Sansão (Sansón Carrasco in the original) agrees to help her, but only if properly compensated. The young aspiring poet alleges that the suddenly famous Don Quixote who constantly appears "no jornal, na televisão . . . deve estar ganhando muita grana" (in the newspapers, on television . . . must be making a lot of dough; II.2.16). If he is to risk his life to return the hidalgo home, Sansão demands a share of the knight's proceeds from his recently acquired celebrity status. As one of the female narrators in the Greek chorus explains directly to the audience, in yet another metaliterary nod, Cervantes' novel portrays the priest and barber as genuinely concerned for Quixano's well-being. However, the narrator continues, in today's "império do lucro global . . . neoliberal" (global, neoliberal for-profit empire), such characters can no longer be rendered sufficiently believable. Instead, the priest and the barber are driven by the same "pequena e suja ganância nossa de cada dia" (everyday petty and dirty greed of ours; I.12.13). Toward the end of the play, they conspire with Sansão to have Quixana

(Quijano in the original) transfer his lands to church ownership for their personal benefit. After all, the priest asks his fellow villagers, why keep so much land in the hands of a madman? (II.10.25). When Quixana ultimately bequeaths everything to his three housekeepers and Sancho Panza, the priest, the barber, and Sansão simply "saem furiosos" (exit in rage; II.15.29). Their hurried stage exit confirms that mere financial gain motivated their actions. Having lost their chance at profiting off the hidalgo, they simply abandon their dying neighbor, while in the original they duly congregate at his deathbed (II.74.935–38).

In stark contrast, fusing once again marginality and metatheater, female and black characters stand out for their positive portrayal in new or oversized roles, often endowed with great literary powers. In fact, it is the protagonist roles accorded to female and Afro-Brazilian actors that sustains the play's metatheatrical structure. First, characters from other Bando de Teatro Olodum plays (thus performed by black actors), such as Jorgete, Professora, and Soldado Leão, populate *Um tal de Dom Quixote*. The intertextuality with other Olodum performances adds metatheatrical depth to a plot that constantly swings back and forth between Cervantes' time and contemporary Brazil, particularly around issues that affect Afro-Brazilians. Second, the female narrators summon famous playwrights to underwrite a (meta)theatrical interpretation of Cervantes' masterpiece. They endorse Cervantes' belief in the Baroque commonplace that the separation between world and stage is but an illusion with similar statements from two other great playwrights: Shakespeare and Bertold Brecht (II.4.17 and II.7.23, respectively). According to narrator D, Don Quixote understands that "todos os homes e mulheres não passam de atores" (all the men and women [are] but actors; II.4.17), as Shakespeare asserts in *As You Like It* (1600). If we are all actors, then theater underwrites social roles, and consequently performative activism may function as a critical tool for transformation.

Um tal de Dom Quixote illustrates how theater companies deeply rooted in their communities transculturate a Spanish classic into contemporary activism in Brazil. The focus on marginality, via characters and themes that emerge out of the everyday realities of today's Brazil, takes a somewhat unexpected turn toward (meta)theatricality via Freire and Boal. In these plays and other appropriations across the Americas, Don Quixote functions as an antidote against exclusion not because of his misguided and meager military skills, but thanks to his fearless, masterful ability to perform a new role for himself and others. In contrast to the two historically prevalent readings of *Don Quixote*, as either an icon for idealism and nation-building or a biting satire of its time, Brazilian plays build their activist interpretation on the revolutionary performance of the main character, the hidalgo Quijano who transforms himself into Don Quixote. In the next chapter, a detailed analysis of these four plays illustrates this new approach to Cervantes' masterpiece, one that opens up uncharted territory in the activist appropriation of a literary classic into the contemporary moment.

CHAPTER 4

The Performative Approach

The Brazilian Third Way of Reading *Don Quixote*

The abundance of original social justice adaptations of *Don Quixote* in the early part of the twenty-first century across the Americas, and particularly in Brazil, points to a potential departure from traditional views on literary classics as canonical works reserved for intellectual and political elites. This new activist appropriation of *Don Quixote* stands in contrast to traditional readings in that it repurposes a Baroque-era text for vulnerable communities, for it not only includes contemporary references to the excluded but also is often performed by and/or for the underserved. On the premise that performance can help anyone, but particularly the disadvantaged, rescript social roles and narratives, *Don Quixote*'s (meta)theatricality becomes a weapon for liberation. This chapter zooms in on precisely the crucial moment in which performance triggers radical personal change in the selected Brazilian stage adaptations of *Don Quixote* and on how this original focus offers a new interpretation, which I will call here performative, of the novel's legacy. How do these theater companies interpret the four-hundred-year-old Spanish classic? And more importantly, how do they aim to transform the lives of both local actors and audiences through their appropriation of a literary hero of such universal dimensions? To answer these questions, I first review the two most influential interpretations of the work, the Romantic and the satirical, which also permeate and conflate in the Brazilian versions.[1] Then I analyze the initial and most critical phase of transformation for the hidalgo Quijano: his consequential creation of the knight-errant. In a book of more than one thousand pages in most editions, the revolutionary renaming of the hidalgo's identity unfolds in chapter 1 over just a handful of pages. Traditionally, critics have regarded Quijano as merely a secondary, dull character whom Don Quixote (thankfully) replaces. In stark contrast, the Brazilian versions underscore the importance of the hidalgo's radical metamorphosis and expand on it in original, sophisticated ways. And finally, I discuss the protagonist's death in Cervantes' text and its adaptations, for in the Brazilian plays Don Quixote's demise functions as the ultimate call for performative activism. In Cervantes' book, the knight falls ill, and the hidalgo reappears in order to renounce his mad actions as Don Quixote, confess his sins, and sign a proper will. In a likely move to allay potential concerns on the part of inquisitorial censors, Cervantes brings back the "sane" hidalgo at the last possible moment so that he can die within the strict social conventions of the time. In the Brazilian adaptations, however, performative activism gives Don Quixote's existence an expansive, liberatory purpose beyond death, as these plays seek to incite individual and social change in their audience. In these activist versions, Quijano never really dies.

From the time of its publication through the end of the twentieth century, *Don Quixote* has been interpreted via two largely opposing views on the qualities of its protagonist.[2] To a great extent, these readings, the Romantic and the satirical, result from diverging views on the creation of Don Quixote and, most importantly, his death. After losing in battle to the Knight of the White Moon, in Cervantes' text the defeated knight-errant returns home one last time. A fever confines him to bed for six days until he falls into a deep sleep from which he awakes only to renounce the "foolishness and the danger" of his chivalric endeavor. He then calls for a priest to hear his confession and composes his last will. Rejecting the quixotic persona that possessed him throughout the entire book, he dies according to the religious and legal mores of the period (II.54.934–36).

In Anthony Close's seminal formulation, the Romantic approach takes Cervantes' crazed hidalgo at his word, for he is regarded as a heroic knight-errant on a mission to right all wrongs. The "real" identity of Alonso Quijano, the hidalgo whose name and place of origin the narrator does "not care to remember" (I.1.19), disappears behind the idealistic hero driven by an indomitable will to better the world through knightly action. Not surprisingly, this Romantic interpretation of Don Quixote has become the most pliable and widely employed throughout the last century. Many political, cultural, and commercial enterprises have exploited the phenomenal appeal of the indefatigable hero who sacrifices his life in pursuit of lofty ideals, however misguided. This kind of hero, to paraphrase Dale Wasserman's widely popular *Man of La Mancha* (1965), dreams the impossible dream and envisions reality not as it is but as it should be. The particulars of Alonso Quijano matter little to the Romantic consumer of the quixotic brand, for madness does not invalidate the knight's quest but rather fuels it. Per this line of interpretation, Quijano's ordinary life pales in comparison with the heroic splendor of the chivalric character. In good logic, then, the Romantic approach repudiates the controversial reversion of Don Quixote back into Alonso Quijano the Good at the end of part II. In a predictable move, the Romantic reading could never accept such a disgraceful ending for an icon of idealism and individual determination of Don Quixote's stature. After all, the insignificant Quijano simply does not possess the legitimacy to replace, much less disavow, the heroic Don Quixote.

In contrast to the Romantic dismissal of the knight's last minute conversion, popular interpretations of *Don Quixote* through at least the eighteenth century in fact paid particular attention to the final death scene. Quijano's sudden denunciation of "detestable books of chivalry" (II.54.935) confirms the explicit narratorial aim of parodying chivalric books formulated in the prologue to part I, in which Cervantes describes his work as simply an "invective against books of chivalry" (8). Peter E. Russell's 1969 article "*Don Quixote* as a Funny Book" recuperated, at least for an academic audience, this predominantly satirical reading of the novel.[3] According to this school of interpretation, the knight-errant functions as a comical conduit, rather than a visionary hero, for the parody of various literary, political, and religious tenets of Cervantes' time. Since the early 1970s, a number of studies, mostly emerging from poststructuralist academic circles, have highlighted the novel's satirical vein in order to dissect the anatomy of its subversive discourse, as James Parr attempts in his well-known 1988 study. In doing so, they update a long-held interpretation of *Don Quixote* as a humorous book whose (anti)hero embodies a parody of old-fashioned ideals and the corrosive effects of literary credulity (Bayliss 391). In other words, Don Quixote is the product of madness, as the hidalgo who originally conceived him admits on his deathbed. If we accept this premise, then, Don Quixote's actions subvert through humor and satire the very principles that he purports to defend. His last-minute conversion and death only confirm the madness of the knight's very existence.

In the end, however, the question of whether Don Quixote is a hero or a fool, in the classic paradox best explored by John Jay Allen, remains critically unanswered. In the text itself, most fellow characters treat Don

Quixote as a fool, either condemning his actions in the strongest terms or fabricating elaborate jokes at his expense. In stark contrast, the hidalgo Quijano himself boasts that he has become a hero of the highest stature, "a knight there could be no greater in all the world" (I.3.31). For most readers and scholars of *Don Quixote*, what creates the character's richness and depth is precisely his fluid oscillation between madness and lucidness (Vieira, "Louco lúcido"). Beyond the book's pages, Cervantes' fool and hero has by all measures become an icon of epic proportions in the global cultural arena, a champion of lost causes and great literature. A fool in the eyes of most fellow characters and readers, as well as a hero for others, the Don's ambiguous qualities intensify the more closely they are scrutinized. Since his heroically foolish or foolishly heroic nature cannot be resolved, as it is intentional and intrinsic to the character, here I hope to shed light instead on the activist dimensions of *Don Quixote*. In this study, I do not aim to discern Don Quixote's textual heroism but to examine Brazilian contemporary interpretations of it. In other words, is Don Quixote a hero or a fool *today*?

To answer this question, activist appropriations of *Don Quixote* in contemporary Brazil hinge on one character that many readers and critics tend to ignore, if not forget altogether: Alonso Quijano. Throughout the novel, Cervantes himself intends to relegate his protagonist to the shadows, while the crazed knight-errant plays a game at once foolish and heroic in the open. The obsessive reader who disregards all kinds of social, biological, and religious norms of his time must conceal himself from the Inquisition and the powers-that-be under layers of lunacy and literary references.[4]

While extolling Don Quixote's fight for justice, Brazilian activists rely even more heavily on Cervantes' performative recipe for transformation, incarnated in the hidalgo Quijano. Abandoning grand national narratives, in their focus on the excluded and the underserved these plays select a different kind of liberation weapon from Don Quixote's arsenal: the power of words, art, and performance. In their reading, it is not the knight-errant Don Quixote who, through the strength of his arm and the threat of his weapons, triggers transformation. On the contrary, change occurs at the moment of the knight's inception, when a bored reader who imagines alternative worlds decides to act them out. His display of creative power conjures a performative vocabulary that, quite literally, makes words happen. As Paulo Freire proposed almost four hundred years later (although to the best of my knowledge he never discussed *Don Quixote* in the context of critical pedagogy), Quijano could well represent the best example of the transformation of the individual and society through the praxis of a new vocabulary of liberation (Ferreira et al.).

The defining contribution of the Brazilian readings of Cervantes' masterpiece thus becomes their focus on the relationship between Quijano (Quixana in the Portuguese-language versions that I examine here) and Don Quixote. The protagonist's character remains in constant flux, as he evolves, changes his name three times, and most markedly undergoes two major transformations. In the first couple pages of Cervantes' book, the hidalgo becomes a presumedly heroic knight-errant; and at the moment of his death, in the last few pages, he reverts to the everyman Quijano. Such radical moments of transformation, which bookend a story of constant personal change, prompt what in the Brazilian appropriations emerges as a key question: Is Don Quixote the glorious creation of a crazy and expendable hidalgo, as most readings suggest, or is Quijano aware of his performative mission to role-play a hero of limited military capabilities but great transformative powers? Ultimately, a significant amount of dialogue and action in these four Brazilian plays ponders the idea of transformation through acting and words, which the dual protagonist embodies more fully than any other character in the story. In order to articulate the message that performance can overcome marginality, the Brazilian appropriations underscore the hidalgo/knight-errant's performative skills and the important role that Sancho and other characters play in this (meta)theatrical process of liberation. Through a rich cast of characters and actors, the making of hybrid identities and the performance of new social roles occur in a transcultural whirlwind that brings together Spanish and Brazilian traditions as well as cultural capital and marginality. If, as Alberto Sandoval-Sánchez and Nancy Saporta Sternbach argue, "theater and performance are the ideal cultural locations to examine transculturation" (33), then these four plays and their treatment of Cervantes' protagonists provide a vantage point from which to analyze the translation of *Don Quixote* into not only the Portuguese language but the Brazilian contemporary activist context as well.[5]

Keenly aware of how relevant Quijano's initial creation of his chivalric persona is, the three São Paulo versions (Valéria di Pietro's *Num lugar de la Mancha*, Telma Dias' *Dom Quixote*, and Andreia de Almeida's *Quixotes*) all commence in a strikingly similar and unexpected way: with actors who play characters on stage. As *Num Lugar de la Mancha*'s third musical interlude demands, to grasp the transformative power of Don Quixote's story it is imperative to "soltar a imaginação" (free your imagination). Embodying this mandate for creative freedom, "Ator Dom Quixote só no palco" (the actor Don Quixote alone on stage) intently states in the first scene of di Pietro's play: "Vou me transformar num outro homem" (I'm going to transform myself into a new man). Behind the subject pronoun of *vou* (*eu*, or I), there is a character, an "actor," who is not yet Don Quixote. In order to become the *outro homem* (the knight-errant), he must undergo a transformational process in a critical first step toward radical individual and social change. From the very beginning, thus, the actor will attempt to pursue a dream armed with only a discursive and performative arsenal. When the priest warns his neighbor against the "grande loucura" (great foolishness) of trying to right all manners of wrong, the actor/Quijano/Quixote imperviously notes that he sees nothing wrong in "melhorar a situação de quem estiver pior" (bettering the situation of those who suffer). As a necessary pre-condition to achieving his lofty goal, however, he compels the priest to call him "a partir de hoje Dom Quixote de la Mancha" (from now on, Don Quixote of La Mancha; 2). His objective as lofty as it is unattainable, Don Quixote brandishes only one effective weapon in his idealistic quest for justice: a performative language that he hopes will turn his unremarkable life into a succession of heroic deeds. By having others call him Don Quixote of La Mancha, he will seek fame through adventures that begin with name-changing and that rely mainly on a voracious appetite for theatricality and the creative (re)writing of the world.

Madness thus plays a lesser role in this adaptation of *Don Quixote*. According to the "Actor" in his opening monologue, the hidalgo does not lose his mind but simply "abandona o incômodo peso da razão" (frees himself from the uncomfortable weight of reason; 1). Significantly, Don Quixote describes the people asleep at the inn in which he intends to spend his first night as "os atores do teatro do mundo e os espectadores . . . ao desconcertante espetáculo da vida" (actors on the world's stage and spectators . . . in the bewildering spectacle of life; 5). If the ordinary people asleep at an inn perform on the world's stage as actors and spectators in Don Quixote's story, theatricality then functions as the great equalizer that unites all of humanity, whether inn guests, Don Quixote, or even ourselves, as spectators of *Num lugar de la Mancha*. The boldness of Don Quixote's proposal is rooted not in madness but in the intrinsic performativity of his revolutionary renaming.

The *Dom Quixote* by Grupo Permanente de Pesquisa, adapted for the stage by Telma Dias and directed by the playwright and Robson Vellado, similarly identifies the multiple and performative nature of the main character as the starting point of Quixote-inspired activism. The play begins with a lone man on stage: "A cena ... começa na penumbra. Vemos um homem magro, velho e cansado perdido em uma imensa biblioteca folheando avidamente livros e mais livros" (The scene ... begins in the dark. We see a thin, tired old man, lost in an immense library avidly leafing through books and more books; 3). Consumed and inspired by his chivalric books, the emaciated old man embodies in this stage direction a new kind of hero for Brazilian youth. Before he engages in any battles to better the world, the old hidalgo must transform himself in a way that relates only literarily to swords and giants. The protagonist's desire to change society starts with his compulsion to read and act out the very process of reading. Much as in Cooperaacs' artivist proposal, here artistic consumption invokes the production of a new social entity.

In a more overt way than in Cervantes' text, Telma Dias' protagonist consciously moves up the social ladder from a lower hidalgo to a higher *caballero* (knight) status: "Hoje mesmo vou me transformar num cavaleiro andante" (Today without delay I am going to transform myself into a knight-errant; 3). The "urgent" (*hoje mesmo*) and deliberate nature of the hidalgo's "transformation" (*vou me transformar*) renders explicit a socially subversive message that echoes García-Guillén's "Vou me transformar num outro homem" in *Num lugar de la Mancha*. In contrast to the hidalgo's willful rise to caballero highlighted in these two plays, Cervantes' original avoids openly challenging the stratified social fabric of the Habsburg regime of his time. The hidalgo's brain simply "dried up [from excessive reading], causing him to lose his mind" to the point of accepting the literal truth of chivalric books (I.1.21). His sanity "completely gone, he had the strangest thought any lunatic in the world ever had, which was ... to become a knight-errant" (I.1.21). With the hidalgo buried under layers of obscurity (we do not know his real name, town, age, or lineage) and madness (his mind is overtaken by insanity and books), Don Quixote's antiheroic façade masks the revolutionary essence of Quijano's discursive rebirth.[6]

The question of whether one can in fact truly reinvent one's social identity remains a thorny one. If social change stems from personal transformation, how can the underprivileged and underrepresented escape stereotyping and social determination in contemporary Brazil? More specifically, how might at-risk youth rewrite the mainstream script that assigns them a subaltern and often criminal role? The prescription for change in Telma Dias' *Dom Quixote* once again presents itself as fully discursive, for the protagonist reinvents himself through words and performance. In his efforts to become a knight-errant, the hidalgo "pega um papel e põe-se a escrever" (grabs a piece of paper and starts writing; 4). Using only his imagination and profound knowledge of chivalric literature, the skinny, nameless, and aged hidalgo rewrites his place in society in order to insert himself into the high-powered world of knight errantry. Significantly, in Telma Dias' *Dom Quixote* the protagonist actually sketches his fictional creation on a piece of paper. Staging the simple act of putting pen to paper foregrounds the literary and self-created nature of the hidalgo's liberation. In contrast to Cervantes, Dias chooses to physically stage the intentional writing exercise that prompts the knight-errant's birth. Moreover, the author takes this physical embodiment of the creative enterprise one step further. As the hidalgo writes his new role, a stage direction calls for three actors to play out Quijano's thought process ("o pensamento do fidalgo") on stage. Brainstorming together, the four "Quixotes" ardously strive to appropriately name the complementary figures to Quijano's new persona: his horse "Rocinante" and lady "Dulcinea." So self-conscious and complex is the hidalgo's scheme that four actors are summoned on stage to deliver the names of his two chivalric creations. In this regard, the writing and staging of the knight's creative birth lays out the elements required to assume control of one's social narrative: a great dose of imagination, a literary education, a fearless attitude, and hard work. In order for at-risk youth to overcome the ominous odds stacked against them, Dias suggests, they must rewrite their social narrative and boldly perform their transformation on the real-life stage. If Don Quixote's ability to change the world relies on his use of words, then Cervantes' proposal to better society hinges on discursive tactics rather than chivalric action.

A still more overt emphasis on the (meta)theatricality of Quixote-inspired activism runs through Andreia de Almeida's *Quixotes*. Drawing substantially on metafictional elements prevalent in Cervantes' original text, the characters in this play are not Don Quixote and Sancho, but a nameless Atriz (Actress) and Ator (Actor) who recount the story of their dramatization of *Don Quixote*. Furthermore, Sancho is performed by a woman, a casting choice that requires, in the tradition of Eugenio Barba's theater anthropology, an overt suspension of disbelief. The spectators of *Quixotes*, at times mere bystanders who happen upon a street performance, witness the work of two actors openly discussing how to play Cervantes' two iconic characters. Both actors and audience become involved in the kind of (meta)fictional process that enabled Alonso Quijano to become Don Quixote in the first place. While they perform a role, they continuously reflect on the act of performing. The whole play unfolds as theater turned

FIGURE 4.1. Performance of *Quixotes* in a public square (Circo Navegador, Andreia de Almeida and Luciano Draetta)

inside out much like *Don Quixote*, the novel, openly discusses the very act of reading (Fuentes, *Cervantes, o la crítica de la lectura*).

As in the other two plays, Don Quixote's madness plays a role only secondary to the hero's theatrical scheme. While discussing how to stage the hidalgo's transformation into knight-errant, the Atriz concludes that Quijano "ficou doidão, e só se metia em confusão" (he went mad, and kept getting in trouble; 2). Then the Ator interjects angrily: "Doidão não! Mas você é cabeça dura mesmo, né? Quando foi que eu te disse que ele era doidão?" (Not crazy! But how silly are you? When did I tell you that he was crazy?; 2). Accepting the actor's reprimand, the actress simply proceeds to dub him a knight-errant, and thus Don Quixote is born out of an actor without Quijano ever having gone mad. From then on, this same deliberate craftsmanship guides the ensuing staging of Don Quixote's adventures. In a telling dialogue around the book's most memorable episode, the charge against the windmills, Don Quixote (the Ator) and the Atriz discuss how to stage the adventure. The Atriz refuses to recreate once more the "passagem mais conhecida da história" (the best-known passage in the book) precisely because everyone knows it already. Don Quixote protests angrily, for this is the story that made him "famoso" (famous). The Atriz responds dryly: "Você não [é] o Dom Quixote" (You're not Don Quixote), never quite letting the Ator get away with his impersonation of Cervantes' hero. By breaking the illusion of theater, this play situates the actor and the act of playing at the forefront of Quijano's heroic enterprise, one based on self-conscious performance more than on the ability to win battles militarily. In the end, the hero is the actor, not the knight-errant.

And lastly, Márcio Meirelles' *Um tal de Dom Quixote* project in Salvador de Bahia, which premiered in 1998, only a few years before the São Paulo versions, also furthers a performative interpretation of Cervantes' masterpiece within a sophisticated metatheatrical structure. After a brief musical introduction, narrator T, one of the seven members of the play's Greek chorus, directly addresses the audience with an "Eis o teatro" (This is theater) that sets the metatheatrical framework upon which the play inscribes itself. In this overtly performative context, actors become "arquitetos de nosso próprio destino, assim como fez certa vez um certo cavaleiro chamado Dom Quixote de la Mancha" (architects of our own destiny, just as once did a certain knight called Don Quixote; I.1.2). The knight-errant is crazy (louco) indeed, but at least his brand of madness, as one of the female narrators underscores, triggers action. In contrast, indifference paralyzes those who, while seemingly sane, foolishly tolerate injustice (I.2.3). Whereas Don Quixote's brand of (in)sanity demands the courage to act, indifference toward inequality is the real madness.

From this first depiction of the main character on, Don Quixote's knightly persona unfolds as a predominantly theatrical experience, a model for other actors who wish to consciously take charge of their own performance. As narrator H pointedly underscores, Quixana's chivalric show commences with the adoption of a new name, Don Quixote. Changing names, she explains, spurs the genesis of the play's protagonist the same way that some animals must shed their skins to grow their bodies. Although directed at the audience, H's comment on the transformative power of naming triggers the reaction of one of the housekeepers, Siomara. In an openly metathetrical exchange, the narrator's allegorical and the character's "realistic" spheres intersect. Following in Quijano's creative footsteps, as he sheds his old hidalgo skin to become a knight-errant, Siomara enthusiastically announces that she wants to join a circus that is performing in town. As in Quijano's case, her radical conversion into a performer will first require a name change: "quando eu for s'imbora com o pessoal do circo, também vou mudar de nome. . . . Vou me chamar Suely Tamara" (when I join the circus crew, I will also change my name. . . . My name will be Suely Tamara; I.2.4). In response to narrator H's observation made directly to the audience about the power of renaming, Siomara finds inspiration in the hidalgo's linguistic transformation into knight-errant to become a performer herself, a renamed Suely Tamara. In *Um tal de Dom Quixote*, thus, it is not only the playwrights who foreground the transformative potential of the hidalgo Quijano's revolutionary performance; now one of the characters exhorts herself to "também" (also) change her persona by abandoning her social location both physically and linguistically through the adoption of a new name.

In contrast to Don Quixote, however, Siomara is a humble female servant who does not enjoy the privileges that come with the old, educated white master's position. In the end, she will not succeed in her intended transformation. In fact, the contrast between an hidalgo with land holdings, three housekeepers, and a black squire versus a timidly dreamy, underprivileged servant intensifies as the plot unfolds. Toward the play's end, the housekeeper again states her intention to leave her master's house renamed as Suely Tamara. Once more, she exhibits the ability to incorporate into her lived reality an allegorical episode that only the audience can observe. When Don Quixote daydreams about a knight-errant's triumphant entry into a city, a small acting ensemble briefly appears onstage to act out the protagonist's narration. Whimsically connected with *Um tal de Dom Quixote*'s metatheatrical and allegorical features, Siomara can also see the play within a play that illustrates Don Quixote's words, and her reaction again parallels the hidalgo's. With renewed enthusiasm, she reiterates her desire to transform herself into Suely Tamara and join this itinerant troupe. Nonetheless, echoing the reaction that the crazed hidalgo elicits from most characters, the other two housekeepers sternly reprimand Siomara for her lack of common sense: "Você está louca?!" (Are you crazy?!), they lash out at her. Without any resistance on her part, the young girl immediately relents in the face of her older peers' scolding. Renouncing her new name, she will stay a servant in the master's house. As Siomara misses her chance to join the acting crew, narrator T admonishes her under allegorical cover for not enacting her dream, in contrast to Don Quixote's resoluteness. "Moral da história," T preaches to the audience: "agarre o seu sonho" (The point of this story: grab hold of your dreams; II.8.24). Although self-admittedly bent on becoming a performer, Siomara poses as a Quijano/Don Quixote simulacrum whose transformation into Suely Tamara never quite materializes. Mainly, she fails because, as her peers pointedly suggest, she lacks land, wealth, literary culture, housekeepers, and a black squire to tend to her material needs. In this regard, thus, *Um tal de Dom Quixote* explicitly underscores the challenges of performative activism for the underprivileged.

Throughout the play, the spotlight remains on Don Quixote, for he has accorded himself a protagonist role in the worldly performance that he so deftly stages. The show must always go on, as Don Quixote's personality exists only when acted out. In this regard, the protagonist has no alternative but to negotiate with his fellow characters the rules of engagement for his theatrical persona. The knight's resulting need to credulously embrace his own fantasy emerges with particular urgency during Sancho's masterful enchantment of Dulcinea (II.8–10 in the original). In Meirelles' version, Don Quixote initially reacts with shock and disbelief to his squire's description of three Rastafari women as Lady Dulcinea and her two maids. Nonetheless, he promptly finds a way to insert Sancho's ingenious trick (an attempt to cover his previous lie) into his own chivalric narrative. In doing so, Don Quixote manages to preserve the theatrical illusion of his enterprise. Some diabolical power must have tampered with his vision, he claims, for he cannot see Dulcinea behind the poorly clad figure of a smoking woman. Rather than challenging Sancho's blatant bluff, Don Quixote maintains the chivalric game by invoking the intervention of evil enchanters. Turning La Mancha and Bahia into an open theater, he twists reality to fit the fictional plot that he so aptly forces upon his largely unaware, often unwilling audience.

Theater has thus, quite literally, overtaken Don Quixote's life; the process of transformation that began with Quijano's radical name change has now reached its apex. Quijano's life unfolds as a continuous performance of a new role that he created for himself, full of adventures and great storytelling. But with his undeniable success, Quijano has also invited other characters into his theatrical game, and these guest performers progressively take charge of Don Quixote's play, as seen in Sancho's enchantment of Dulcinea. With the increasingly disruptive performances that populate part II of the original book in particular, the protagonist starts to lose control over his own script, a process that culminates at the end of the novel with his passing.

The key question about Don Quixote's death remains whether Quijano went mad at the beginning of the story and then returned to sanity hours before his death; or whether he, on the contrary, consciously enacted a role that evolves but ends back where it all began, at Quijano's home. The former characterizes the Romantic approach; the latter would imply that performance might function as a tool for social change and that acting proves a potentially empowering strategy for the common individual.[7] Settling the issue, Edward H. Friedman has intelligently reframed the question of Don Quixote's conversion in the original text by asking not what the character believes at the moment of his passing (is he sincere in his repudiation of chivalry?), but what remains after he expires ("Executing the Will" 121). And the answer to this question appears indisputable: what remains is literary fame. Both in the book and outside it, after the protagonist's death several important fellow characters, as well as the novel's readers and critics over the last four hundred years, battle "for the control of [Don Quixote's] life story" (R. Schmidt 115), for his literary afterlife. His legacy does not hinge on a discussion of madness and repentance but rather on who will continue the hidalgo's literary and performative enterprise, and how.

In the few final pages of Cervantes' book, Don Quixote's illness and subsequent death provoke a frenzy of authorship claims. Many characters want a piece of the heroic protagonist's anticipated literary fame: the Arabic "historian" Cide Hamete, who narrates his story (he even cites his pen's warning to future writers that the story "is reserved only for me"; II.74.939); Sancho Panza, who in a display of literary and personal loyalty offers to continue performing his master's fantasy; Sansón Carrasco, who wholeheartedly enters Don Quixote's chivalric game to the point of risking his own life by battling the knight-errant; and Cervantes himself in the prologue to part II, as he discredits the apocryphal 1614 "Avellaneda" continuation of *Don Quixote*. The fact that so many characters, including the author himself, lay claim to the story attests to the protagonist's success in achieving not eternal life in a religious sense, but perpetual literary fame. In a world that functions as a stage or *theatrum mundi*, the curtain never falls on heroes whose deeds are continuously told and enacted (Friedman, "Making Amends" 13, "Executing the Will" 115). Crucially for his performative scheme, Quijano's death does not represent a Christian conversion or a sincere repudiation of chivalry but "an ironic change of modus operandi" to achieve an undying literary existence (R. Schmidt 122, 112). At the time of his death, Quijano must relinquish authority and renounce the madness of his enterprise but not before having won his greatest victory: literary fame. In passing the performative baton to others, the hidalgo ensures that his life's mission remains continually enacted after his death by "communities of imaginative expansion" (Brewer 22) that extend themselves from the pages of the book through contemporary Brazil and beyond.[8]

This is the very performative strategy that Brazilian activist adaptations underscore as Cervantes' paramount contribution to the betterment of society. In the end, it is all about retaining some control over the performative process, especially for those on the fringes of society. In these plays, the possibility emerges of writing and performing a role different from the one imposed by an oppressive society as the ultimate weapon for liberation. In keeping with the self-consciously theatrical birth of Don Quixote, in the Brazilian adaptations Alonso Quijano could not simply renounce his acting role and revert back to the obscure commoner from a village whose name the narrator does not remember. While the four plays offer varied solutions to the story's final conundrum, they all emphasize the ongoing performative nature of the dual protagonist.

In the three São Paulo-based plays, the initial transformation of the hidalgo elicits much more attention and onstage time than his death, which feels somewhat rushed. For all the emphasis on the process of conscious self-transformation that enables an old hidalgo to rewrite a protagonist role for himself, the undoing of a theatrical project of such magnitude unfolds swiftly, as if the authors felt reluctantly compelled to stage the protagonist's death. In the São Paulo versions, the main character stumbles upon death much like a play comes to its close: with the expectation that it will be staged again the following day. Far from final, death presents itself as a way to wrap up a performance that will nonetheless renew itself. By foregrounding the performative aspects of Don Quixote's demise, these three Brazilian adaptations endorse the literary nature of the protagonist's project, as well as the activist potential of his theatrical legacy to better today's society.

In Valéria di Pietro's *Num lugar de la Mancha*, the protagonist's passing differs from Cervantes' text in that the hidalgo Quijano never renounces Don Quixote, a paramount and controversial moment in the original book.[9] In an improvised funeral march, the cast sings to "Dom Quixote, um louco heroi" (Don Quixote, a mad hero) as a prelude to the final and illuminating dialogue between a student and Dulcinea. Upon the student's invitation to contemplate the hero's corpse, Dulcinea responds that a man died, but not Don Quixote. Embodied here by an actress with a physical presence on stage (in Cervantes' text Dulcinea never appears in the flesh), the knight's lady refuses to accept Don Quixote's death. As the student calls her *moça* (girl), she corrects him and, reminiscent of the ending of Wasserman's *Man of La Mancha*, proudly proclaims her transformation: "Meu nome é Dulcinéa" (My name is Dulcinea). Then, a final song closes the performance with a call, once again, to "soltar a imaginação" (free your imagination; 13). The final words in the play reveal how fellow characters, and in particular the peasant girl whom the fictitious knight-errant renamed Dulcinea, regard

Don Quixote. An exercise in freeing the imagination, Don Quixote's adventures endure thanks to fellow characters like Dulcinea and Sancho Panza, who craft a new role for themselves through acting and renaming. In somewhat contradictory ways, this adaptation stages the protagonist's passing but makes it clear that Don Quixote will not die as long as others continue to free their imagination in order to transform themselves and society.

The ending of Telma Dias' adaptation also condenses in a matter of just a few minutes the creative frenzy that the quixotic enterprise entails. Don Quixote appears distressed by the duke and duchess' malevolent theatrical practices. He leaves their court "tendo no peito uma tristeza profunda e sem explicação aparente" (feeling deeply sad for no apparent reason; 26). As in the original, Don Quixote is then defeated by the Knight of the White Moon, but here the victorious knight immediately takes his helmet off to reveal himself as Sansón Carrasco (27). In Cervantes' book, Sansón only shares his secret with Don Antonio Moreno, not with the leading characters (II.65.888). In contrast, in Dias' version Sansón reveals his social identity at once, turning his military victory over Don Quixote into an even more devastating theatrical defeat. With the knight-errant subjugated both militarily and theatrically, as the "real" identity of his adversary is revealed, the curtain closes on the hidalgo's performance. Mocked and defeated, Don Quixote quits a performance that others have corrupted. Exhausted, he passes the performative baton to the audience and dies. Rather than repent, he refuses to act in a play that he no longer directs.

Andreia de Almeida's *Quixotes* departs from Cervantes' original text in even more significant ways than di Pietro's and Dias' versions do. The play's performative protagonists, an Ator and an Atriz, strive not to enact chivalry and correct social wrongs but to stage Cervantes' story, an epic theatrical challenge in its own right. In this play, the actors become the true *Quixotes*, in the plural form in the title. In consonance with the other two São Paulo versions, Don Quixote never reverts back to "Alonso Quixano the Good" before expiring (II.64.935 in the original). Purposefully, the performer passes away on stage while staying in character, embodying the persona that he so painstakingly created throughout the play. When the Atriz announces that "morreu Dom Quixote, como todos os homens" (Don Quixote died, like we all will; 14), the actor/hidalgo still clings to his dream role. Death takes the man but not his performance. In contrast to Cervantes' repentant and obscure hidalgo, who at the end of the original book renounces Don Quixote as the product of his madness, de Almeida lets her protagonist, who never lost his sanity in the first place, die as Don

Quixote. Yet, what remains of the knight-errant is not his military deeds or concrete accomplishments. His body expires, "Mas suas palavras não! Há 400 anos as palavras desta estória se proliferam pelo mundo todo!" (But not his words! For four hundred years the words of this story have proliferated around the world!; 14). As the Ator celebrates Don Quixote's wordly and worldly legacy, he encourages the Atriz to pursue the hidalgo's theatrical and discursive mission: "Vamos correr mundo, contar essas estórias em outras praças!" (Let's travel the world over, let's tell these stories everywhere!; 14). In a self-conscious endorsement of Don Quixote's own theatrical mission, the actors state their intention to share "these stories" with audiences in public squares and on stages throughout the world. By the beginning of 2019, in fact, Circo Navegador continues to perform *Quixotes* fourteen years after its premiere.

What *Quixotes* proposes, thus, diverges a great deal from Don Quixote's knightly ambitions to right wrongs through armed intervention and military heroism. In their playful and simultaneously uncanny metatheater, the actors in *Quixotes* carry out a performance that above all celebrates the act of performing itself. Like the hidalgo Quijano, the actors embody the very continuum of reading, writing, and acting that calls for ordinary people to actively engage in individual and collective change. Employing the plural form, "Quixotes," in the title functions as an activist call for audience members to become performers themselves. Against absolutist societies, both Cervantes and the Brazilian playwrights who adapt *Don Quixote* for the stage invite us all to exercise our innate right to enact transformation through play. The book's potential for social change emanates from its considerable literary powers, not only because its words still proliferate four hundred years later, but also because *Don Quixote*'s protagonists utilize naming and acting as their main weapon for liberation. If as Freire proclaims, "Human existence cannot be silent" (69), the hidalgo/knight-errant's story then becomes profoundly human and humanitarian, for it reveals that even an obscure everyman in the twilight of his life can achieve personal as well as social transformation through storytelling and performance.

Lastly, although written and performed a few years earlier, Meirelles' *Um tal de Dom Quixote* develops the metatheatrical potential of the demise of Cervantes' protagonist in the most explicit and elaborate of ways. Increasingly, as was the case in the São Paulo versions, in this play the protagonist is forced to fight not to right wrongs but mainly to retain control of his performance. Toward the end, a variety of characters attempt to enter Don Quixote's game on their own terms (Sancho's clever rendering of Dulcinea is only the first instance of this growing menace for the protagonist). In a series of (meta)theatrical events, several main characters put their lives at risk as they seek Don Quixote's military but also theatrical surrender and subsequent return to his home. While trying to secure the hidalgo's defeat, these characters endeavor to usurp Don Quixote's control over the story.

With Quijano's performative project under increasing threat, narrator D quickly steps out of the Greek chorus' allegorical sphere to reflect on Don Quixote's conundrum. As she explains directly to the spectators, Don Quixote acts not only as the apt director and protagonist of a phenomenal knightly show, but he also embodies its most devoted and credulous spectator. In reality, characters such as Sancho leave him no choice but to accept the stories that they increasingly script, direct, and incorporate into the hidalgo's own play. Caught by surprise, narrator D elaborates, "não podia esperar que Sancho Pança deixasse o seu papel de escudeiro para se meter a diretor da cena" (he could not anticipate that Sancho Panza would leave his role as squire and become instead stage director; II.4.17). Consequently, D points out, Don Quixote has to adopt a new role in the ongoing performance of his chivalric world: "nosso triste cavaleiro [é] o espectador ideal: ele deseja antes de tudo crer no encantamento" (our sad knight-errant [is] the ideal spectator: he wants more than anything to believe in [Dulcinea's] enchantment; II.4.19). Ensnared in Sancho's performance, Quixana/Don Quixote can either close the curtain on his chivalric fantasy or embrace it wholeheartedly, thus accepting Sancho into the select circle of playwrights who at one point or another dictate the script of his life in both the original book and the Brazilian adaptations. Of course, the hidalgo turned knight-errant opts to lose himself in the unpredictable, potentially never-ending show he has started. His gullible attitude toward the performances directed by others has become a weapon of necessity rather than choice. Credulity, after all, breathes life into his self-described heroic persona and guides his erratic grand mission. In this scene, he adopts the same posture that he demands from the bewildered spectators who witness his self-created adventures: the will to believe and the courage to participate in an insanely volatile play.

For this reason, Don Quixote's ending takes an unprecedented though fully coherent turn in this adaptation. The knight does not suffer a fever and slip into a deep sleep, as in Cervantes' text, from which he awakens to reclaim his former identity of Alonso Quixano the Good (II.74.935). Rather, a series of incidents marshal the action toward a much more explicitly theatrical denouement. First, Don Quixote loses to Sansão in his Knight of the Mirrors disguise. While in chapter 14 of Cervantes' part II Don Quixote wins this joust, here he seems to face the decline of his own performing self in the reflection of his opponent's mirrors (a similar scene takes place in Wasserman's *Man of La Mancha*, although in our personal communications Meirelles never brought up the Broadway musical as a direct source of inspiration for his adaptation). In fact, the protagonist seamlessly accepts his defeat at the hands of the Knight of the Mirrors by calling his chivalric adventure to an abrupt and conscious end. As he renounces Don Quixote, another mirror, this time figurative, is placed in front of him. Riding a wooden horse, a *louco* (madman) claiming to be Don Quixote rapidly cruises and exits the stage. The knight-errant witnesses with sadness the ridiculous performance of his outlandish copycat and shouts "Basta" (Enough). Out of exhaustion, seemingly fed up with the volatility of his endeavor, he drops the curtain on his chivalric performance. Don Quixote immediately reverts back to Alonso Quixana (Quijano in the original) as he forsakes "o personagem que . . . eu estava destinado a representar" (the character . . . that I was destined to perform; II.15.29). Fully conscious of his theatrical mission, the hidalgo/knight-errant deliberately relinquishes the role that he originally felt called to play.

A few scenes earlier, narrators T and S have already anticipated Don Quixote's final defeat at the hands of the two characters who perversely mirror the knight's performance, the Knight of the Mirrors and the louco, or madman. Since the function of theater is to hold a mirror up to everyday life, T and S explain, it seems only fitting for Don Quixote to suffer defeat "por um golpe de teatro. Melhor ainda: por um truque de espelhos" (from a theatrical blow. Even better: through a prank involving mirrors). A mirror can be dangerous in the hands of mean-spirited individuals and those unconscious of its powers, narrator H warns (II.12.27). The Knight of the Mirrors and the louco who claims to be Don Quixote turn theater against its most devoted practitioner by respectively defeating him in battle and embodying the very madness that tarnishes his heroic persona. The theatrical mirror now offers Don Quixote a distorted image of himself and of his imagined worlds, which he can no longer endure. After taking care of his finances, he only wishes "ir para casa, para morrer em paz" (to go home to die in peace; II.15.29). In the most explicit of parallels, the end of his performance equates for Don Quixote the end of his life.

Significantly, however, it is once again up to the female narrators and, in the last scene, Sancho Panza to adopt a protagonist role in order to perpetuate the revolutionary metatheatrical motion that the hidalgo initiated. Before a now hopeless Quixana, narrator A proclaims that the hidalgo/knight-errant is "um de nós! Seres mutáveis, encantados!" (one of us! Mutable, enchanted beings!), whose performance takes place "no vasto palco do planeta" (on the vast stage called planet Earth; II.16.31). Once again, the play's metatheatrical and "realistic" spheres intersect as Don Quixote becomes "one of us"—that is, one of the chorus-like narrators who direct their commentary on the ongoing play to the audience in an openly self-referential way. Aware of their performative mission, Don Quixote and the narrators occupy a similar location in and out of the play, for their self-professed condition as actors connects them to the inner fictional worlds of the play as much as to the outer spheres of the audience and the world beyond the Vila Velha theater.

Immediately preceding Don Quixote's defeat, the female chorus ponders the very essence of the quixotic enterprise. Against the most extended interpretation of Cervantes' work, the Romantic dreaming of the impossible dream, the narrators state that the mere act of pursuing an ideal fails to guarantee a just outcome: "Não estamos aqui pra fazer a apologia do sonho. Mesmo porque existem sonhos insanos, nefastos" (We're not here to make the case for dreaming. Particularly, because some dreams are dangerous, toxic; II.12.27). Dreams can yield positive or negative outcomes depending on their motivation and effects. As a contemporary example, narrator C points to those who dream of enriching themselves through political corruption and profiteering. From the chorus' point of view, thus, a purely Romantic approach to *Don Quixote* proves insufficient as an agent of social betterment, for idealism alone does not necessarily lead to positive change. In a play focused on social justice, then, what lessons on equality may the knight-errant's story teach its audience if not the romanticized pursuit of lofty goals, of the elusive impossible dream? For the female narrators, Don Quixote's true contribution to individual and collective transformation is his ability to perform. More than just a dreamer, "Dom Quixote é um conhecedor do teatro. . . . É mais que um ator, é um ator consciente que escolheu sua personagem, escreveu sua própria peça e fez do mundo seu palco" (Don Quixote is a theater connoisseur. . . . More than an actor, he is a conscious actor who created his character, wrote his own play, and turned the world into his stage; II.12.27). In an overtly metatheatrical interpretation of Cervantes' *Don Quixote*, the protagonist in Meirelles' play shows himself as an actor who consciously crafts his role and takes his performance out into the world. At the end of the play, consequently, Don Quixote does not die, for his theatrical mission can never conclude. Instead, he witnesses with pride how other characters joyously take up the performance of his life story while simultaneously celebrating, in yet another metatheatrical reference, the reopening of the Vila Velha theater. This perpetual cycle of theater and performance all but guarantees Don Quixote's immortality.

In an attempt to preserve and foreground Don Quixote's performative mission, the entire conversion and death scene in Cervantes' original is not solely repurposed in *Um tal de Dom Quixote*, as in the São Paulo adaptations, but rather reformulated altogether. True to the play's metaliterary character, the buildup to its conclusion benefits from an intensifying erasure of the lines that separate reality from fiction as well as the inside and the outside of the theater (the building) itself. Throughout the play, various female narrators as well as a silent Dulcinea waving a Vila Velha flag from a balcony constantly remind the audience that *Um tal de Dom Quixote* celebrates the reopening of a local cultural and political landmark. With its boundless Quixote-themed space, the interior and exterior of the Vila Velha building physically replicate the same theatrical whirlpool that in the play engulfs participants in the knight-errant's performative scheme. A complex web of characters taken from Cervantes' text, the contemporary Brazilian context, and previous Bando de Teatro Olodum plays interacts with Don Quixote under the attentive stance and careful guidance of a loquacious Greek chorus. The female narrators thread together a succession of disjointed episodes taking place in different eras and featuring a multitude of characters from various racial, class, and gender backgrounds. Most significantly, however, they place the main character in the metatheatrical framework that legitimizes and explains his performative and activist mission. As the narrators go to great lengths to explain, Don Quixote *is* theater. And from this perspective, the Vila Velha and Don Quixote are two manifestations of the same performative phenomenon.

If Don Quixote embodies theater, he of course cannot die. In a clear echo of the initial "Eis o teatro" (Here's theater), toward the end of the play narrator A proclaims, "o Teatro está pronto" (The theater is ready). Such "theater" is none other than the Vila Velha whose reopening prompted the performance of *Um tal de Dom Quixote*; and so the story has come full circle.

It begins with the cheerful proclamation "Eis o teatro" and ends where it all began: with the inauguration of the new Teatro Vila Velha. Despite Don Quixote's successive theatrical defeats, the hidalgo who performs Don Quixote will not die on stage because the theater (the building, the act itself of performing) has now been brought back to life in the Maciel-Pelourinho neighborhood. When the protagonist admits defeat, fellow characters pick up his performative baton and celebrate his theatrical triumph by singing and dancing a final samba. In an endless whirlwind of acting and transformation, the line that separates actors from audience blurs, just as the inside and the outside of the theater (the building itself) become one indivisible stage presided over by Don Quixote's overflowing performance.

In the last scene, Sancho Panza makes a final appearance as *puxador de samba* (lead singer in a samba crew), with his wife and daughter (here Joana and Sanchica) taking on the role of *passistas*, or dancers. Sancho sings that "somente os dementes, os loucos, os teatros . . . podem vencer os dragões" (only the demented, the crazy, theater . . . can beat dragons). In a festive ending, the song is directed at an audience who entered the building via a ramp whose adjacent wall features a mosaic of Don Quixote charging at a dragon. Theater (the act of performing, the building) and Don Quixote have merged into one, the all-encompassing "teatro do ator que recria Quixotes de Espanha, la Mancha e Bahia" (the show/theater building of an actor who recreates Quixotes of Spain, La Mancha, and Bahia). Sancho's samba quite literally inscribes Cervantes' character into the building's very structure, and not just because he stands next to Don Quixote in the gigantic tile mosaic at the entrance ramp. More significantly, the squire reaffirms the conflation of the knight's on-stage presence with the reappearance in Salvador's cultural scene of the latest iteration of the Vila Velha. While Quixana/Don Quixote passively observes the samba finale from an armchair, Sancho invites the audience with his jubilant tune to fill the theater night after night, for there the spectators can find "Quixote no Vila Velha: Quixote vem adorar" (Don Quixote at the Vila Velha: come adore Don Quixote; II.16.31–32). Ultimately theater, and particularly the Vila Velha, provides the marginalized—Afro-Brazilians, women, an old hidalgo, theater lovers, former militants against the dictatorship—with a space where they can develop agency. Pointedly, Don Quixote offers a model of performative courage that benefits from, but simultaneously undermines racial, gender, and class privilege. As narrator A and Sancho conclude, marginality and (meta)theater, acting in concert, maximize the transformative potential of performance. By becoming self-reflective and critically aware of oppression, theater turns itself and its practice into a powerful weapon for liberation.

Neither solely a Romantic embodiment of ideals such as justice, nationalism, or religious righteousness nor, on the other hand, a mere satire of chivalric literature and old-fashioned ideals, *Don Quixote* inhabits politically and culturally distinct coordinates in contemporary Brazilian Quixote-inspired activism. The stage adaptations examined here point to a third way of interpreting the book, one that offers equal doses of idealism, satire, and activism deployed at the community and street levels. *Don Quixote* adaptations often target underprivileged audiences or involve disadvantaged performers who have presumably not read the book, and may never read it, at least in its entirety. While maximizing the advancement of their social justice mission, playwrights and directors must thus condense the novel's complexity for expedient theatrical consumption. Enhancing the iconic and visual qualities of the protagonist pair, they inevitably offer a romanticized version of the hero as a champion for the betterment of society, a victorious fighter against the monstrous evil of inequality. At the same time that they adopt this Romantic approach, however, they do not wield "the impossible dream" to uphold or even glorify an idea, whether nationalism or any other ideologically malleable concept such as justice or individualism, or a particular partisan agenda. Rather, the Brazilian stage adaptations present Don Quixote as a symbol of progressive social change, a critical exposé of the social disowning of underprivileged communities. Instead of submitting a prescribed, pre-packaged solution to social wrongs, these Brazilian plays offer a roadmap that situates words and performance at the core of Quixote-inspired activism. If social change derives from personal transformation, then the hidalgo Quijano gives an invaluable lesson in radical metamorphosis—or, in broader terms, systemic social change. Cervantes' protagonist gains depth as a character who does not strive to uphold long-established ideals but, on the contrary, encourages subversion.

Don Quixote's cultural and political location within Brazilian community theater thus exposes the simultaneous presence and playful interconnectivity of the Romantic and satirical lines of interpretation. This hybrid approach points to a peculiarly Brazilian, and more broadly American, third way of interpreting *Don Quixote*, one that combines two seemingly contradictory readings into a unified transformative strategy that promotes social change through words and theater. Is Don Quixote a chivalric hero in pursuit of lofty ideals or an outcast who embodies a satire of old values and absolutist political systems? In Brazilian social justice activism, he is both, and this alone represents a unique, fresh reading of the four-hundred-year-old character. Furthermore, Brazilian social justice-oriented interpretations place a renewed emphasis on the hidalgo Quijano, who consciously decides to rewrite and enact a new social role for himself, thus endowing words and performance with the power to effect individual and collective transformation. Shifting away from the idealistic, if delusional, warrior tilting at windmills, these adaptations shine the spotlight on the writer and actor who purposely utilizes discursive weapons to fight ideological complacency. At the beginning of the story, he creates and performs himself consciously; at the end, even when defeated, his theatrical legacy survives on the stages of Brazil, for his story continues to be retold as audiences repeatedly flood in to see the hidalgo, once again, transform himself into Don Quixote.

PART III
Urban Quixotes
Performative Activism and Citizenship in Contemporary Brazil

"A cultura é o principal instrumento da mudança"
"Culture is the main instrument for change"
BANDA AFROREGGAE, *Cara Nova* (2006)

CHAPTER 5

"A Place of Hope"

Performing Citizenship in Contemporary Brazil

Since the end of the twentieth century, a number of stage adaptations across the Americas and particularly in Brazil have formulated a groundbreaking interpretation of *Don Quixote* as a handbook for performing a new form of citizenship. As we have seen in the two previous chapters, these plays transculturate the Spanish classic into an activist proposal that aims to rescript and enact new individual and collective roles, particularly for the underserved and the excluded, in order to change mainstream social narratives. Neither solely an individualistic Romantic hero nor a satirical emblem of the decadence of imperial Spain, as traditional European readings suggested, Cervantes' protagonist emerges in recent original adaptations as a hero of performance who embodies both idealism and social critique. A consummate actor, Quijano consciously rewrites and performs a new protagonist role for himself as an antidote to the rigid social narrative that boxed him into a subordinate role. Through chivalric literature and a deep knowledge of theater, the hidalgo Quijano transforms himself into the presumedly heroic knight-errant Don Quixote, thus challenging the social and religious status quo of his time at the most fundamental of levels. Simultaneously, adding a social dimension to his quest, he also sparks change in others by engaging many fellow characters in his revolutionary, performative project.

With such awesome activist potential, the Cervantes-inspired performative dream of altering the role of individuals at the community level has not been limited to theatrical and public stages. Rather expansively, a number of community-engaged and activist initiatives employ *Don Quixote* as a model for a new performance of citizenship, particularly in Brazil. Here I focus mainly on three activist nonprofits in the city of São Paulo, the country's financial and cultural capital: the Instituto Religare, the Espaço Comunitário Quixote, and the Projeto Quixote (I already examined Cooperaacs in Chapter 1). Taking direct inspiration from *Don Quixote*, their community-based cultural work connects with broader grassroots efforts throughout the country that aim to redefine the performance of citizenship at the local and national levels.

In this chapter, I investigate the vibrant socio-political and cultural context within which Quixote-inspired performative activism has thrived. Without understanding how citizenship is challenged and performed in Brazil from an activist perspective, the close examination of initiatives based on Cervantes' classic, which I undertake in Chapter 6, could seem arbitrary or, worse yet, inconsequential. First, this chapter defines the concepts of performance and performative activism as the building blocks for the ensuing analysis. I then examine two recent Brazilian grassroots efforts of historical significance: the nationwide protests during the Brazilian Autumn in 2013 and the cultural activism of the Grupo Cultural AfroReggae in Rio de Janeiro. Following my probe into these two ways of performing citizenship in contemporary Brazil, the final section of this chapter establishes parallels and reveals the context within which Quixote-inspired activism carries out its own performative vision.

According to their mission statements, the ultimate goal of Quixote-inspired activist organizations is to provide the excluded and the invisible with the tools to perform a new concept of citizenship. These nonprofits act on the unwavering belief that through words, art, and performance, marginalized populations can become more visible and less stigmatized in the collective imaginary by taking on a protagonist role in their families and society at large. As Peterson Xavier, the actor who played Quijano/Don Quixote in *Num lugar de la Mancha*, explains, his protagonist role transformed his life on and off stage because "o teatro não forma artista; forma cidadão" (theater does not educate artists; it educates citizens; dos Santos 17). A critical influence in Xavier's citizen education, playwright and theater director Valéria di Pietro explicitly founded her Quixote-inspired Instituto Religare (the Reconnect Institute, or what in the United States would be called "Re-entry") as a bridge between the artistic and the social stages, as young participants in *Num Lugar de la Mancha* ended their internment at the FEBEM. In their efforts to reconnect underprivileged youth with self, society, and family, Religare aims to cultivate through art and theater "um cidadão [que] consegue enfrentar com mais clareza a complexidade da sua vida e qualifica-se para aprender a reivindicar melhor a sua participação na sociedade" (a citizen [who] succeeds at confronting with greater clarity the complexity of their life and learns to better assert their participation in society; Instituto Religare, "Arte aos quatro ventos"). When the excluded and the marginalized perform citizenship through a less prejudiced distribution of social roles, positive change for all can ensue.[1] According to the mission statement of de Almeida's Quixote Espaço Comunitário, cultural work of a social justice persuasion "garante espaço de convivência e formação para a cidadania" (secures a space for harmonious coexistence and educates citizens). Within that new understanding and performance of equal citizenship, the *Projeto Quixote* in São Paulo adopted "Another Story" (*Uma outra história*) as its motto. The organization contends that mainstream stories about at-risk children and youth typically condemn them to a life of marginalization as potential criminals or passive victims. According to this NGO, social betterment for at-risk youth depends first and foremost on the recasting of their individual and societal roles in the collective imagination. Because this transformation begins at the discursive level, mainstream society needs to hear the stories from the Other, the outcast, the silenced, and the ignored in their own words. Most critically, these new narratives from the margins must be performed publicly and acted upon to effectively bring about a more egalitarian practice of citizenship.

Understanding performative activism requires first a discussion of the concept of performance, which lacks proper translation into both Portuguese and Spanish and is, even in the English language, a rather multilayered notion (Bishop-Sanchez 23). In his 1956 *The Presentation of Self in Everyday Life*, Canadian sociologist Erving Goffman described performance in the context of social exchanges as "the activity of a given participant on a given occasion which serves to influence in any way any of the other participants" (15). At the core of social relations, Goffman continues, the repetition of a participant's performance produces social roles, or "the enactment of rights and duties attached to a given status" (16). In relation specifically to gender, Judith Butler honed Goffman's very broad notion of performance into an effective instrument for understanding how (gender) identity works. In two of her major books, *Gender Trouble* (1990) and *Bodies That Matter* (1993), Butler employs the term *performativity* to describe everyday actions that, often unconsciously, both define and are a consequence of our gender roles. In contrast, Butler uses *performance* only to describe self-aware attempts at playacting and exaggerating a given gender role, such as the concept of femininity dramatically staged by a performer in a drag queen show. In this book I favor the word *performance* over *performativity* because, as Sarah E. Chinn writes, in the end the two "speak to each other" in less antagonistic than complementary ways (294). If the distinction between the two lies mostly in the varying degree of self-awareness and theatricality, I find it particularly difficult to make a determination as to when an individual (much less a fictional character) exercises performance or performativity. Additionally, as I further document below, one of the main traits of performative activism is the self-conscious nature of its practice, which for Butler would constitute in any event an act of performance, not performativity.

Even if we settle on the use of *performance* to describe the brand of self-conscious activism promoted by Quixote-inspired organizations, the concept itself eludes a one-dimensional definition. The idea of performance suggests an intentional artistic intervention *on* a given space and time. Through a richly compact formula, Diana Taylor describes performance as "a doing to, a thing done to and with the spectator" (*Performance* 86). In Taylor's conceptualization, performance functions as an action directed at someone and something ("a doing to") that requires the spectator's engagement ("a thing done to and with the spectator"). Thus, the idea of activism lies within the very concept of performance, for the artist requires a response, explicit or implicit, from a spectator, who should not only be passively interpellated but also become actively engaged. Far from producing a normative process or a predictable response, performance thrives in its volatility. Kathryn Bishop-Sanchez explains this "inherently unstable" nature of performance because of its hybrid, in-between status across genres, cultures, and disciplines (16–17). Inextricably attached to the specific location and time in which it takes place, performance does not confine itself to any one setting, such as a stage or museum, or any one form of art (theater, painting, dance, or any other); it can and does occur potentially anywhere and through an endless combination of possibilities. Ephemeral and subjective, it embodies ideas with which the audience must contend and react to in the moment. Counter-intuitively, Bishop-Sanchez describes performance as a "site of invisibility and disappearance rather than unproblematic visibility and presence" (21). Although a performance certainly provides visibility and presence by staging an idea or an identity through some form of intervention, the act of performing begins and ends as it unfolds. Precisely because of its ephemeral nature, performance makes us aware of the (in)visibility of its subject. Confronted with a fleeting and typically thought-provoking act, spectators witness a process of destabilizing meanings and identities, which in turn makes us more self-aware of the very nature of representation. As spectators and coparticipants, we must reflect not only on what happens during a performance but also on how and where it happens, for what purpose, who takes a leading role and who does not, and whether and how audience engagement, including our own, takes place.

Self-conscious, ephemeral, open to interpretation, and actively engaging, performance adequately lends itself to activist interventions. Nonetheless, the term *performative activism* and its variants remain widely under-utilized and under-studied. Its most accomplished definition and application may still be Barbara Green's 1997 study of performative activism in the context of the suffrage movement (1905–1938). Green defines the term on the basis of Austin's premise that performative utterances such as "I do" in a marriage ceremony or the sentence read by a judge "reveal the word as act" (16). Through speeches which included performative statements like "Votes for Women!" but also via "repeated rituals and gestures" such as wearing suffrage colors and badges, activists "mapped new meanings . . . onto the metropolis" (15). More recently, in 2016 L. M. Bogad coined the term "tactical performance" to describe "the use of performance techniques, tactics, and aesthetics in social-movement campaigns" such as the Zapatistas in Chiapas, Mexico (2). However, if we are to study both large-scale movements and community-based initiatives, the concept of performative activism remains more broadly applicable than tactical performance, for it best captures everyday resistance tactics as well as the logistics of mass protest. Because change can and must occur at the individual and collective levels, performative activism seeks to permeate public discourse from mass interventions or national demonstrations down to the quotidian and the street level. As Daphna Ben-Shaul describes in her study of Public Movement, the Israeli duo of performance artists Dana Yahalomi and Omer Krieger, performative activism imbues public life with art in order to spur and facilitate "participation in the choreography of change" (130). In the realm of community activism, Quixote-inspired organizations seek to equip mainly youth in vulnerable situations with the performative tools to effect change. Through artistic and pedagogical interventions, the Brazilian nonprofits examined here aim to activate children's potential for taking on a leading role in the choreography that fuels social progress.

Both choreographed and inherently unpredictable, performative activism constantly and paradoxically lives on the edge of provocation and irrelevance, engagement and indifference, meaningful change and mere posturing. In fact, the leap from personal to structural change that Quixote-inspired organizations are predicated on is anything but a sure occurrence. Is personal transformation, in fact, even a precondition to broader social betterment? This question profoundly concerned activists already in the 1960s. As George Lipsitz warns in relation to the 1960s and 1970s counterculture movement in the United States, personal self-awareness alone may not do enough to interrogate power structures and thus may fail to effect deep social change. In his study of Brazil's own *contracultura* movement, however, Christopher Dunn addresses the notion of change from the opposite perspective. As Dunn explains through his application of Félix Guattari's concept of molecular revolution, without "a kind of mutation among people" carried out in the everyday through individual "practices of change," no meaningful social change can occur (203). Ultimately, the circularity of transformation between the individual and the collective may best be described as two sides of the same coin. Regardless of which one takes precedence, personal and social change must occur simultaneously at some point in order to achieve far-reaching and meaningful results without oversimplifying an issue as complex as marginalization or oppression.[2] Ephemeral and uncontrollable, performative activism walks the razor edge between deep transformation, ineffectiveness, and even frivolity.

In Brazil, cultural activism has traditionally been understood as a critical tool in the performance of citizenship, partly because the federal government itself has always given culture a preeminent role in the configuration of the national self both within its borders and abroad. Already in the 1930s, under the influential presidency of nationalist and populist Getúlio Vargas, government regarded public culture as a key tool in the consolidation of modern Brazilian identity (McCann). Although constantly evolving under successive administrations, each with their particular ideology and political interests, culture has traditionally acted in Brazil as "a state project of citizenship and a viable industry for export" (Pardue, "Taking Stock" 4). The best-known example of the intersection between culture, citizenship, and export value remains the Tropicália or Tropicalism movement.[3] Spearheaded by Caetano Veloso and Gilberto Gil, Tropicália both protested the 1964 coup d'état and simultaneously popularized Brazilian music around the world by blending (or cannibalizing, as Oswald de Andrade would have preferred) rock and roll and other foreign influences with local, mostly Afro-Brazilian rhythms.

When union leader Lula da Silva became president in 2003, cultural citizenship performed from the margins by nonprofits and minority cultural movements moved to a central position in the country's government. By naming Gilberto Gil the country's minister of culture, President Lula brought the Tropicália movement full circle from its location of resistance against the military junta in the 1960s and 1970s to the highest office in national cultural politics. Through a program called Pontos de Cultura (Cultural Points), Gil's ministry awarded approximately 120 million US dollars to over one thousand community centers around the country (Pardue, "Taking Stock" 7), including the Quixote-inspired Instituto Religare. Thanks in part to the financial support from federal and local governments, and with one of the Tropicália founders at the helm of Brazil's official cultural agenda, artivism flourished and turned urban spaces across the country into a "laboratório de criação" (a laboratory of [artistic] creation; Benassi 1536) with a social conscience. Against the harmful effects of neoliberalism and consumerism on particularly the most vulnerable populations, a heterogeneous "fenômeno do coletivismo artístico e ativista" (phenomenon of artistic and activist collectivism) offered a plethora of cultural methods of intervention in public physical and virtual spaces, from open mic sessions in underserved neighborhoods to graffiti, public art, or the digital remixing of television commercials (Mazetti 107). At the community level, numerous nonprofits attempted to promote urban development and equality "from the standpoint of the margin" (Pardue, "Reversal of Fortunes?" 40).

Two recent examples in Brazil best illustrate new forms of performing citizenship through bottom-up street activism at both the national and community levels. In my two case studies, the 2013 Brazilian Autumn and the Grupo Cultural AfroReggae (GCA), the practice of alternative forms of citizenship that go counter to mainstream and elite narratives is deployed at the street level through performative activism. First, I examine the nationwide efforts to recast the country's identity through the 2013 mass protests that became known as the Brazilian Autumn (the *Outono brasileiro*). Then I probe into the street activism that a cultural organization such as the GCA deploys among marginalized favela populations. To some extent, the distinction between the nation-building and community-based efforts described here is more gradual and complementary than clear-cut or antagonistic. The 2013 mass demonstrations, or *protestos*, exposed not only collective demands but also personal and highly localized grievances, such as references to specific individuals or neighborhood projects affected by the government's inefficiency. Conversely, community-based efforts equally denounce problems and perform a type of citizenship that, while rooted in the case of GCA in the Vigário Geral favela in Rio de Janeiro, can be extrapolated to the collective construction of an alternative practice of Brazilian national identity.

In June 2013, millions of people across Brazil took to the streets to tell another story about their country. After almost a decade of robust economic growth, the mass demonstrations known as the Brazilian Autumn, a direct reference to the Arab Spring that toppled authoritarian governments in various Middle Eastern and North African countries between 2011 and 2012, constituted a relatively spontaneous and collective effort to change the nation's story against the official discourse of prosperity. Abruptly, a six-year economic expansion (2004–2010) had turned into a contraction in 2011 and then a full-scale recession by 2014, while the impending celebration of the 2014 FIFA World Cup and the 2016 Olympic Games inched forward plagued by corruption and delays. Increasingly, the official narrative of economic and social progress articulated by the country's business, media, and political elites did not correspond to the everyday realities of common citizens. In a matter of a few turbulent weeks, the Brazilian Autumn drew a stark contrast between the elite-driven fantasy of a country on the cusp of greatness and the daily hardships endured by most Brazilians.[4]

In early June, before the movement blew up to a national scale, the previously little-known São Paulo organization Movimento Passe Livre or MPL (Free Pass Movement, in reference to public transportation) organized the first street protests. As the movement expanded throughout the country, MPL spokespeople (they refuse to call themselves leaders) cited the Zapatista movement in Chiapas, Mexico, and particularly its best-known spokesperson, Subcomandante Marcos, as their main ideological and tactical compass for their leaderless mass revolt (Farah). Subcomandante Marcos' well-documented passion for *Don Quixote*, in his view the most important book on political theory ever written ("The Punch Card"), bears mention here, for his activism has also been described as performative (Gómez Peña; de la Colina). In fact, the collection significantly titled *Our Word is Our Weapon* remains Subcomandante Marcos' best-known anthology of texts. During the Brazilian Autumn, in the largest demonstrations in Brazilian history since the pro-democracy campaign that ended the military dictatorship in the early 1980s, ordinary people also used performance and words as weapons to radically rewrite the country's official narrative of order and prosperity. Collectively, by performing their activism in the streets and online, common citizens exposed what the political and economic powers would rather keep out of the public eye: corruption, poverty, inequality, and inefficiency.

Public discourse and the streets, particularly in urban centers, quickly became the main conduit for the performance of a new form of activist citizenship across Brazil. In their rewriting of the national storyline, demonstrators articulated a counter-narrative against the official storyline by heavily relying not on a literary classic, as in my Quixote-inspired case studies, but on popular culture, including sports and most notably advertising. Two commercials in particular, "O gigante acordou" (The giant has awoken) by British whisky distillery Johnnie Walker and "Vem pra rua" (Come to the street) by Italian carmaker FIAT, best captured the discursive and performative nature of the clash between elite-driven, top-down and street-level, bottom-up activist efforts to construct the image of the national self. Given their outsized role in the Brazilian Autumn *protestos*, these two extremely popular television ads warrant careful analysis.

In the 2011 "O gigante acordou" commercial, the iconic Sugarloaf Mountain in Rio de Janeiro arises in the shape of a giant. A serene piano melody first provides the musical background for a mystical landscape: the Sugarloaf reigns over a foggy panoramic view of Rio de Janeiro. In sharp contrast, a close-up of the mountain's surface suddenly fills the screen as a massive crack splits the rock in two. In the next frame, large debris rolls down the mountainside. In shock, Rio residents look up but do not panic. As a full orchestra amplifies the piano melody via an inspiring tune in constant crescendo, a stone giant separates first its head and torso and then its legs from the monolithic mountain and finally begins to rise up. With broad smiles on their faces, people from across the city run toward windows and balconies and flood the streets in order to catch a glimpse of the moving giant. As it stands up, the giant casts his shade on entire neighborhoods, but sunshine stills showers a city paralyzed with joy. In a reassuring climax, the giant walks toward the water after safely depositing on the ground a cable car full of tourists (after all, the Sugarloaf summit remains one of Brazil's main tourist attractions). Against the backdrop of a bright blue sky, the walking giant once again towers over a foggy Rio lying at its feet. In the final frame, the following phrase fades in: "O gigante não está mais adormecido" (The giant no longer sleeps). As the music suddenly stops, the screen goes black, and in large font we read "Keep Walking, Brazil" in English, followed by the Johnnie Walker logo.

Figuratively, the commercial celebrates Brazil's transformation from a global sleeping giant of great resources but disappointing performance into a full-blown world titan.[5] Accordingly, the Johnnie Walker commercial touches on the country's nationalistic fibers at deep-rooted levels. As the Brazilian legend goes, the mountains that surround Rio de Janeiro materialized when a sleeping giant, the Guanabara Bay titan, petrified. From the opposite coast of Niterói, the Pedra da Gávea Mountain that towers over the city represents the giant's head, and the Sugarloaf peak symbolizes its feet. So ingrained remains this legend in the Brazilian imaginary that the national anthem includes in its first stanza a reference to this "impávido colosso" (fearless colossus). In celebration of Rio's gorgeous natural setting, the second stanza describes the giant "Deitado eternamente no berço esplêndido / Ao som do mar e à luz do céu profundo" (Eternally lying on a splendid cradle / To the sound of the sea and under deep sky light).

In the Johnnie Walker commercial, the reclining giant placidly enjoying "the sound of the sea" under the sun has now arisen and walks decisively toward the ocean, a metaphor for the country's active participation in the international scene. Instead of passively relishing its privileged environment, the Brazilian giant goes to work. At a symbolic level, this advertisement captures the booming national pride of a nascent world super-power, a sentiment that peaked around 2011 as Brazil's economic boom prompted the rewriting of its geopolitical and cultural role on the global scene. For Scotch whiskey brand Johnnie Walker, the campaign also acknowledged Brazil as its top international customer through a full one-minute commercial dedicated, for the first time in the company's history, to just one country. As the video, a collaboration between the Brazilian advertising agency NEOGAMA/BBH and English and US film-production companies, comes to a close, the word "Brazil" (spelled in English with a z instead of the Portuguese s) is cunningly added to the company's motto, "Keep Walking." In an unprecedented move, the company celebrates Brazil by fusing its international rising-star status with Johnnie Walker's own leading position in the domestic market. With the giant now fully awake and consuming vast amounts of Scotch, the company encourages the country to "Keep Walking, Brazil" (Penteado).[6]

During the prosperous first decade of the twenty-first century, Brazil indeed rewrote for itself a protagonist role in the global theater, most notably through its newfound position as an international sports-event host. For decades, Brazil's global profile relied almost exclusively on its touristic allure and a wealth of legendary artists and sport figures. The organization of the 2013 Confederations Cup, the 2014 FIFA World Cup, and the 2016 Olympic Games was intended to prove that Brazil could not only win international sporting events elsewhere; the sleeping giant, finally awoken, could now host them, as well. In May 2013, one month before the Confederations Cup, Italian carmaker FIAT released their "Vem pra rua" (Come to the street) advertising campaign. With more than eighteen million hits on YouTube alone, the centerpiece of this campaign was a one-minute video of simple but effective format: images of people dancing in the street, with several close-ups of attractive women looking mischievously into the camera, a catchy soundtrack, and many Brazilian flags. Produced by the Leo Burnett Tailor Made agency in São Paulo, the ad masked its commercial nature by subliminally displaying FIAT cars among a mass of people seemingly celebrating a victory by the Brazilian soccer team. Cunningly, this top car-seller in Brazil for over a decade did not directly sponsor the Confederations Cup, and the commercial does not display the FIAT brand until the very last three seconds of footage. In only a few weeks, however, this ad became the most watched car commercial ever as well as the most watched video about the Confederations Cup on YouTube ("Vem pra rua").

Against a simple drumbeat, the video begins with images of empty streets and an eerie calmness in an unnamed city. Then a vivacious instrumental melody erupts, providing the cheerful musical backdrop to close-ups of people of all genders, races, and ages biting their nails while intently watching a soccer match. As if celebrating a victory, people start jumping up and down in a burst of collective hysteria. Simultaneously, a male voice (the lead performer of the popular afro-reggae/funk band O Rappa, Marcelo Falcão) sings an invitation for all Brazilians to come out to the street. In the first stanza, the lyrics echo the rhetoric of awakening giants that Johnnie Walker had so successfully exploited: "o Brasil vai tá gigante / Grande como nunca se viu" (Brazil will be a giant, larger [greater] than ever before). Although we do not see soccer stadiums or clear images of a match or any particular player, people appear to celebrate Brazil's victory in the streets through an exuberant display of nationalistic symbols, such as flags and t-shirts of the national soccer team, amid mostly slow-moving or stopped FIATs. If Johnnie Walker's giant arises to triumphantly stride onto the international scene, FIAT's call to flood the streets prompts Brazilians to celebrate their country's good fortunes in their own cities as well.

In contrast to the contagious optimism conveyed by these two popular commercials, the public performance of citizenship in Brazil took a radically different and activist turn in 2013. In the months prior to the

Confederations Cup, deep cracks appeared in this glowing national façade of awakening giants and street jubilation. In fact, public rage had been brewing for some time.[7] Mass protests in reaction to public-transportation fare increases had already begun at the local level in 2012 in several major cities, including Natal's Revolta do Busão, or Bus Revolution, as well as marches in Porto Alegre and Rio (Gutiérrez 41). Yet, the intensity of the June 2013 demonstrations and the speed with which the #BRevolução, as it was labeled in one of its most popular hashtag forms, irradiated from São Paulo to the rest of the country took everyone by surprise. Millions of disgruntled citizens took to the streets to alter the glowing national narrative that failed to recognize the sudden, dramatic fall of the Brazilian giant into economic recession and political mayhem.

On June 13, after a few days of growing demonstrations due to a hike in São Paulo's public-transportation fares, the police acted with such blind brutality against protesters that even numerous journalists covering the protests sustained serious injuries. Consequently, mainstream media such as the independent *Folha de São Paulo* and the conservative *Globo Rede* conglomerate reversed their initially critical stance against the demonstrators and began to recognize the legitimacy of their cause (Moraes 144–46). A video account on YouTube of a June 13 incident in which a young female *Folha* journalist, Giulana Vallone, was hit in the eye with a rubber bullet was viewed almost two million times within only a few days of the incident. With mainstream media now also outraged at the government response, between June 17 and 21, millions of Brazilians flooded the streets across the country; 1.4 million people marched on June 20 alone. Through this performance of citizenship, previous elite narratives of economic growth and social equality crashed head-on with a leaderless oppositional movement powered by mass participation and social media. In less than two weeks, the oppositional movement that was sweeping Brazil forced President Dilma Rousseff and Congress to swiftly pass robust anticorruption and socially progressive laws. In two televised appearances on June 21 and 24, President Rousseff acknowledged her government's mistakes and corrected the country's course through several substantial legislative initiatives. Lacking in homogenous ideology and partisan identification, the *protestos* articulated a collective effort to rewrite the national discourse from the bottom up.

The #BRevolução declared itself political, not partisan; chose not to appoint any visible leaders; and coalesced around mainly abstract demands (Quixote-inspired organizations operate on similar terms, as Chapter 6 documents.) Most protesters did oppose transportation-fare hikes and a handful of policy proposals under review at the time, from legalizing therapies to "cure" homosexual behavior (PDL 234) to a constitutional amendment limiting the power of the judicial branch to investigate political corruption (PEC 37). But to politicians' dismay, the movement resisted ideological, generational, racial, and class-based identification. With no concrete alternative to current political parties and forms of government, protesters broadly defended their right to express their grievances in public and, more specifically, to receive adequate public services. In this regard, the Brazilian Autumn functioned as what Michael Hardt and Toni Negri define as a "multitude" of heterogeneous voices, rather than as a traditionally homogenous "mass movement," in which participants coalesce around a single ideology or political party. In its powerful use of "the networked space between the digital space and the urban space," the Brazilian Autumn operated as a leaderless movement of people engaged in the public expression of outrage and hope (Castells 11, 222–28).[8]

In his 1985 article entitled "The Symbolic Challenge of Contemporary Movements," Italian sociologist Alberto Melucci elucidated the modus operandi of popular protests of his time, and in doing so he foretold the social media-enhanced mass movements of today. In fact, the theoretical framework Melucci outlined reveals the discursive underpinnings of the Brazilian Autumn as well as those of Quixote-inspired activism. Although not explicitly influenced by Paulo Freire's *Pedagogy of the Oppressed*, in a section of his article entitled "Naming the World" Melucci identifies (re)naming as a critical tool for challenging power structures. In this subheading, he identifies "the fight for symbolic and cultural stakes" as the defining characteristic of contemporary social movements (797). With the ultimate goal to reverse "symbolic systems embodied in power relationships," late twentieth-century demonstrators prioritize "form" and discursive resistance over partisan identification and concrete policy proposals (809, 813). While confronting traditional political systems (parties, laws, dictatorships), contemporary protests do not seek their institutionalization and do not draw from traditional actors, such as opposition parties or even NGOs. Instead, Melucci argues, demonstrators aim to publicly share "their messages and translate these messages into political decision making" (815), a process which the Brazilian Autumn culminated in less than two weeks by forcing President Roussef and Congress to pass a battery of anticorruption and fiscally progressive laws.

In specific reference to social media-enhanced protests, Manuel Castells confirmed some twenty years later Melucci's assertion that current oppositional movements do not revolve around singular ideological issues but center on "the battle for the construction of meaning in the minds of people" (5). In June 2013, the symbolic challenge theorized by Melucci and Castells turned the Brazilian streets into a discursive battlefield upon which common citizens, traditionally mere spectators of the political spectacle, became its defining actors and writers. Occupying the streets as well as virtual spaces, ordinary Brazilian citizens entered the fray over the control of meaning with a discursive arsenal capable of, without guns or violence, rewriting Brazil's narrative. In their symbolic challenge to power, then, how did the protesters achieve so much in such a short period of time? How did the Brazilian people rescript and perform their citizenship through bottom-up street activism?

In the battle for control over the national story, Brazilians resorted to creativity over ideology and prioritized symbolic actions over concrete policy proposals. While the Internet proved an invaluable tool, the achievements of the Brazilian Autumn cannot be attributed solely nor even primarily to social media. Although Facebook, Twitter, and the like helped facilitate, articulate, and disseminate social movements both domestically and internationally, the protestos succeeded because demonstrators deployed discursive tactics not only virtually, but also via the physical act of handwriting protest signs and chanting slogans in the streets.[9] Significantly, a large handwritten banner heading the June 17 mass demonstration in Rio de Janeiro asserted "Somos a rede social" (We are the social network). In this march a wall of demonstrators embodied the human quality of the social network that took over the country. As Luisa Martín Rojo explains, the cycle of "viral replication of messages" moving back and forth between virtual and physical spaces in fact often starts and ends in the street. Demands shouted by demonstrators are written onto signs and placards before becoming images circulated online, feeding further chants and signs in subsequent marches (9–10). A popular sign that apologized for the chaos in the streets while Brazilians rebuilt the country ("Desculpe o trastorno, estamos mudando o país"; Pardon our appearance, we are changing the country) became a particularly telling illustration of the fluidity between street and virtual spaces. Amply circulated online, a technology-influenced version of this slogan also became highly visible across many marches: "Desculpe o trastorno, estamos *formatando* o país" (Pardon our appearance, we are *formatting* [*resetting*] the country; my emphasis). In this playful and effective convergence between handwritten personal messages and social media, signs and banners constituted the main channel of expression for protestors even when they claimed to be

A Place of Hope | 139

FIGURE 5.1. Handwritten signs in public protest in Porto Alegre, Brazil (June 18, 2013). Photograph by Isaias Ramos

resetting or formatting the country. In this regard, online resistance complemented and magnified but never replaced street activism by facilitating the organization and dissemination of mass protests (Farias and Alves 156, 158; Gohn 368; Arruda and Moreira).

Enhanced by the savvy use of social media, the success of the Brazilian Autumn rested on the discursive strategies by which people (the human "social network") rescripted the mainstream version of the contemporary Brazilian story articulated by politicians and business conglomerates such as Johnnie Walker or FIAT. In only a matter of days, the #BRevolução would awake its own alternative version of the Brazilian giant, one who not only walks, but now also talks, and rather loudly. Conquering the streets of the entire nation, this vociferous titan, in contrast to Johnnie Walker's silent colossus, channeled myriad individualized messages publicly performed (written, chanted, enacted, posted, and shared) by ordinary citizens.

Through the tens of thousands of handwritten signs and placards in hundreds of marches across the country, another story (the stories of many Others) began to emerge. Together, signs and the physical act of protest wove a narrative that proved deeply political and utterly performative. With the message quite literally embodied in the marching demonstrators who wrote and chanted their demands, signs acted as linguistic, bodily extensions of people's outrage and hope.[10] Intertwined in a symbiotic relationship, the stories told through signs and banners cannot be separated from the person or people who wrote, waived, and chanted them. In this consequential synthesis of discourse and action, of performative transformation and social change, I identify the same brand of activism that I later examine as the main feature of Quixote-inspired Brazilian organizations.

In lieu of the silent giant digitally created by an advertising agency for a multinational liquor company, the titanic Brazilian body that for a few days towered over government and economic elites consisted of millions of anonymous citizens engaged hands-on in the mass rescripting of the national narrative. While Quixote-inspired activism leans on a literary giant to guide their subversive act of rewriting, the Brazilian Autumn instead appropriated the two videos that had arguably best captured the nation's newfound role as a world titan in the collective imaginary: Johnnie Walker's awakening "gigante" and FIAT's "Vem pra rua." By repurposing these two commercials, ordinary people drew from decades-long oppositional tactics that take full advantage of the ubiquity of advertising in conjunction with the potential of the Internet for mass mobilization.[11]

In recent years, wide access to digital remixing technology via inexpensive or free editing software and applications rendered the popular Johnnie Walker and FIAT advertisements, albeit unintentionally, into ideal targets for the subversive imagination of a network of anonymous citizens. As Henrique Mazetti pointed out already in 2008, artistic and activist collectives in Brazil have incorporated into their arsenal "sabotagens midiáticas e guerrilha semiótica, em paródias ou adulterações da publicidade comercial" (media sabotage and semiotics guerrilla warfare, via parodies or edited versions of commercials; 108). With experience accumulated over at least a decade, by 2013 activists were well versed in *sabotagens* of commercials disseminated through social media. During the protests, and according to Brandviewer (a company that monitors social-media usage), the hashtag #VemPraRua impacted more than eighty million Twitter users in Brazil alone, followed by #OGiganteAcordou, with over sixty million. On Instagram, each of these two hashtags respectively stored around 650,000 and 455,000 images related to the protests (Mariano and Lopes; Fordelone). Technologically unsophisticated but brandishing a high emotional charge, anonymously remixed versions of the "O gigante acordou" and "Vem pra rua" campaigns appeared on YouTube and rapidly spread via social media. Because these videos are often posted, tweeted, and shared under different titles and by thousands of users across multiple platforms, including Facebook, Twitter, and Instagram, I cannot provide exact data on how many versions circulated and how many times each was viewed. Thus, I will only analyze two generic examples of the kinds of appropriation that these popular commercials underwent as activists turned them into the two chief symbolic pillars of the Brazilian Autumn. First, I examine remixed political videos or RPVs (Horwatt 78) in support of the demonstrations, and then I analyze protest songs based on the most popular slogans seen and heard at the marches.

Numerous RPVs adapted the two ads by remixing images of Johnnie Walker's awakening giant, FIAT's effervescent soundtrack, and actual street demonstrations. While some clips reveal police brutality, others oscillate between panoramic views of the protests and close-ups of people chanting and holding signs or banners. A particularly popular video, lasting around three minutes, begins with Geraldo Alckmin, governor of the state of São Paulo at the time, describing to reporters on June 12, 2013, the budding *movimento* as politically motivated and *pequeno* (small). Parodying the governor's statement, the word *pequeno* is replayed several times in rapid succession. Immediately after, we see a widening crack on Sugarloaf Mountain, taken from the moment in the Johnnie Walker commercial that announces the rise of the awakening giant. Accompanying these hopeful images, the vivacious soundtrack from FIAT's "Vem pra rua" replaces Governor Alckmin's ominous voice and provides a blissful musical background to the images of street demonstrations and the rising giant that follow.

After the first image of the splintering Sugarloaf, a particularly popular version of this video, "estrelando qualquer brasileiro disposto a mudar" (starring any Brazilian willing to change [the country]), credits Atitude Records as its producer. I have not been able to find any information about an Atitude Records production company or group, and the rudimentary editorial quality points to the hand of amateurs, not a professional company. Atitude Records gives this video the title "Um pouco de troco," which roughly and appropriately translates as "A little change." Around the two-minute mark, the song comes to an end when the Johnnie Walker commercial's final image of the Brazilian giant walking into the ocean materializes with the words "The giant is no longer asleep" (*O gigante não está mais adormecido*) written across the sky. Instead of following this last frame with the company's "Keep Walking, Brazil" slogan, however, the editors insert the following modified plea, also in English: "Keep Fighting, Brazil." The video continues for about one minute more, initially with a voiceover against a black screen of an unidentified woman asserting the people's right to fight for Brazil. Lastly, the "Vem pra rua" song starts over while slides reminiscent of memes underscore how former soccer players were more committed to social causes than current Brazilian stars. The video ends with the #VemPraRua hashtag written in large font across the screen.[12]

Corporate commercials unintentionally provided the imagery and sound for the protests, but only after they underwent a creative process of transformation akin to the change (*troco, mudança, formateo*) protestors demanded for the entire country. Tech-savvy anonymous editors remixed the Johnnie Walker and FIAT commercials into a giant that spoke for the people through images of street protests and a cheerful musical call to "come to the street." With the twofold purpose of disseminating information and calling for action, these RPVs infused two lighthearted commercials with the gravity of the mass outrage expressed during the unprecedented nationwide demonstrations. In order to change the country's narrative, however, the new stories emerging from the streets and online, whether personal grievances or social values (anticorruption, equality, progressive fiscal policies), had to be enacted. The demonstrators called for words that ultimately "do things," for their activism rooted itself in performativity. In the streets and online, the Brazilian Autumn demanded that the people's written, chanted, and posted national stories be translated into actual legislative and political change.

Second in popularity only to the remixing of television commercials, the other main discursive tactic of the Brazilian Autumn consisted of weaving protest slogans together into songs explicitly composed in support of the marches. While FIAT's "Vem pra rua" jingle served as the protests' unofficial anthem, several well-known Brazilian singers incorporated the "Vem pra rua" and "O gigante acordou" themes into their own original songs. Perhaps most notably, Thiago Correa created "Brasil em cartaz," a song that plays with the double meaning of the word *cartaz* in Portuguese, roughly translated as "sign" and "in theaters" (i.e., "Brazil through protest signs," "Brazil in theaters now," or more literally, "Brazil in the spotlight" or "on stage"). With over 206,000 views on YouTube, the lyrics of this song consist of an amalgam of popular protest signs, including "Saimos do Facebook" and "Vem pra rua." By recording a soundtrack that showcases some of the most popular slogans chanted and displayed in the streets, Correa reinforces the notion that art and performance (the act of rewriting, editing, shouting, demonstrating) can articulate a message that is ideologically and ethno-racially diverse yet also cohesive in terms of its purpose and tactics. Through the multitude of voices that flooded the streets and inspired Correa's hit song, ordinary citizens boldly affirmed the performance of their citizenship. The protestors' clamor, Brazil's true awakening giant, rose over deceitful political as well as commercial narratives and ultimately forced Congress to effect significant legislative change.

In his more personal take on the Brazilian Autumn, São Paulo native MC Daleste officially released "O gigante acordou" (The giant awoke) on June 23, 2013; he was only twenty years old at the time. Viewed over eighteen million times on YouTube, in the two-and-a-half-minute video MC Daleste stands in front of a microphone in a seemingly modest studio, reading his lyrics off a cell phone with only a sound engineer seated in his proximity. In the first three seconds, an undulating Brazilian flag fills the screen with a female voiceover proclaiming the historical nature of the 2013 demonstrations, for in June the national *gigante acordou*. We then see Daleste from behind wearing a yellow polo with the word *Brazil* (in the English spelling) embroidered in green across the shoulders. Significantly, Daleste does not wear the official equipment of the national soccer team but an unbranded polo with the national colors (yellow and green) and the country's name on the back. Implicitly, thus, he disavows the soccer-fueled impetus for national jubilation that FIAT's "Vem pra rua" celebrates. Before Daleste begins recording his song in front of a studio microphone, the video plays short clips from the June protests. The lyrics of "O gigante acordou" include a number of slogans chanted at demonstrations and handwritten on signs that articulate a familiar narrative demanding an end to corruption and the improvement of public services. Together with the call "vem, vem pra rua" (come, come to the street), the references to the Brazilian giant abound. In yet another explicit attempt to reframe Brazilian nationalism, Daleste updates the national anthem line that describes the giant "deitado em berço esplêndido" (lying on a splendid cradle) by claiming that now "the povo acordou do coma" (the people woke up from a coma). In the chorus, the singer repeats several times "O gigante Brasil acordou / Sem violência, eu quero mudança" (The Brazilian giant awoke / Without [resorting to] violence, I demand change). With a Brazilian giant now fully awake and renouncing violence, Daleste summarizes in his call for change the people's aspiration for a significant shift in the way government administers Brazil's wealth. Through his succinct but forceful call for broad, non-prescriptive *mudança*, Daleste captures the unifying sentiment and underlying strategy of the Brazilian Autumn, which broadly coincide with the purpose and tactics of *Quixote*-inspired organizations. Intrinsically performative, their activism presents itself as open-ended but nonetheless utters words that aim to "do things," that demand change. Seemingly, protestors and activists can cope with ambiguity but will not tolerate inaction.[13]

The composition and goals of both the 2013 mass demonstrations and the modestly sized organizations that employ *Don Quixote* in their community work prove far-reaching, non-prescriptive, and ultimately open-ended. Instead of offering detailed proposals and setting concrete goals, Brazilian performative activism seeks to influence and ultimately transform public discourse by rescripting elite-driven symbolic systems in politics, business, and media. Concerned mainly with the transformation of society through the rewriting of personal and social narratives, the national wave of protests that flooded the country's streets in 2013 mirrors community-based efforts such as the Quixote-inspired organizations that utilize cultural instruments, including art and theater, as weapons for liberation. Chief among Brazilian cultural organizations, the Grupo Cultural AfroReggae (GCA) serves as a perfect segue between the large-scale mass protests of the Brazilian Autumn and the neighborhood-level activism of Quixote-inspired nonprofits.

Among the civil-society efforts to change spaces of marginalization into visible cultural centers, the most prominent and arguably most successful NGO in Brazil remains the GCA. Although unrelated to *Don Quixote* organizations, GCA also works with at-risk youth populations and employs a similarly performative and artivist approach to that of my Cervantes-based case studies. The enormously successful Rio de Janeiro organization found in the award-winning documentary film *Favela Rising* (Matt Mochary and Jeff Zimbalist, 2005) an effective medium to enhance its by-then already significant international recognition. *Favela Rising* tells the story of the nonprofit through the eyes of one of its founders, Anderson Sá, whose life dramatically changed on August 29, 1993, when the Vigário Geral favela of Rio de Janeiro where he resides suffered a brutal police attack. In retribution for the murder of four officers who were notorious for their regular extortion attempts on both drug traffickers and residents, twenty-one innocent bystanders were indiscriminately massacred by police officers in a central street of the favela. As Sá recounts in the film, his own brother was among the victims. Overcoming his anger, fear, and resentment, Sá managed to cope with this traumatic experience by taking on a leading role in the GCA, and particularly in its flagship initiative, the Banda AfroReggae, which I discuss below.

While the documentary has been criticized for its oversimplification and melodramatic emphasis on one personal story over the structural causes of poverty and violence (Larkins; Cala Buendía 105), *Favela Rising* no doubt helped introduce the GCA to a larger, mostly English-speaking audience. Partly inspired by the Olodum organization in Salvador de Bahia (which also looms large over the Bando de Teatro Olodum that staged Márcio Meirelles' *Um tal de Dom Quixote*), the GCA has received near universal praise for its artivist intervention in the favela space. Over its twenty-five years of continued operation, and partly thanks to substantial support from private sponsors and both local and federal government, the organization has expanded its cultural offerings from hip-hop, percussion, capoeira, and dance to theater, circus, classical music, graffiti, literacy, and other forms of artistic expression and social intervention, such as waste recycling, public-health campaigns, and career training. When considered as a whole, the cultural and social enterprise promoted by AfroReggae demonstrates that, as the English subtitles to one of their songs excerpted toward the end of the film proclaim, "Within music and culture, a new movement exists."[14]

The favelas or slums in major Brazilian cities, but most pointedly in Rio de Janeiro, function as ever-evolving urban areas with very localized idiosyncrasies and particular circumstances. Although inhabited by Brazilian citizens by birth, favela dwellings sit for the most part in illegal settlements, and the lives of their populations remain often exposed to the brutality of the pervasive and violent drug trade as well as severe police corruption. As Teresa Caldeira and James Holston denounced back in 1999, many favela dwellers "suffer systematic violations of their rights" in a blatant example of a disjunctive democracy that treats its citizens very differently based on their zip code, income, and skin color (692). For most favela dwellers, as is the case with participants in Quixote-inspired projects in São Paulo, the situation has not changed much since then. While most of its inhabitants are low income and live under varying degrees of precariousness, some favelas, or at least parts of them, may be much more developed than others, and their socio-economic fabric can be rather diverse. Alongside the ever-present drug trafficking across urban centers worldwide, a wide variety of businesses, tourism, and cultural production flourishes within some parts of the favelas. However, economic activity appears vulnerable to severe disruptions caused by wars among rival drug gangs, police corruption, and other forms of violence. Given the deficit in infrastructure and social services, residents have organized in groups such as GCA in Vigário Geral, which constitutes but one particularly successful example in a larger artivist trend in Brazil that articulates its pursuit of social justice around art and performance. In April 2003, journalist Juliana Monachesi had already documented "A explosão do a(r)tivismo" (An explosion of a(r)tivism) across the country, which updated for the twenty-first century politically engaged art movements of the 1960s and 1970s, including the influential Tropicália spearheaded by Caetano Velhoso and Gilberto Gil.

Artivist groups working with vulnerable populations in favelas, the São Paulo *periferia* (literally, periphery, or shanty towns around the city proper), or the downtown of many Brazilian urban centers face a certainly daunting task. (I do not include rural areas here, for their challenges and opportunities differ significantly from those of major cities and would require a separate study.) Following a steep upward trajectory during the Lula presidency, around 2012 the global recession coupled with political instability in Brazil caused a sudden and ongoing collapse of all major indicators of progress, which as I have discussed above triggered the Brazilian Autumn. Predictably, the economic situation very directly affects vulnerable populations in a country where violence, especially among and against underprivileged youth, has historically been devastatingly high. As the data demonstrate, youth crime feeds itself from socio-economic exclusion and proves much more lethal for marginalized youth themselves than for the broader population. Since the economic crisis started, and amid Brazil's hosting of the FIFA World Cup in 2014 and the Olympic Games in 2016, the situation has deteriorated alarmingly. In 2016 Brazil suffered 61,600 homicides compared to 17,000 in the United States, which boasts a population of 110 million more inhabitants, and the police killed 4,224 people, a whole 20 percent of them in Rio alone. Of these police victims, 76 percent were black and 80 percent between the ages of twelve and twenty-nine. Police officers have also been killed in record numbers: more than four hundred died in the line of duty in 2016 alone (Waldron). After the Olympic Games, the spiral of violence only worsened, and in February 2018 the military took control of the Rio de Janeiro police forces (Prengaman and DiLorenzo). To make matters worse, critics of police brutality and corruption are frequently targeted, as in the still-unresolved murder in March 2018 of iconic Afro-Brazilian and LGBTQ activist Marielle Franco, a city councilwoman born and raised in Rio de Janeiro's Maré favela. With the recent election in October 2018 of far-right, retired military officer Jair Bolsonaro, who ran on a law-and-order platform, the situation is likely to worsen, at least in the short term. (President Bolsonaro wants to grant immunity to police who kill suspected criminals in the line of duty.)

With challenges of such magnitude, how do artivist nonprofits and performative activists in general, whether inspired by *Don Quixote* or not, articulate their mission and deploy their cultural tactics? As with the nationwide protests during the Brazilian Autumn, the theme of transformation underscores the community-based work of both Quixote-inspired organizations and the well-documented case of GCA in Rio de Janeiro. If the hidalgo Quijano embodies change for the São Paulo nonprofits, for GCA it is the god-monster Shiva who symbolizes the transformative power that cultural production can trigger. According to one of its main co-founders, José Junior, AfroReggae's mission takes inspiration from the extraordinary being that in the Hindu tradition explicitly embraces its dual and ever-evolving nature. Governed by what its leaders call "the Shiva effect," AfroReggae garners the god's destructive powers to promote transformation and rebirth; out of chaos and suffering, CGA breeds a new society through cultural expression. For Junior and Anderson Sá, it is the Shiva effect that enables them to utilize culture (music, theater, dance, art) to rebuild society out of the ashes of Brazil's inequality, violence, and corruption (Neate and Platt 27).

On the margins of society, unfortunately, inspiration often arises from Shiva's destructive chaos. In the film *Favela Rising*, Anderson Sá describes a childhood steeped in the surrounding, suffocating violence and the frequent sound of gunshots. Out of this harsh environment, CGA created the Banda AfroReggae, arguably the most successful and well-known brand of the CGA organization. Sonically, the Banda AfroReggae employs a combination of rap and Afro-Brazilian drumming, together with choreographed acrobatic dancing, to reproduce the chaotic, enormously dynamic nature of an urban and racialized space in transition. While globally influenced by, among other genres, US rap and hip-hop, the Banda remains deeply rooted in its local circumstances. As Sá recounts, the group initially sought to transform the brutal noise of machine guns and death into rhythmic percussion performances in the Afro-Brazilian tradition of batucadas, popularized worldwide by Bahian musician Carlinhos Brown. With borrowed or improvised percussion instruments and an instructor from outside of Vigário Geral, AfroReggae began its non-violent activism with the goal to provide black role models to children whose point of reference for a functioning organization was almost exclusively the local and wildly successful narcotics trade. As the group's activities and outreach within the community grew, they gained the respect of fellow favela dwellers and started receiving external support from private and public entities. With a "hammer in one hand, a pencil in the other," as a song featured in the film claims (00:44:55), their visibility increased exponentially in both the domestic and international arenas.[15] Through a local government program called Urban Connections, for example, AfroReggae offered a number of free concerts in Vigário Geral and other favelas with the highest production values. Intentionally, the top quality of these free concerts in terms of sound, staging, and lighting aimed to reinforce the portrayal and visibility of favela residents as worthy producers and consumers of culture in their own eyes and in the eyes of mainstream society. Through lyrics that speak of the everyday and show a deep respect for favela dwellers, Banda AfroReggae models transformation for their communities through their own actions, by performing a new model of citizenship. Its members sign a pledge to not use or deal drugs and to function as favela ambassadors for good work ethics and social commitment. As the group sings in "Iguais sobrepondo iguais" (Like dominating like), from their *Cara nova* album (2006), "a cultura é o principal instrumento da mudança" (culture is the main instrument for change), a motto that band members themselves embody in the flesh.

The same principle fuels Quixote-inspired organizations in their fight against exclusion. Both the GCA in Rio and *Don Quixote* nonprofits in São Paulo seek to change urban spaces plagued by poverty and violence through a creative whirlwind of artistic and performative activism. Quixote-inspired initiatives overlap with AfroReggae's not ony in their radically pacifist attitude, but also in their shared goal of bringing the cultural identities of the excluded to the forefront. Through collective authorship and transculturation, urban transformation occurs in well-defined physical and social spaces whose identity and public image may be significantly altered via art and performance rather than police intervention or gun violence. Even if deeply connected to larger national and global trends, artivist groups seek the "ativação do espaço público" (the activation of public space; Benassi 1535) that may transform individuals and communities at the neighborhood and street levels. The transformative effect that organizations in underserved communities promote revolves around "The Importance of Being 'Gente,'" as Janice Perlman titles chapter 12 of her *Favela: Four Decades of Living on the Edge in Rio de Janeiro*. Being *gente* roughly translates into counting as a person, being recognized socially as more than a second-class citizen, or one with no rights at all. Through this broad notion of being gente, organizations such as AfroReggae or the Quixote-inspired nonprofits go beyond any one marker of identity, including race, gender, or class, in their efforts to promote the performance of citizenship by and for underserved communities. Instead of stressing one defining aspect of identity, they aim to change the discourse of marginalization through self-transformation and by modifying the social imaginary about both people and places. According to José Junior, since AfroReggae consolidated its presence in the community via a very rich, varied, and now extremely popular local cultural production, the favela Vigário Geral became no longer just the location of the 1993 massacre but "a place of hope" (*Favela Rising* 1:03:35).

In this complex process of (self)mutation, favela or *periferia* residents, at-risk children and youth, and street-connected populations aim to raise their public profile as citizens with full rights and responsibilities who deserve a dignified and free-of-prejudice role in the social narrative. Two key issues hinder their efforts: the rigidity with which mainstream society identifies individual and collective roles, especially among the underprivileged; and concurrently, the lack of public visibility of vulnerable communities as anything other than either criminals or victims. Rooted in spaces of deep marginalization, AfroReggae skillfully negotiates the tensions between fixed and fluid identities in order to develop a practice of citizenship that the government does not seem to care or be able to cultivate.

A consequential tactic for the identity of the underprivileged, particularly, as Paulo Freire already noted in his *Pedagogy of the Oppressed*, remains the choice between using legal or street names. The issue of naming may determine to a significant extent the performance of one's citizenship, as I previously discussed in relation to Brazilian stage adaptations of Cervantes' classic. In *Don Quixote*, we find a deliberate and comprehensive effort to use (re)naming in life-changing ways. At the beginning of the novel itself, the narrator and main characters fail to provide Don Quixote's legal name or family origins, as if the lack of social determination unlocked his imagination and triggered the enactment of his radical performative proposal. Only as his adventure comes to a close does the character himself disclose his official name in order to die within the legal and religious parameters of his time. In contrast, for many excluded from society it is the act of actually reclaiming one's legal name that may spark liberation. In fact, the two GCA leaders, José Junior and Anderson Sá, use only their legal names in the film, as if boldly affirming their visibility and full-fledged citizenship while representing underserved favela communities.[16]

In a revealing instance of the consequential nature of this interplay between legal and street names, *Favela Rising* captures the dramatic conversation between Anderson Sá and a boy, around ten years old, who claims to dream about the day he can quit school to join a drug gang. In a casual but firm tone, Sá insists on the importance of doing well in school and presents culture and art as a far better alternative to a life of crime. Unpersuaded, however, the boy declines Sá's invitation to join AfroReggae. When Sá asks his name, the boy answers "Richard," but a friend laughingly corrects him: his name is Murilio. When the kid bitterly protests his friend's unsolicited intervention, Anderson simply calls him "Richard Murilio," fully recognizing the boy's fluctuating stage in his identity formation. With a similar impetus, as I discussed in Chapter 3, Sancho Panza tries to settle the dispute between Don Quixote and a barber over the famous basin-helm (I.44.390), a unique prodigy that superimposes the chivalric world of epic heroes onto the humble work of a barber in early seventeenth-century Spain. Out of the chaotic discussion over the basin-helm, Sancho transforms a modest utensil into a hybrid of fluid meaning and ever-shifting social function. Similarly, out of his destructive desire to join a drug gang, "Richard Murilio" has been invested by Sá with a new name and social role, that of either a gangster or an artist in the making. At any point, the boy's identity in flux could turn to either or both cultural production and crime. In a characteristically happy-ending fashion, *Favela Rising* announces at the end of the film that five months after his conversation with Anderson Sá, "Richard Murilio" joined AfroReggae. Shiva has done it again, as out of chaos emerges order and artistic expression.

Parallel to the interplay between legal and street names, AfroReggae embraces and uses to its advantage the visibility afforded by mainstream audiences' fascination with the favelas, even if from a distance. Although most local residents work and live within the law, favelas conjure in the public imaginary both a sense of deep fear and an attraction to its untamed, mysterious nature. Gigantic settlements constantly growing outside official urban planning, the ever-mutating favelas have generated a cultural and touristic industry that Erika Larkins calls a "Favela, Inc." of global dimensions. As a consequence of the public fascination with these intriguingly edgy urban creatures, a conglomerate of revenue-generating activities has invaded the safer parts of the urban margins, including organized favela tourism and the production of popular television shows and movies such as *Cidade de Deus* (2002). Of course, in most cases the revenue generated is not invested locally (Sneed 27), but the attention that favelas elicit, even when for the most abject of reasons (violence, murder, drugs), affords a public platform from which AfroReggae attempts to change perceptions both inside and outside the slum, at the domestic as well as international levels.[17]

The productive tension between outside and local initiatives goes beyond the representation of Brazilian favelas for domestic and foreign consumption. Community-based cultural initiatives transform external cultural influences in music, cinema, literature, and art into a product tailored specifically for local residents, which in cases such as AfroReggae might then become a global phenomenon in their own right. In fact, the manifold cultural manifestations of AfroReggae turned out to be a resounding success within Rio, in Brazil, and internationally. As early as 1997, the band embarked on their first European tour, with many other performances in a variety of countries to follow. The Universal label offered them their first international record deal in 2002, several years before *Favela Rising* was even released. The "glocal" (global + local) nature of community-based artivist movements such as GCA manifests itself internally through a process akin to the very transculturation of *Don Quixote*. In GCA's approach to cultural creation, the Shiva effect that destroys to produce something new out of chaos replicates the transcultural process that Oswald de Andrade described with cannibalistic terms in his foundational "Manifesto antropófago" (1928). Key to their social and artistic project, in their song "Capa de revista" the Banda AfroReggae celebrates the endless, revolutionary potential of transformation: "Tudo vai mudar, vai mudar, vai mudar" (everything is going to change, change, change; quoted in Yúdice 151). As with Quixote-inspired activism, the war cry of "change" guides a process of reinvention based on the rewriting and performing of new identities. This radical metamorphosis starts with a creative enterprise that transculturates different influences (African, Caribbean, North American, European) into a new Brazilian hybrid by the name of AfroReggae. Drawing on Oswald de Andrade's call for a cannibalistic attitude toward the production of a genuinely Brazilian culture, John T. Maddox interprets AfroReggae as an exercise in the "sublimation of 'savagery' . . . as a source of uniquely Brazilian creativity" (463). Through this complex process of conscious and risky play with the notion of the "savage," the god monster Shiva inspires AfroReggae "to turn *soldados* [drug soldiers] . . . of the favelas into something new, evolving, protean" (472), god monsters themselves born out of a cannibalistic process of cultural frenzy.[18]

In conclusion, performative activism at the community level seeks the transformation of spaces of hardship and violence, both real (in the streets, institutions, and homes) and in the public imaginary (prejudices, stereotypes, and racism), into places where cultural productivity can flourish and actually alter the social narrative. In this "place of hope," as José Junior of GCA describes Vigário Geral, a new practice of citizenship that revolves around artistic discourse and community organizing transforms the role of youth from presumed criminals into producers and consumers of culture thanks to the Shiva (or Don Quixote, we could equally say) effect. At the nationwide level, ordinary citizens have also deployed performative activism in the streets and online to modify the national storyline produced by political and business elites, as in the case of the 2013 protestos. In both the Brazilian Autumn and the GCA, performative activism aims to confer a protagonist role to the Other, whether the commoner ignored by the ruling elites or the deeply marginalized youth in street situations. Through tactics such as self-naming, rewriting, and performing in public, the destabilization of institutionally sanctioned and fixed identities proves a critical step for the excluded to rescript their social role in their own words. Furthermore, ignored, misrepresented, or even vilified individuals may be able through art and performance to turn themselves into quite literally spectacular beings who elicit the attention of mainstream audiences, thus increasing their social visibility. Through a process of renaming and performance, whether we take Shiva or Quijano/Quixote as our model, urban spaces in Brazil continue to deeply transform the ways in which they script and enact their identity both at the national and neighborhood levels.

CHAPTER 6

"Quixotinhos Urbanos"

Performative Activism and
Urban Transformation in São Paulo

Four hundred years after its publication, Cervantes' *Don Quixote* serves today as an icon for individual and social transformation in activist projects throughout the Americas, and most commonly in Brazil. Several social justice initiatives around the country, but mainly in the financial and cultural hub of São Paulo, deploy a form of activism inspired by Cervantes' classic that employs (re)writing, art, and performance in order to change social narratives that marginalize particularly children and youth in high-risk situations such as homelessness, poverty, abuse, and mental illness. This type of Quixote-inspired activism anchors itself in concrete geographical and socio-economic locations, in the cases studied here both urban and underserved. Keenly aware of the disconnect that vulnerable youth experience from their families, schools, government, and their own selves because of drug use or mental illness, these organizations locate their participants' struggles and aspirations in very concrete though highly creative and ever-evolving spaces. In contrast to stage adaptations of *Don Quixote*, performative activism occurs at the street level without the possibility of rehearsing scenes or drawing a curtain if things do not go as planned. In community and street activism, the stakes are high, and risks abound, for the reading and application of *Don Quixote* occur within a complex and long-standing web of structural inequities and challenging personal circumstances. To counter the family, socio-economic, and political pressures that breed marginalization, activists focus on the rather expansive, vague notion that equality demands the deliberate (re)writing and performance of new individual stories for the vulnerable, which in turn will cumulatively produce a new social narrative. While Quixote-inspired organizations also tend to the material needs (from food to shelter or job training) of their participants, they strive to change the way in which underprivileged children and youth imagine themselves and the way in which society sees them. Through performative activism, they seek to proactively cultivate in their young project participants the self-awareness of their role as members of society with full rights and obligations. By honing artistic expression and theatrical skills, the theory goes, children and adolescents in vulnerable situations may resort to self-conscious performance to free themselves from the notion that their life story is predetermined by poverty and violence or, in its most racist version, by character flaws inherent to their socio-economic or racial identity. Through play and art, young project participants who in their quotidian lives must often take on adult responsibilities, such as securing food or seeking protection from abuse, can again experience age-appropriate psychological and emotional development. By analyzing these organizations' printed and online materials, available data, research publications, and artistic production, and through participant observations and multiple personal conversations, in this chapter I examine how community activists deploy Cervantes' masterpiece in Brazilian underserved urban spaces in order to transform personal and social narratives into stories of greater equality and opportunity.

For the sake of space, here I limit the scope of my research to long-term activist efforts in São Paulo, Brazil's financial and cultural capital, that have produced meaningful and somewhat measurable results, including the Instituto Religare (Reconnect or Reentry Institute) in Barra Funda, the Quixote Espaço Comunitário (Quixote Community Space) in Ipiranga, and the Projeto Quixote (Quixote Project) in Vila Mariana, all located in distinct neighborhoods of São Paulo.[1] The Instituto and the Quixote Espaço Comunitário (QEC) were founded by two of the playwrights and directors discussed in Chapters 3 and 4, Valéria di Pietro and Andreia de Almeida, respectively. Initially conceived in 2002 as a reentry program and community center, the Instituto Religare provided job training in theater and artistic careers as well as a space for participants to write and perform their own plays.[2] Founded in 2008, the QEC offers in the Ipiranga neighborhood free art-based workshops, ranging from acting to circus, writing, singing, capoeira, and dance, for about three hundred children and adolescents every month. Since 1996 the Projeto Quixote, the longest standing and largest of all São Paulo-based Cervantine organizations, has served more than fifteen thousand children (1,185 in 2017 alone, as quoted on their website) and consolidated its presence in the Vila Mariana neighborhood with a new building inaugurated in 2010.[3]

My analysis first probes the premise that rescripting and performing "another story," as the Projeto Quixote motto ("Uma outra história") demands, may have a positive and long-term impact on at-risk youth who often experience severe material and emotional deprivation. Next I examine three tactics that are central to Quixote-inspired activism: the process of (re)naming; the destabilization of fixed identity categories; and the tending to material needs, including the transformation of physical spaces inhabited by at-risk youth. I investigate these tactics first in Cervantes' own book, as the primary source of inspiration for the Brazilian organizations, and then in the Instituto Religare, the Quixote Espaço Comunitário, and the Projeto Quixote, in ascending order of size and impact, the Projeto being the largest and longest-lived of the three. A commentary on the limited assessment practices adopted by these organizations ensues, for the lack of clear outcomes and data on rates of success remains in my view the most significant shortcoming in Brazilian Quixote-inspired activism. As a final example that sums up in one dramatic scene the essence and methods of Brazilian Cervantes-based activism, I review the 2006 documentary film *Exilados do mundão* by the Projeto Quixote. This filmic project leads me to conclude with a revised definition of performative activism, a theoretical concept and praxis applicable beyond Brazil and beyond *Don Quixote*. More than simply the performance of discontent in public demonstrations, this type of cultural activism deploys words and performance as key instruments of individual and collective change in community-based contexts.

The vehement call for transformation that fuels social justice and Quixote-inspired activism emerges from the urge to modify a reality that breeds insufferable inequalities for the underserved, which often result in trauma and isolation. Under these extreme circumstances, according to the organizations I examine here, *Don Quixote* provides a model for youth to deploy a performative and literary arsenal against injustice. As Valéria di Pietro told me in a personal conversation, one of the FEBEM interns who participated in the staging of *Num lugar de la Mancha* captured in a particularly telling way the plight of at-risk youth in relation to Don Quixote's story. While Cervantes' knight-errant tilted at windmills as if they were giants, a young actor in the play explained, children in high-risk social situations charge at giants as if they were windmills. In their daily fight against a "monstruosa injusticia social" (monstrous social injustice, as described on the Projeto Quixote website), the life and death situations that street-connected and at-risk children are forced to face may include abuse, addiction, severe health issues, and hunger. Tilting at the actual giants and monsters of violence and despair, the adolescents become "quixotinhos urbanos" (little urban Quixotes, in the Projeto Quixote's illuminating phrase) who, often, cannot see an alternative story to that of their own marginalization. For this reason Andreia de Almeida, the author of the play *Quixotes* analyzed in Chapter 2, poses Quijano and not the often-belligerent Don Quixote as the ideal model for a new practice of citizenship for at-risk youth based on the self-conscious rescripting and performance of new roles. After all, as she claims, it was the hidalgo Quijano who one day "deixou de ser somente mais um espectador" (quit being simply a spectator) and left his home in search of adventure and a better world. For many, she continues, Quijano "tornara-se doidão. Pra nós Dom Quixote não" (Quijano went crazy. For us, Don Quixote is not [crazy]; *Quixote* 8–9). In Brazilian social justice appropriations of Cervantes' character, Don Quixote is not the product of madness but of a conscious acting statement by a modest hidalgo who, far from simply losing his mind, takes on an active role in the performance of his social persona. Fulfilling Augusto Boal's famous plea for spectators to turn themselves into actors or spect-actors, Quijano becomes in de Almeida's reading an early example of an outcast who, via a real-world performance, enacts a new form of citizenry.

In search of "Uma outra história" (Another story), Projeto Quixote's founder, Dr. Auro Lescher, goes back to Cervantes to find inspiration for his art-based mission, and in the process identifies the true protagonists of these new narratives. Through his immortal character, Dr. Lescher claims, Cervantes "mostrou que cada um de nós escreve sua própria história" (showed that each one of us writes our own story; "Miguel de Cervantes"). If "each one of us" can rescript our role in public discourse, how does an organization foster and facilitate this process? Who conceives and performs these new tales in the Projeto Quixote, project leaders or the children themselves? Who are the true Quixotes in these stories? As Dr. Lescher and his team recognized early on, the staff act not as Don Quixotes but rather as Sanchos, who accompany and attempt to bring back to a more caring reality São Paulo's urban knight-errants: the true *quixotinhos urbanos* (little urban quixotes). According to Dr. Lescher, children and youth suffocated by deprivation and violence wander like Don Quixotes in a journey "para o centro da cidade em busca de outra história para si mesmas" (into the city downtown in search for another story for themselves; Projeto Quixote, *Quixote* 46). And much like the loquacious hidalgo Quijano himself, practitioners of Quixote-inspired performative activism do not shy away from sharing their urban experiences, their "another story," if given a chance. Over my four trips to Brazil in preparation for this book, and despite the logical reservations that many children and youth may have held toward a white male Spanish professor who lives in the United States and speaks Portuguese with a foreign accent, many project participants often voluntarily shared their experiences with me through informal conversations. After a short period of trust-building and ice-breaking, some *quixotinhos urbanos* in fact proved eager to share at least a piece of their "other story," even if anecdotally. In a more formal fashion, numerous testimonials have also been published in print as part of either activist projects or academic studies on youth nonprofits. These publicly accessible stories about and by the Other constitute the basis for most of the ensuing analysis.

Of course, the application of artivism and performance to social justice projects with youth in vulnerable situations is not exclusive to Brazilian organizations modeled after *Don Quixote*. In fact, storytelling and role-playing have recently taken center stage in street-connected youth activism around the world. Working out of a space of trauma and extreme otherness, Uruguayan psychoanalyst Marcelo Viñar created his Montevideo-based Grupo de Palabras (literally, Group of words) to open up channels of expression for street-connected children and youth. According to Viñar, who has also participated in a number of Brazilian projects, his nonprofit provides a space for at-risk youth to safely share their frequently traumatic stories so that, in the end, "o horror fale uma palavra transformadora" (out of horror emerges a transformative word; "Uma utopia" 13). Noticed only when they inspire fear or pity, but ignored and silenced otherwise, at-risk youth are often deprived of basic feelings associated with "being *gente*" (loosely translated as "being someone, feeling human"), such as affection, recognition, and self-esteem (Perlman, ch. 12). Wandering the most extreme and dangerous margins of society, children and youth in high-risk social situations cry out for expressive outlets through which they can (re)define themselves personally and collectively as more than simply victims or aggressors *(Street Children: A Mapping* 13).

In a study conducted in 2016 in Rio de Janeiro by Elinor Milne and Eloïse Di Gianni for the Consortium for Street Children, thirty-seven current and former street-connected youth between the ages of eleven and twenty-two gathered to discuss their needs and aspirations. Representing a variety of countries, including Brazil as the host nation, the children and youth were asked to offer input and recommendations to the UN Committee on the Rights of the Child. Despite the extreme deprivation of basic resources they experience in the streets, their suggestions had little to do with material needs. Most of their comments centered on the idea of enabling children and youth to narrate and perform their own personal and social identity. According to a fifteen-year-old Brazilian boy, what street-connected children need the most is not just food or shelter but recognition: "it's not about getting them off the streets and into shelters, it's about giving them a status" (Milne and Di Gianni 11). Many other participants also demanded from politicians, police, and community residents to be seen and treated "as a person," in the words of a girl from Mozambique (5). As an eighteen-year-old male from Rio de Janeiro summed up, all that street-connected youth ask from adults is "the opportunity to change our story" (11). Inserted into a new storyline of their own making, the Projeto Quixote would claim, at-risk children cultivate through their own words a "sentimento de pertencer, participar, ser protagonista" (a feeling of belonging, participating, being protagonist; *Quixote* 27) that can facilitate social inclusion.

In recent years, scholars in the field have emphasized the need for capturing the stories told by at-risk youth populations through focus groups and one-on-one interviews (*Street Children: A Mapping* 17). More and more, researchers draw from the everyday work and methods of activists, as they are beginning to accept the reliability and authenticity of the outcomes achieved through participatory action research (PAR). Often, PAR resorts to the kind of exercises that nonprofits such as Quixote-inspired organizations employ, including "role-playing, drama improvisation" and other forms of performative and artistic expression, from drawing and dancing to mapping (*Street Children: A Mapping* 18). One such pioneering and rather thorough study remains Udi Mandel Butler's 2009 "Freedom, Revolt, and 'Citizenship': Three Pillars of Identity for Youngsters Living in the Streets of Rio de Janeiro." Through one-on-one interviews with ninety-two children and youth between ages eleven and mid twenties, Butler reports that her research subjects self-identified as "active participants in shaping their destinies" (12, 14). Besides their urge to free themselves from oppressive households and revolt against the injustices that forced them into the streets in the first place, most often extreme poverty and abuse, the idea of citizenship in the broad sense of "being like everyone else" emerged as a recurring, central theme (24–26). Similar to what other studies and Quixote-inspired organizations confirm, Butler found that street-connected youth ask mainly to be "treated as a 'person,' a 'citizen,' or just like anyone else" (24). For them, transitioning into or out of the streets is only a phase in their journey out of extreme marginalization. Urban refugees in their own country, as the Projeto Quixote claims, they demand their participation in a citizenry that rests less on legal documents or access to rights than on the collective recognition of their personhood and human worth. They want to tell their stories in their own words, and they want to be heard.

A critical step toward a more egalitarian practice of citizenship remains the act of naming, one of the most powerful triggers and manifestations of change in Quijano's story as well as in Paulo Freire's influential *Pedagogy of the Oppressed* (69). Behind a name lies an individual's story and social perception, as evidenced by the complex relationship between street and legal names that so many at-risk youth navigate on a daily basis. For most mainstream identities, a nickname functions mostly within domestic or artistic spaces, while legal identity typically dominates professional and public life. However, for children and youth in high-risk social situations the choice of name is less straightforward and more consequential, for to a significant extent it shapes their societal role and their storyline. In order to examine how Quixote-inspired organizations harness the potential of self-naming to enact change, I first investigate the issue in Cervantes' classic and then review the tactics of name changing in contemporary Brazilian nonprofits.

A master of (re)naming in his own right, the hidalgo Quijano offers valuable insights into a process that can trigger deep transformation. In *Don Quixote*'s first pages, the narrator gives us hardly any information about the hidalgo's last name and place of origin, as I analyzed more extensively in Chapters 3 and 4. While he does "not care to remember" the protagonist's hometown, both the narrator and several characters speculate on the possible legal identity of this mysterious John Doe: was his last name Quixada, Quexada, or Quexana? (I.1.19–20). Within a few paragraphs and through a purely literary genesis, freed from the strictures of a legal identity and ancestry, the hidalgo changes his social persona into that of the extravagant knight-errant Don Quixote. Incarnated into his new chivalric creation, he then proceeds to rename the world around him, including Dulcinea, Rocinante, giants (instead of windmills), or armies (in reality sheep). As his adventures unfold, Don Quixote yet again metamorphoses into newly minted characters, depending on the context and outcomes of his latest exploits. He becomes the Knight of the Sad Face or Sorrowful

Countenance, the Knight of the Lions, the shepherd Quixotiz, and then again Alonso Quijano the Good. At the end of the book, as he faces death, the protagonist himself confirms his legal identity in his own words, for he intends to write a will and confess before passing away (II.74.935).

Devoid of genealogical and biographical detail, the protagonist of the greatest novel of all time acts as a blank canvas for self-transformation, which gradually and at times chaotically unfolds over the book's approximately one thousand pages. As early on as chapter 5 of part I, in fact, the character makes a foundational declaration of intent on his radical creative freedom. Concealed under a scene of defeat and disorientation, this revolutionary statement actually constitutes the open-ended creed that will fundamentally guide the hidalgo/knight-errant's extreme endeavors, as well as the equally bold social justice work of Quixote-inspired organizations today. In chapter 4 of part I, Don Quixote encounters a group of merchants on their way to Toledo and asks that they "confess" that Dulcinea stands as the most beautiful "empress of La Mancha" (39). When the merchants naïvely require proof of what the strange-looking mounted figure requests of them, Don Quixote becomes enraged at their lack of faith in his chivalric world and furiously charges them. In characteristic fashion, however, his horse Rocinante trips, and both fall hard to the ground. Chapter 5 opens with Quijano lying on the floor, badly wounded and delirious. By chance, his neighbor and farmer Pedro Alonso encounters him on his way to the village, offers to accompany him home, but Don Quixote mistakes him for an epic ballad character (the Marquis of Mantua), and appoints himself as its protagonist, Valdovinos. Moments later he will also call himself Abindarráez, the hero of a famous 1559 pastoral novel, the *Diana*, by Jorge de Montemayor. As a whirlwind of fictional identities possesses a fallen Don Quixote, Pedro Alonso simply interpolates him as "Señor Quijana," a new last name that the narrator had not included in his previous list of the hidalgo's possible legal identities. Quick to highlight the potentially serious consequences of restricting Don Quixote's freewheeling identity by means of a legal surname, the narrator half-jokingly comments that Señor Quijana "must have been his name when he was in his right mind" (42). Of course, the narrator's speculation ("must have been") only confuses the reader further, for this is the fourth possible last name offered to the reader in five short chapters. Hiding in plain sight within a maze of possible identities, the character's freedom to be whomever he wants must be preserved despite his neighbor's potentially devastating identity recognition. Threatened doubly by his chivalric incompetence and a neighbor who may have just betrayed his "real" name, Quijano/Quixote realizes the gravity of the moment. Reaching deeper into his creative arsenal, he then declares solemnly, "I know who I am . . . and I know I can be not only those I have mentioned [Valdovinos and Abindarráez], but the Twelve Peers of France as well, and even all the nine Paragons of Fame" (I.5.43). Liberated from a constraining social identity, the nameless and obscure hidalgo boldly affirms not only that he knows who he is but also, most importantly, that he can be whoever he wishes.

Quijano's radical literary and performative actions do not aim to establish exactly who he was or will be, for he claims several (fictional) identities in a matter of only a few sentences. Rather, he expresses his inalienable right to effectively write and perform whatever storyline he may choose for himself. Instead of a narrative of origins and a clear goal or point of arrival, performative activists such as Quijano/Quixote strive to develop a *method* for social change based on a never-ending, revolutionary process of rescripting and performing. If we think of society as a puzzle where the different pieces (individual and collective identities, institutions, laws, interpersonal relations) follow an order within a carefully crafted social storyline, typically determined by the elites, performative activism continuously deconstructs the puzzle to put it back together anew. Without a stated end goal, specific benchmarks, or predetermined models beyond the vague idea of equality and fairness, performance itself becomes the key instrument of change, the true "weapon for liberation," in Augusto Boal's phrase, for an endlessly mutating social narrative.

Youth nonprofits, including the Quixote-inspired organizations, typically recognize and use nicknames in the everyday, but they also seek to bring their participants' legal identities out into the open. In order for the invisible and the excluded to claim a new protagonist role outside of marginalized or criminal networks, our organizations all encourage young participants to disclose, embrace, and deploy their institutional identities in order to activate their participation in public citizenry. In the process of unlocking their public persona, children and youth in Quixote-inspired organizations utilize writing and theater as chief conduits for rescripting their own role.

With its official denomination as Ponto de Cultura (Cultural point) from the Ministry of Culture, the original, Cervantes-based Instituto Religare served socially vulnerable young residents in the downtown neighborhood of Barra Funda. Religare presented itself as a center for "Reciclagem Cultural e Social" (Cultural and social recycling), particularly for youth recently released from incarceration or internment. Tellingly, the organization's official logo was a spiral, which symbolizes the circularity in the process of recycling. A constant in social justice discourse in Brazilian cultural nonprofits, the concept of individual recycling and collective transformation also materialized in Religare's motto: "Embora eles levem consigo o que eram, partem em busca do que poderão ser" (While they [young participants] take with them who they were, they sally forth in search of who they can be). In this process of becoming, fueled by theater and art, participants embark on the adventure of reimagining themselves as who they could or would like to be, not just who they have been. Visually, Religare's promotional materials employed an image of Don Quixote and Sancho riding on horseback toward the horizon. Like the hidalgo Quijano who left behind his previous social role, these young performative heroes in the Barra Funda district of São Paulo search for who they can and want to be. Through "o contato com as emoções e . . . os sentimentos" (the contact with emotions and feelings), di Pietro includes "a autocrítica e a auto-estima" (self-critique and self-esteem) in the recipe for transformation that she prescribes for youth who often have a criminal record and/or come from broken families.

In di Pietro's Instituto Religare, one project in particular, Peterson Xavier's *Mutatis* (2006), illustrates this comprehensive sense of personal change that relies on cultural and emotional affirmation as well as on career preparation. A FEBEM intern at the time, Xavier starred in di Pietro's version of *Num Lugar de la Mancha*, as discussed in Chapter 3, and followed his performative mentor to the Instituto Religare. Since then, Xavier has described himself as a cultural educator and promoter who has released hip-hop albums, performed in a variety of theatrical productions, and participated in community-based initiatives in numerous Brazilian cities and abroad. At Religare, he staged a play directed by Valéria di Pietro based on his own poems, with music by Célio Pires, Jarbas Mariz, and Edvaldo Santana. Significantly, the title of his work, *Mutatis*, is the past participle of the Latin verb *Mutare*, to change, and thus translates as "changed," or "having been changed." In a cultural blog, Célio Pires describes the play as a story by and about a group of former FEBEM interns "desde os 'tempos sombrios' (privados de liberdade) até os 'tempos de transformação' (a partir da arte)" (from the "dark times" [incarceration] to the "times of transformation" [through art]). According to Pires, the stage adaptation of *Don Quixote* gave Xavier, in a most Freirean manner, a new vocabulary of liberation that included words such as "sonho, ideal, objetivo" (dream, ideal, goal). Previously absent from their everyday lexicon, these concepts offered the former FEBEM interns an alternative to marginalization, "um projeto de vida, um projeto de futuro" (a life project, a project for a better future; Pires). Characteristically, the text is overtly political. Through hip-hop, dance, performance, and poetry, it discusses contemporary issues such as the group's opposition to lowering the legal age for incarceration and the denunciation of marginalization and poverty as primary causes of violence (a video of the performance can be found on YouTube).

The artistic expression of the process by which former FEBEM interns claimed to have been *Mutatis* (changed) reached deep into their self-consciousness, as reflected in the interplay between their nicknames, street names, and legal identities. In a book published in 2006 by the Fundação Telefônica (Telefónica, or Telefônica in its Portuguese version, is the Spanish telecommunications giant, which dominates the Brazilian market), around twenty children and youth in high-risk social situations and as many adult respondents discuss their experiences in accessing services legally guaranteed by the 1990 Estatuto da Criança e do Adolescente or ECA (the Brazilian Child and Adolescent Rights Act). Appropriately, the first and richest section of the book describes ECA as "instrumento de transformação de vida" (instrument for life transformation), and one of its most illustrative examples owes much, by his own account, to Don Quixote. The protagonist of a radical transformation, Peterson Xavier went from budding criminal with convictions for robbery and drug trafficking before age eighteen (Dimenstein) to professional educator and artist upon the realization that he wanted to "Viver para representar!" (Live to perform!; 67–70). After the FEBEM's 2007 closure and re-foundation as Fundação CASA (The home foundation), in early 2010 Xavier returned to the institution to lead theater and cultural workshops for the interns. In March of the same year, he gave an extensive interview to the *CASA em revista* magazine, in which the word *transformation* and its variations appear in almost every paragraph over the eight-page piece. In her introduction, journalist Rosemary dos Santos sets a lofty tone for the ensuing conversation by stating that the challenge for excluded and criminal youth remains the achievement of "a liberdade pela transformação" (freedom through transformation; 12). With the stakes so high, Xavier identifies art and theater as "a maior ferramenta de transformação, não só pessoal, mas também . . . na comunidade em que você vive" (the greatest instrument of transformation, not only personal but also . . . for the community in which one lives; 14). In this particular form of militant artivism, which extends to all

Quixote-inspired and other artivist organizations such as GCA, art and various kinds of performance (theater, dance, music, video) can potentially trigger personal transformation against the social imaginary's deterministic forces that portray vulnerable youth as mere criminals or victims. By performing as Don Quixote on stage, Peterson Xavier showed his worth as an artist, his potential to shatter the stereotype of a young male from the *periferia* (the marginal neighborhoods in the outskirts of São Paulo) that seemingly condemned him to a life of crime in his own mind and in the minds of others. By altering first his own performance through onstage acting, Xavier hoped to also mutate the broader social narrative.[4]

Conversely, social transformation can also precede personal change, as José Valmir Gomes demonstrates in a story simply entitled "Transformação," published in the same collection about the transformative virtues of ECA where Xavier's "Viver para representar!" appeared. Writing in the third person, Valmir Gomes recounts how Zeca (possibly his nickname in real life, and in any event his alter ego in this short piece) turned his life around when the new 1988 Constitution and the ensuing 1990 ECA banned child labor. Since age eleven, he had been working at a local brickyard to help his adoptive grandparents. At sixteen days old, his biological mother abandoned him, and his beloved adoptive mother died when he was only ten. Freed from work after the passing of ECA, Zeca went back to school. Later in life, he involved himself in local governance to monitor the implementation of ECA rights for children with experiences similar to his own. Eventually, he took a government job and earned a college degree in history. By telling his life story, which includes abandonment, extreme poverty, and the love of an adoptive family, Valmir Gomes offers a revealing picture of how a legislative initiative and support from family can turn a life around. Personal and collective change feed into each other in ways that may end up causing a whirlwind of transformation. The personal and the social often go hand in hand, with one facilitating or impeding the other, and cannot be dissociated. In some cases, such as in Xavier's, personal transformation preceded the larger dismantling and re-founding of the institution where he was interned, while in others, such as in Valmir Gomes' story, change occurred as a result of progressive legislation and the care of an adoptive family.

For both Xavier and Gomes, furthermore, the act of renaming functioned as trigger and evidence of individual as well as collective change. After his first stay in the infamous detention center, Peterson Xavier recounts that in his native Itaquera, a low-income neighborhood in São Paulo's periferia, he was often scolded with the nickname FEBEM. After he experienced self-transformation through theater, however, people would frequently refer to him in admiration as Dom Quixote (Dimenstein). In this regard, nicknames prove more malleable than legal names and thus best reflect the fluctuating quality of an ever-evolving identity. As mentioned in Chapter 3, to mark his own momentous identity-changing moment, Xavier published under his legal name and in at least two different media (an online blog and a print essay) the chronicle of his self-transformation into "o dom Quixote das ruas ... eu Peterson Xavier Quixote de la Mancha" (the Don Quixote of the streets ... I, Peterson Xavier Quixote of La Mancha; "Dom Quixote das ruas"). Molding and expressing his identity via different names, either self-chosen (Don Quixote of the streets), uttered by others (FEBEM and Dom Quixote), or sanctioned by law (Peterson Xavier), the young actor and author culminated his transition from young criminal to performative activist on a mission to educate underprivileged children and youth.[5]

At the Projeto Quixote the rewriting and performing of one's own story exposes from its very initial stages the complex interplay between visibility and concealment triggered by the revelation and public exposure of one's legal identity. After all, names function as "atos políticos" (political acts), as graffiti artists at the Projeto proclaim with regards to the importance of choosing a signature for their urban artworks (*Por trás dos muros* 40, 43). Indeed, for anyone who attempts to move from a position of exclusion and otherness into a central role endowed with some degree of agency, identity raises a number of vital and contradictory questions. In theory at least, and particularly for children and youth in street situations, establishing a legal identity may provide access to rights and privileges such as constitutional protection and social services. At the same time, however, a legal identity may expose the child to disciplinary powers or abusive environments such as dysfunctional government orphanages or biological and adoptive families plagued with domestic violence and/or addiction.

In a clear exposé of the inherent tensions in the political act of naming, children and youth in vulnerable situations contend during the Projeto Quixote admission protocols with the fear and potential benefits of disclosing their legal identities. Project participants at risk due to addiction, dysfunctional families, or behavioral disorders are generally referred to the Projeto Quixote by schools and governmental institutions, and in other, fewer cases, street-connected children are approached directly in the central neighborhoods of São Paulo. In a first phase, youth are introduced to the program via a rather unstructured welcome session called "Acolhimento" (Welcoming), centered on the idea that play will enable participants to feel like children again (*Mundo do Trabalho* 20; "O enfrentamento da problemática" 16–17). For many at-risk children, their everyday realities often require them to act as adults, as they procure for themselves food and protection from abuse and/or de facto parent younger siblings. The guiding principle in these sessions remains the notion that the Projeto should foster *uma outra história*, "um ambiente que não é o lugar conhecido, que já foi vivido, experimentado" (an unknown space, an environment that is yet to be lived and experienced by the participant; *Quixote* 109). Board games, artistic expression, and loose conversation between educators and participants create a cordial atmosphere, an "espaço brincante quixotesco e libertador" (playful and liberating quixotic space; *Quixote* 127) where children and youth are not forced to follow any particular agenda or provide any specific information. On occasion, educators at the Projeto have used children's or comic versions of *Don Quixote* as inspiration for drawing or playing games (I myself led one such session), but acolhimentos work best when they are less guided and children have a say on the type of game or project they want to carry out. As several staff members told me, many participants in the program, naturally suspicious of institutions and other kids, often do not provide their legal name at first, only a nickname or a street name. In the case of young females in street situations, it is not unusual for them to adopt a masculine name and identity for self-protection. For instance, an educator shared with me that a boy revealed herself to be a girl only after more than six months of continuous participation in the program. Typically, in fact, it takes multiple acolhimento sessions for participants to feel comfortable enough with the staff to engage with them at a deeper personal level. Often, youth who do not open up after one or a few acolhimentos, or whose family circumstances change for one reason or another, simply quit the program, for participation is entirely voluntary.

If and when trust does ultimately develop, a therapist or social worker takes a detailed intake report that lists the specific issues affecting the child; most often problems are family-related, the product of addiction, or psychological in nature. Then the Projeto staff member writes with the participant a confidential "Projeto da vida" or "Life project," described as "a tentativa de realização de sonhos e desejos" (a plan for the achievement of [their] dreams and wishes; *Mundo do Trabalho* 131). At this point, the child's legal identity (and thus information about his or her family, home address, or school) might still not be known or recorded, particularly if the child comes from a street situation. Throughout the entire process, there exists a clear and present tension between making visible the source of the issues affecting project participants, which often requires legal and clinical interventions, and the child's own sense of protection or safety from abusive relatives or institutions.

Even when their legal identities are concealed under a street name, however, participants undergo a profound transformation at the Projeto Quixote, through which their inner lives start to reveal themselves. Somewhere during this process, which typically leads to the reclaiming of their institutional persona, participants produce a new narrative, an oral and written trail of a life story previously hidden or ignored by the official discourse. The Projeto experience culminates with the efforts to reconnect participants with their families in what they have termed *rematriamento* (for re-mothering, in the sense of returning to one's motherland or home), which again requires the child or youth to volunteer their legal identity and home address. In general, then, the Projeto seeks to reveal the youth's "real" identity in order to unlock their access to state services and biological or adoptive family, provided that they can offer a safe environment for the child. As teens navigate the tensions between using legal or street names, at any rate, the Projeto helps its participants become self-aware of the malleability of identity as part of the larger process of individual and collective change.

As a marker that reflects and triggers change, naming in fact reveals the ever-shifting nature of identity as an ongoing process of becoming. Focused on transformation, particularly at the discursive and performative level, Quixote-inspired organizations find in Cervantes' classic a rich model for the notion that identity categories are far more permeable and supple than prejudices and misconceptions about the Other might make us think. As *Don Quixote* amply demonstrates, ambivalence and complexity complicate the simplistic antagonism between good and evil, right and wrong.

Despite the prevalent Romantic interpretation of Don Quixote as a champion for justice and the oppressed (Close) or even a sanctified hero (Ziolkowsky), moral ambiguity plagues the actions of the self-proclaimed knight-errant who longs first and foremost to gain "eternal renown and everlasting fame" (I.1.21). In fact, the adjective *quixotic* carries in the English language negative connotations as foolish, excessive, and impractical, according to standard dictionaries such as the *Merriam-Webster*. In the name of justice and freedom, or simply seeking fame to aggrandize his status as aspiring knight-errant, Don Quixote attacks innocents and destroys property on numerous occasions, most frequently while still attempting to consolidate and make visible his new identity in part I (there are numerous examples in chapters 3, 4, 8, 9, 15, 18, 19, 20, 21, and 22, among many others). Throughout the book, he pushes himself and others to commit illegal or reckless acts from which he escapes unharmed only because of luck, as when he irresponsibly confronts a lion that simply turns its back on him (II.17), or thanks to the support of powerful people who see him as a madman deserving of sympathy, mockery, or even pity, as in the resolution of the fight over a barber's modest basin that Don Quixote mistakes for a famous helmet (I.45).

Unprovoked, our (anti)hero often charges against members of the clergy and law officers, including a group of Saint Benedict friars in I.8 and a handful of guards escorting convicted criminals on their way to the galleys in I.22. On at least two occasions, Don Quixote flirts with excommunication or expulsion from the Church, the harshest religious punishment possible in the fervently Catholic society of the time. Alarmed by Quijano's foolish impersonation of Don Quixote, his niece and the housekeeper urge the town's priest to purge and burn the hidalgo's books in a bonfire. Obviously, Cervantes references in this scene the *autos de fe* (literally, acts of faith) which the Inquisition staged to publicly punish and often burn convicted heretics at the stake (I.6). In part II the knight-errant accepts a duel with the footman Tosilos, a doctrinal offense that the Council of Trent, which ended its deliberations in 1563, punished with outright excommunication (II.56). As early as chapter 19 of part I, Don Quixote is in fact explicitly excommunicated by a cleric for attacking a funeral march (I.19.140). On too many occasions to list here, our protagonist is called satanic or a demon by several different characters, including Sancho himself (Miñana, *Monstruos que hablan* 173–77).

Despite the mounting evidence, I am by no means denying the stated good intentions of the character, nor Don Quixote's extraordinary appeal as a champion of the oppressed for generations of readers and fans, including the organizations I study here. Rather, I am exploring the ambiguity and contradictions that add multiple layers of depth to the arguably greatest literary character of all time, for he too, as a proper (anti)hero, embodies hyperbole, embraces contradiction, and thrives on extreme opposites. Unfortunately for him, most characters in the book don't see him as hero, but rather as fool or even a dangerous madman. Even though the mantle of madness and his self-proclaimed lofty intentions often save Don Quixote from total demise, throughout the book the old man is severely beaten, caged, and scorned nearly more times than one can count. In the "real world" of contemporary Brazil, the consequences of visibility, self-naming, and role-playing can no doubt be even direr, particularly for the excluded.

At the core of Don Quixote's performative adventures thus lies an urge to profoundly challenge and rewrite sacrosanct laws and time-honored customs of his time, which in good logic would make him a moral and social outcast in the eyes of mainstream society. Likely for that reason, Cervantes depicted his towering character as a madman, for as Catholic reformist Erasmus of Rotterdam famously wrote in his *In Praise of Folly* (1511), fools and children are more capable of telling truths than adults, who operate within the social order. Rather than a dangerous revolutionary, Cervantes' foolish Don Quixote would pass in the eyes of inquisitorial censors for an old crazy man worthy of some degree of compassion and laughter. In order to rescript his place in society, Quijano/Quixote pursues a deliberate performative strategy, as he plays an outlandish role (that of the knight-errant Don Quixote) that allows him to subvert societal and religious rules in plain sight. Even if perceived as a madman or a monster, Don Quixote accesses a public platform from which he can launch his all-out attack against his legally and socially sanctioned persona, that of a modest hidalgo in the twilight of his life. After acquiring sufficient literary and theatrical knowledge from books, the old hidalgo chooses to break away from his reality and instead rescript and perform a newly minted heroic identity for himself. Such is Don Quixote's thirst for visibility that he continuously risks his physical well-being (and worse, that of the many innocents whom he often attacks) in a myriad of gratuitous skirmishes and eccentric performances.[6]

Putting oneself in the public spotlight, as the case of Don Quixote proves, comes with its own risks. More often than not, closely watched with fear and mistrust, the underprivileged pay a high price for their exposure. However, visibility through art and performance may also afford our *quixotinhos urbanos*, typically denied a voice in public discourse, a unique chance to safely speak for themselves, to be seen and heard. While public exposure renders marginal subjects more vulnerable to the disciplinary actions of power (Foucault, *Discipline and Punish* 187), it may also on the other hand provide outcasts with a unique opportunity to change the lens through which society and even the authorities perceive them. The 2000 premiere of *Num lugar de la Mancha*, which I described more thoroughly in Chapter 3, best captures the tensions and ambiguity intrinsic to the visibility afforded by theatrical performance. The play featured 140 FEBEM interns on stage at the Memorial de Latino América, a large

FIGURE 6.1. "Workshops for adolescents who seek transformation," Quixote Espaço Comunitário, São Paulo

event that mobilized an extensive security detail with dozens of police vehicles, agents, and even helicopters. The play's protagonist, Peterson Xavier, acknowledged that the extreme preventive measures responded to the fact that "o que todos esperam da Febem são monstros e não artistas" (what everyone expects from the FEBEM are monsters, not artists; "Dom Quixote das ruas"). Remarkably successful nonetheless, the performance brought together officers, families, and interns in celebration. The tensions surrounding the identity of the prisoners/artists abated under thunderous applause, as a newfound admiration toward the performers erupted on and off stage among tears, hugs, and words of encouragement and appreciation. By courtesy of *Don Quixote* and the magic of theater, the stigmatized young criminals had transformed themselves into actors and producers of culture, and thus their feared criminal persona (the "monster" in Xavier's words) had crossed over into a state of artistic worth. Even if only for the duration of the play, the individuals generating public discourse on stage were no longer the authorities but the dispossessed and the locked away, for they had taken control, in the most literal of terms, of their own performance.

On the same premise that identity fluctuates and is multilayered, Andreia de Almeida founded in 2008 the Quixote Espaço Comunitário (QEC) in the Ipiranga district, a mixed neighborhood where middle- and even upper middle-class and low-income families live side by side. Mirroring the neighborhood's hybrid social fabric, the QEC offers free cultural workshops without explicitly aiming its activities at youth in vulnerable social situations. In fact, the individual and social change that de Almeida promotes hinges on the unmarking of the vulnerable as a population in need of help from mainstream society. Instead, she uses art and performance to encourage anyone and everyone to rescript his or her story and that of the broader society and to do so together, learning and experimenting in tandem. In this true "community space," all are welcome, and all interact as one regardless of their social provenance, race, or education. In personal conversations, de Almeida explained to me that in her mind the transformative power of art predicates itself on its egalitarian nature, a space of creative power that can erase social and racial boundaries and present both the elites and the excluded as equally capable of producing art.

In sum, deep personal and collective transformation, particularly for vulnerable populations, requires not only the liberating act of renaming and an enhanced public visibility, but also the loosening or elimination of rigid boundaries and stereotypes around identity markers such as class, race, gender, and sexual orientation. Only if these categories become sufficiently porous can the underprivileged and the underserved effectively alter the mainstream social narrative that boxes them into marginalization. Pliability and hybridity thus become hallmarks of Quixote-inspired performative activism, for employing clear-cut labels to catalog people goes against both Cervantes' novel itself, which takes place in the gray areas between fantasy and reality or chivalry and callousness, and the contemporary activist organizations that it inspires. Performative activism does not elude moral ambiguity but rather builds on it as it weaves complex life narratives through a combination of art, hard work, and often therapy. Tellingly, none of the nonprofits I study here naïvely denies the potential duality of street-connected and at-risk youth as both "vítimas e agressores" (victims and aggressors; *Conceitos* 69–77), in a revealing phrase by Fátima Dinis Rigato, a staff member at the Project Quixote. As documented in the published texts and interviews with many of the youth cited throughout this study, participants in *Don Quixote* projects often have criminal records and/or experience serious behavioral and psychological challenges. Consequently, Quixote-inspired activism neither masks identities nor blurs them; rather, it nurtures the porousness and fluidity of the self against stereotyping and social determination. Through theater and art, complex individuals such as Quijano/Don Quixote or Xavier/Dom Quixote das ruas employ (re)naming and performance to rehearse and implement deep change in their lifes. And with their own self-transformation, they aim to turn society into a fairer playing field in which collective narratives allow for even the excluded and the underserved to rescript and perform their stories in their own terms.

The importance of underrepresented populations' performative needs and aspirations cannot and should not cloud the serious threats that many of them face on a daily basis against their material and physical well-being. Millions of children and teenagers in Brazil and in the Americas at large are forced to confront every day almost insurmountable adversities as extreme as abandonment, hunger, abuse, and domestic or street violence. From this point of view, can a four-hundred-year-old, Spanish-language classic offer any tangible benefits to its practitioners?[7] To address this question, the practice of Quixote-inspired performative activism not only revolves around the discursive aspects of identification and belonging but also, in fact, recognizes that underprivileged populations are often deprived of consistent access to basic needs such as food, healthcare, and safety. In general, due to either lack of funds or expertise, Quixote-inspired organizations do not offer long-term strategies to improve the system, such as lobbying the government or proposing new policies. However, at a smaller scale, organizations with sufficient means do take meaningful steps to complement their performative work with quantifiable efforts to increase their project participants' chances to secure food and shelter.

The largest and best-funded nonprofit of all the Cervantes-inspired entities examined here, the Projeto Quixote tends to the material needs of its participants in three fundamental ways. First, it ensures that all participants who sign up for its activities eat a meal in the building, have access to healthcare, including psychiatric and psychological evaluation and treatment, and undergo some form of professional training. These benefits are built into the program rather than delivered through charity work. A long-term healthcare plan is designed as part of the "Projeto da vida" or "Life Project" that ensues the initial acolhimento phase. During the subsequent *atendimento* phase (roughly, treatment), the Projeto offers clinical and educational programs tailored to their young participants. Besides art-based workshops and therapy sessions as prescribed, professional training workshops help youth build a resume, hone their public presentation skills, and develop their technological abilities (Cooperaacs and the Instituto Religare, for instance, also provided on-the-job career preparation). As income-generating programs, the Agência Quixote Spray Arte (Quixote Spray Art Agency) and Usina de Imagem (Image Workshop) formally employ Projeto Quixote staff and young participants to deliver graffiti and video production services, respectively. Frequent clients include companies, schools, and other institutions such as hospitals. Through sponsors such as UK-headquartered PricewaterhouseCoopers, paid internships are also available for a limited number of participants. Lastly, parents and relatives can participate in crafting artisan products (purses, t-shirts, pillows, rugs, bags, etc.) that they can then sell at the Loja Quixote, or Quixote Store, located in the main building.

A second pillar of the Projeto Quixote's attention to the material needs of its participants is their Formação e Pesquisa (Training and Research) program. In parallel to the activities developed for and with young participants at their headquarters and branches in São Paulo, Projeto staff also lead workshops around the country for professionals in the area of addiction treatment and youth activism. Additionally, they consult for a variety of entities and government agencies and publish studies typically based on the Projeto's own programs, several of which are cited throughout this book and listed in the bibliography.

Third, the Quixote-inspired adventure of transformation physically materializes in the spaces occupied by the Projeto. Through the visual and material adaptation of Cervantes' masterpiece, the organization advances its mission in concrete geographical as well as social locations, altering the urban landscape and its imaginary in the process. Throughout the central area of São Paulo, the Projeto Quixote has over the years transformed several urban spaces via a Cervantes-inspired, playful imagery of books, knights, and windmills predicated on the idea of recycling, change, and alternative storytelling. Within logical legal constraints, the Projeto understands public space as collective property potentially open to artistic intervention (*Por trás dos muros* 52). Particularly through its graffiti-based Agência Quixote Spray Arte, the organization has intervened in marginalized spaces such as neighborhoods with high rates of homelessness, schools in low-income areas, and psychiatric hospitals (60–63). As an "espaço visível" (space of visibility), the streets become embellished areas that facilitate the encounter not only between individuals but also between everyday realities and the alternative worlds imagined by the Projeto artists themselves (*Conceitos e estratégias* 12). This philosophy extends to the very physical spaces occupied by the Projeto Quixote itself. On October 16, 2010, the building that currently houses the organization in the downtown neighborhood of Vila Mariana opened, replacing the two smaller houses in adjacent Vila Clementino that they had previously occupied. All of the spaces out of which the nonprofit implements its social mission offer the same playful recreation of a Cervantes-inspired world, with graffiti, drawings, murals, and artistic objects modeled after *Don Quixote*'s fictional universe displayed throughout the space.

No building embodies the transculturation of *Don Quixote* into a concrete space of personal and collective transformation better than the centrally located Moinho do Bixiga, or Bixiga Windmill. Encompassing several city districts, the large downtown area of São Paulo includes areas of extreme poverty and a high concentration of children and youth in transition between the streets, government institutions, and their family homes. The Luz neighborhood within the Bom Retiro district houses Cracolândia, a few city blocks of abject poverty and rampant drug usage that at any given time may rank from three hundred to four hundred children and youth among its homeless population. In this and neighboring areas, urban *Quixotinhos* (little Quixotes) roam the streets in a desperate effort for survival. As the Projeto Quixote explains, children and youth who are forced from their family homes by poverty and/or violence thus feel like "estrangeiros em sua própria pátria" (foreigners in their own homeland; *Quixote* 98). Beginning in 2006, local government under then Secretary of Social Development Floriano Pesaro dotted the urban landscape with a number

FIGURE 6.2. Bixiga Windmill Shelter, São Paulo. Photograph by Rogelio Miñana

of CRECAs, or Centros de Referência da Criança e do Adolescente (Referral centers for children and adolescents), which provide shelter for up to two months to street-connected children and youth under eighteen years of age. In the central neighborhood of Bela Vista, also known as Bixiga, the Projeto Quixote opened in May 2007 one of the CRECA shelters closest to Crackolândia. Due to a lack of sufficient resources to continuously staff such a complex, around-the-clock operation, the Projeto terminated their partnership with the CRECA network two years later. Nonetheless, while the Projeto Quixote remained in charge, the Bixiga Windmill embraced the Cervantes-inspired idea of performance and transformation to its fullest.

Before opening its doors to children and youth in need of temporary shelter, the building had to metamorphose itself in order to physically embody Cervantes' literary masterpiece. Under the Projeto Quixote's management, the gorgeous turn-of-the-century, freestanding house did not become one more CRECA with a number attached to it (the fourteenth in the city at the time). Rather, the shelter presented itself to its residents as a Quixote-inspired adventure by the name of Bixiga Windmill. For such material and literary transformation to occur, the Projeto commissioned the renovations through local architect and art director Gert Seewald, who specialized in stage design for children's shows in both television and theater (Rocha Barroso, "Arquitetura"). The building's façade is comprised of a three-story square tower attached to a two-story, slightly bulkier structure that features the main entrance to the house with a balcony on top of it. While the tower has two semicircular windows on the third floor, the main structure's second-floor balcony is enclosed by three similarly sized windows. Cleverly, the tower represents a slim Don Quixote while the two-story, plumper structure stands for Sancho. Both façades feature eyebrows on top of the windows, painted pupils attached to the glass (blue for the knight, brown for the squire), and a moustache drawn above the doors on the lower floor. In Sancho's face, a red metallic platform resembling a clown's nose protrudes from the balcony's stone baluster right below the middle window. Playfully, a fire pole runs through a hole on the red platform for those brave enough to slide from the second story down to the ground. Through a collaboration between the Projeto, the city government, artist Gert Seewald, and the sponsorship of Banco Safra, Don Quixote and Sancho found temporary shelter as they continued their travels from La Mancha to the heart of São Paulo in their quest to transform the stories of its most excluded and vulnerable inhabitants.

In more meaningful ways than a decidedly enchanting façade, the transculturation of the Quixote-inspired ideal of change permeates the building. First, the renovation transformed an old house into an environmentally friendly building where furniture and décor are made mostly of recycled materials. Solar panels and a small wind turbine generate electricity for the building, and rainwater is collected on site. A large room serves as a space for cultural activities such as graffiti or hip-hop but also as a workshop for creating artistic and household objects out of recycled materials. According to Dr. Auro Lescher, Paulo Freire's notion that the pairing of aesthetics and ethics can prompt radical social change inspires the architectural and scenographic intervention on the building's physical space (Rocha Barroso, "Arquitetura"). Highly visible from the street, the Bixiga Windmill, which houses up to twenty residents at a time, presents itself as a playful, inviting space where the Projeto offers children in street situations beauty as well as integrity. In the same way as the building recycles its resources, society metaphorically gives excluded youth a second chance to engage in age-appropriate activities, for while in the streets these children and teens must fend for themselves like adults striving for their own survival. During their stay in the Bixiga Windmill, residents eat regular meals, shower, study, and play on a daily basis. They do not have to concern themselves with securing food, shelter, and protection from violence and abuse. Through a radical and immediate change in the day-to-day routines of the residents, the Bixiga Windmill aims to foster the appropriate conditions for a radical transformation to occur. Under the most strenuous of circumstances, residents as young as eight years old arrive in the shelter after severing ties partially or entirely with their families, typically due to violence and deprivation at home caused by extreme poverty, addiction, and/or physical, sexual, or psychological abuse. These urban refugees, as the Projeto Quixote calls them, have experienced at a very young age a traumatic disconnect from their families as well as from their own childhood, as they fend for themselves in extreme situations that would appear insufferable even for full-grown adults.

From the moment they set foot in the Bixiga Windmill they enter a Quixote-inspired world that encourages the rewriting and performance of *uma outra história* by and for themselves. An extensive staff of educators, social workers, and therapists works with residents and their families to collectively author a different narrative and reimagine a different scenario for the child. As new residents enter the building, the staff explains that they must commit to a process of rescripting their lives in order to transform their story. First, new residents who are physically able and so wish pass through a hexagonal window on a wall to the left of the main entrance, which symbolically marks the beginning of their new storytelling process. As I can attest myself, the act of jumping through this opening on the wall is no minor feat, a symbol perhaps of the hardships ahead for these children who face an uphill battle against poverty, abuse, and marginalization. Based on the results of meticulous evaluations, residents then go through the educational and therapeutic programs designed by the staff, from health check-ups to pedagogical sessions and treatments for addiction or mental illness when necessary. After completing the two-month program, if not earlier, residents who so desire can leave the house by sliding down the fire pole from Sancho's nose back down to the main entrance. Through this spectacular exit, the transformation that began by passing through a "magic" window culminates in an exhilarating descent back into the street. At the ground level, however, family members, staff, and other residents now await and cheer for the children and youth that have transformed their stories of exclusion into narratives of hope and potential. Ideally, those who leave the windmill return to a more functional home life where they can continue their development in an age-appropriate and safe manner. In other cases, program participants are placed in institutions based on their individual circumstances and needs. Throughout their stay, residents play and learn in rooms decorated with Don Quixote graffiti and drawings, and they experience first-hand the value of transformation as objects around them are recycled and converted into utensils or art.

As in the case of Cooperaacs discussed in Chapter 1, the Brazilian tradition of recycling waste into art and the very transculturation of *Don Quixote* once again converge, this time into a windmill-shelter in Bixiga that aims to provide children with another chance at a nurturing adolescence. A temporary dwelling for no longer than two months, the Bixiga Windmill strives to enable residents and their biological or adoptive families to create an age-appropriate environment where children can safely develop upon leaving the shelter (*Conceitos e estratégias* 8). Via artistic expression and performance, young project participants recover their sense of self as they experiment with their budding identities. Borrowing the term from Argentinian writer Ernesto Sábato, Dr. Auro Lescher describes this comforting space of personal growth as a "mátria" (motherland in English), an amalgam of home, safety, and adequate care that provides a healthy space for development. Through rematriamento, children and youth at the Projeto transition out of the streets into a mátria with their biological family or, if not possible or advisable, with an adoptive family or appropriate government institution (Rocha Barroso, "Trabalho"; *Quixote* 38, 98–101).

This extreme rescue from the streets, which sets off the radical rewriting of the lives of the most excluded youth, begins at the street level with the playful and casual actions of *educadores terapêuticos* (ETs or therapeutical educators) equipped with "mochilas lúdicas," ludic or playful backpacks filled with board games, soccer balls, and other forms of entertainment (*Quixote* 72). If the urban refugees roam the streets as true *quixotinhos urbanos*, Dr. Lescher contends, ETs then function as Sanchos who bring the children, often traumatized and intoxicated, back to reality. In this sense, the ETs function as "uma espécie de ego auxiliar, uma ponte entre a ficção, o delírio e a realidade" (a sort of auxiliary ego, a bridge between fiction, delirium, and reality; "Uma ilha para Sancho"). In the streets, the ludic backpacks replicate the sense of acolhimento offered in the Projeto's facilities through relatively unstructured, playful sessions. Inspired by the relationship between Don Quixote and Sancho, the Projeto's interventions do not mean to simply insert participants back into the disciplinary, abusive, or uncaring society that caused them severe disruptions in their childhood in the first place. For Dr. Lescher, rematriamento features a distinct literary quality, for it functions as the "matéria-prima da narrativa do sujeito como um ser autônomo, único, que tece sua vida como uma linha que não separa, aliena nem esquarteja, mas alinhava, define e protege" (raw material for autonomous, unique individuals to weave their life narratives with a thread that does not separate, alienate, or quarter, but rather bastes, defines, and protects; "Da terra do crack"). Through the Projeto's programs, the children and youths' true transformation occurs when, in a most Quixote-like manner, they become "o narrador da própria história" (narrator of their own stories; "Da terra do crack"). Equipped with the skills and courage of the hidalgo Quijano, children and youth reinvent their identities and social roles to become protagonists and storytellers in control of their own narratives. A first step toward liberation and healing, "poder falar sobre o que nos aflige transforma as narrativas e indica caminhos" (being able to talk about what hurts us transforms narratives and reveals new paths; *Quixote* 129). As those narratives of transformation emerge in the public eye, they begin to form a new mosaic of collective stories.

The attention to project participants' material and physical needs that these organizations provide can be somewhat quantified in the form of meals delivered or buildings restored. For instance, the Projeto Quixote publishes on its website the exact number of participants who have been welcomed at their centers as well as their budget expenditures (this is not necessarily the case with other, smaller Quixote-inspired nonprofits, for which I have not been able to find published data). However, much more challenging remains the assessment of the less tangible outcomes of Quixote-inspired performative activism. How can we measure the success of socio-discursive, cultural, and performative enterprises? In one of the major flaws of all of the organizations studied here, defining success, setting benchmarks, and developing metrics to assess effectiveness are for the most part lacking beyond the anecdotal evidence of participants who, for one reason or another, remain in contact with the organization. Those testimonials, such as Peterson Xavier's trail of published statements or some of the quotes from Projeto Quixote participants posted on their website, offer a first-person account of the impact of Quixote-inspired activism. Beyond these individual cases, circumstances as varied and unpredictable as family relations, health issues, the often-itinerant life of street-connected and vulnerable populations, or even the weather can deeply affect our ability to observe and evaluate performative interventions. Anecdotally, I witnessed first-hand the effect of a cloudy sky on a promising performance that was carefully prepared by a subset of the Quixote Espaço Comunitário (QEC) crew. Within the QEC, de Almeida created in 2014 an amateur theater group called Trupe Quixotesca (Quixotesque troupe), which takes the organization's performative mission out of their headquarters in Ipiranga into the broader metropolitan area. Typically, on weekends, the Trupe travels to community centers and schools in São Paulo and its *periferia* to perform plays created or adapted by participants under de Almeida's guidance. Even if not direct adaptations of *Don Quixote*, their plays focus on the same messages of recycling, transformation, and performative activism that fuel the QEC and other Cervantes-based organizations. On a Sunday in July 2015, I accompanied the Trupe quixotesca to a public park in Vila Mariana, the downtown neighborhood where the Projeto Quixote is located, for an improvised performance for a group of street-connected youth who frequently congregate there. As often happens with artivist interventions such as this one, however, that day (cloudy, threatening rain) the Trupe's target audience was nowhere to be found and thus the unannounced public performance never took place. Notably, the transformative potential of performance that the QEC intended to trigger that day was disrupted by just a cloud-filled sky. Transformation never comes in a linear, predictable fashion.

Better financed, planned, and executed efforts to track the success of performative activism do not necessarily produce more reliable results either. In July 2007, the Projeto Quixote completed production of the short documentary *Refugiados urbanos*, a filmic project that illustrates the limited capabilities of nonprofits to document and disseminate the real-life outcomes of rematriamentos. *Refugiados* follows three Projeto Quixote residents at their Bixiga Windmill shelter as they return to their families. Once home, they are given cameras to film their own quotidian lives in a process that replicates the exercise undertaken by other Projeto Quixote youth in *Exilados do mundão* (2006), a film that I discuss below. (In fact, the filming and editing of *Refugiados* are credited to two of the six *Exilados* participants, Washington Luiz Aguiar and Hélio Lopes.) The youngest child in this video, Wesley, was nine years old at the time and has an amputated leg below the knee from an unspecified accident. After only one week with his family, he returned to the Projeto Quixote because his family could not properly tend to him. Another of the three protagonists, a teenager by the name of Bruno, initially reported an improved relationship with his father. However, a few months after the completion of this video Projeto Quixote staff found him living again in the streets to escape his violent father. Intoxicated at the time he was seen, he refused reentry into the Projeto program because, he claimed, he missed the freedom of life in the streets. I could not gather any further information about the third youth in the video (Jefferson), for often the Projeto staff logically loses contact with the thousands of children and youth who, with different degrees of involvement, participate in their programs.

Led by Graziela Bedoian, the Projeto research staff has also undertaken at least one project to quantitatively measure the success rates of rematriamento. For twelve months between 2010 and 2011, they interviewed children and youth who were tended to at any of their facilities in the Crackolândia area. Out of 209 children and youth up to twenty-five years of age, 136 were male and 73 female. Most reported being in the streets because of negligence and abandonment of their parents (37 percent), physical abuse (18 percent), and sexual abuse (15 percent). Fifty-eight out of 209 were "re-matriated" back with their biological or adoptive families (42) or shelters (16), with the rest "in process" of "being re-matriated" ("Refugiados urbanos"). While the figures offer valuable information on the protagonists of these dramatic urban stories, the data unfortunately lacks context and interpretation. The report does not address what methods of rematriamento were used, whether and how they were effective, or what factors may contribute to long-term rematriamentos. Among the many Projeto Quixote publications I have consulted, I have not found any such studies on rematriamento, or any additional data or information.

The challenges of tracking and measuring the success of rematriamento efforts loom large not only for the Projeto Quixote, but for any similar youth organization. In the broader field of activism with street-connected youth, as Melissa S. Harris and her collaborators point out, very few studies have been conducted on the success rate and quality of social reinsertion of children and youth. With a small sample from just two organizations (one in the São Paulo state municipality of Campinas and the other in Lima, Peru), Harris' team identified, based on interviews with the staff and program participants, three predictors of effective rematriamento: a healthy and safe family environment; a longer stay with the organization, usually involving vocational training; and the level of formal education with which participants entered the program (723, 728). Although these three predictors may also apply to the Projeto Quixote, we lack reliable and comprehensive data for our São Paulo-based nonprofits. Besides the methodological and ethical questions about what information to gather and how to do so, the other impediment for data collection remains the fact that nonprofits tend to expend their limited resources on providing services rather than assessing them. Inevitably, thus, performative activism often functions for many organizations as an idealistic process that in a Quixote-appropriate manner fails to back with evidence how many former residents in fact took a protagonist role in their rescripted story. Even from a strictly literary standpoint, assessing whether and how successfully project participants "narrate" their own life stories may be extremely difficult if not impossible to define.

Furthermore, the reality of everyday narratives for underserved children is often as obstinate as harsh, which might make even measurable success a short-lived occurrence. Despite the many years of intervention, for instance, the downtown Crackôlandia area persists as a neighborhood highly populated by the most excluded members of society, including street-connected children and youth. The then mayor of São Paulo, João Doria, nicknamed the Brazilian Trump for his role in the local version of *The Apprentice*, vowed in January 2017 to eradicate Crackôlandia. Needless to say, soon after bulldozers leveled improvised tents and open-air drug markets in May 2017, addicts and dealers simply congregated in other downtown neighborhoods. In late 2018, they continued to have a significant presence in the Crackolândia area, for the underlying issues of poverty and violence behind the decades-long crack epidemic remain unresolved and, if anything, have aggravated in recent years (Cowie). In this endless cycle of poverty and addiction, it is legitimate to ask: did the Projeto Quixote's Bixiga Windmill or the smaller Luz and República spaces make a dent in the tragic plot unfolding daily for so many children and youth in Crackolândia? We simply have no hard evidence of how many participants in any of their programs were successfully rematriated and, if so, for how long and under what conditions. Furthermore, it is even harder to track whether "another story" transformed the lives of participants in the Projeto Quixote or other Cervantes-based initiatives. The windmills that Don Quixote tilted at in São Paulo have certainly proven giants.

Nonetheless, the success of the Projeto Quixote remains remarkable and measurable if we consider its longevity (more than twenty years of continued operations), the number of children and youth attended to (more than fifteen thousand), as well as their numerous publications, seminars, sponsorships, awards, and other recognitions. Beyond the gathering of quantifiable data, which smaller organizations such as Cooperaacs, the Instituto Religare, or the QEC may not even have the capabilities or interest to gather, it is the individual examples of significant personal and collective transformation that enable us to assess the ability of Quixote-inspired organizations to effectively promote change. Most importantly, those daily stories of progress and triumph over adversity are what keep the staff going, despite the typically low salaries and emotionally charged workloads. Among such real-life testimonials, one last example from the Projeto Quixote best illustrates how performative tactics, in all of their complexity and limitations, can coalesce into powerful, even if precarious, moments of deep personal and collective change.

Between 2005 and 2006, Chilean filmmaker Daniel Rubio directed the *Exilados do Mundão* (*Exiled from the World*, 2006) documentary project under the auspices of a partnership between the Projeto Quixote, UNI-FESP (the Federal University of São Paulo), and two Canadian universities (McMaster and Calgary). The film presents its audience with a slice of the everyday life of recently released FEBEM interns as they reenter society. To that effect, the film's producers gave small video cameras to six youth (five male and one female) with the deceivingly simple charge to record their quotidian lives through their own eyes. In the next few pages, I probe how this social justice experiment transforms a classic literary piece such as *Don Quixote* into a process by which six ex-FEBEM interns seek transformation themselves with simply a small video camera in their hands.

In a preparatory meeting with the young participants and other Projeto Quixote educators, Dr. Lescher argues that *Don Quixote*'s most revolutionary proposal remains the different *olhar* (roughly, a different way of looking) with which he views reality. In an editing choice that symbolically highlights the importance of this new olhar, the background in the opening credits of the forty-five-minute film features a close-up of the six project participants' eyes in a mosaic-like still composition. From the beginning of this movie, spectators participate in an attempt to look at everyday reality in and from the margins, for we as viewers add our own pair of eyes to the mosaic that fills the screen. Expounding on the premise of a different olhar, Dr. Auro Lescher explains the artivist rationale behind the project. Although Cervantes' hero becomes a knight-errant in order to right wrongs, Dr. Lescher argues, his truly transformative act rests on the fresh look he takes at windmills, farmers, prostitutes, and modest inns through the literary eyes of chivalric thrill. As the knightly character Don Quixote emerges out of the imagination of the hidalgo Quijano, the invention of his new persona engenders a new vocabulary to describe a lackluster society in epic terms. Armed with words and his chivalric performance, Don Quixote seeks to achieve a fairer society by daring to take a different look at people and things, which in turn facilitates new forms of storytelling about oneself and the world. While Don Quixote's military capabilities are profoundly inadequate and often misguided, his powerful mind succeeds at drawing numerous fellow characters and countless generations of readers into a story of radical metamorphosis. As Dr. Lescher remarks in the film, in order to achieve meaningful liberation, the social roles that oppress us can and should be replaced with a different narrative born out of our own imagination and artistry.

Out of the six young participants in the project, a nineteen-year-old male by the name of Michael interpreted the assignment in a most daring way: he swapped his handgun for a camera in order to take a fresh, inside look at youth crime in his neighborhood. One night, he ventured into a dangerous section of his *bairro* and interviewed a group of armed teens. Although Michael has likely neither read nor will ever read *Don Quixote*, his audacious interpretation of the new olhar at the core of the *Exilados* filmic experiment offers new insights into a Brazilian-activist reading of Cervantes' masterpiece. Armed with only his knowledge of chivalric literature, Alonso Quijano had already embarked on a similarly foolish adventure four hundred years earlier. In preparation for staging his revolutionary performance of chivalry, the hidalgo did restore family relics covered in dust (a sword, lance, and body armor), but his weapons proved as old and half-broken as his own aged body and the squalid nag he took as a steed. His military adventures almost always end up in ridiculous defeats with catastrophic consequences for himself and, frequently, others. Rather than his null chivalric capabilities, it is his language and acting that appear infectious, as more and more characters voluntarily enter his performative game, radically changing their lives in the process. In the shadows since the first few pages of the book, it is the modest hidalgo surrounded by books who offers a new revolutionary way of looking at reality, a new olhar. Through art, words, and a different performance from what social expectations dictate, the transformation of self and others can happen through a sophisticated and potentially dangerous exercise in rendering the invisible visible. In a brilliant if risky application of this daring olhar, Michael held an exhilarating conversation with a gang of armed and intoxicated youth, who typically move in the shadows of illegal activity, with the help of just his bold artistic mindset and a small video camera. Young soldiers in the drug wars, the most invisible and expendable of populations, became visible as they took a protagonist role in their own story.

Some time past midnight in late 2005 or early 2006, Michael approaches a group of four masked and heavily armed youth. The encounter takes place in a dangerous section of Michael's neighborhood in São Paulo's *periferia*, the favela-like settlements around the city's urban center. Holding a camera rather than a gun, Michael starts filming once the four youth have consented to being recorded and covered their faces. During the first frames of footage, nonetheless, they still casually point their guns at him. Agitated, they show clear signs of intoxication. Michael reassures them again and again that he is a local resident whose only intention is to capture on camera a conversation about their everyday life. As Michael continues filming, the masked youth finally loosen up and confess on camera to having just robbed a store. While casually wielding high caliber shotguns and pistols, they remain talkative. Moreover, they behave cordially with a fellow resident, Michael, who seemingly shares much of their life experience. Born in the municipality of Santo André, adjacent to São Paulo, Michael dos Santos was nineteen years old at the time and has eleven siblings (by 2006 his mother had been married to six different men, he explains on camera). Both Michael and all of the armed youth had been incarcerated at the FEBEM, and they all bitterly complained about the brutality of the experience. As Michael states, it was not his traumatic stay at the FEBEM that changed his life for the better. Rather, it was the *Exilados* project that prompted him to trade his gun for a camera, a simple but radical act that transformed his life: "Foi a troca que mudou a vida" (It was this change that turned my life around).

With his camera, Michael exposes the film's audience to unexpected behaviors and new characters, including his own, in a rarely seen social narrative that fundamentally diverges from mainstream portrayals of at-risk and criminal youth. For these children and adolescents, historically deprived of the means to self-represent their interests and aspirations, the narrative around who they are and what they want is typically written by those who control mainstream media and political discourse. How often, if ever, do we see stories narrated or images recorded by the underprivileged? Approaching unknown gang members in the dark, Michael risks his life with the ultimate objective not to rob a store or buy drugs but to record the story of masked, adolescent criminals (one of them claims to be twelve years old). In this scene, Michael and the low-rank soldiers in São Paulo's never-ending drug war have cast themselves as not only protagonists *in* but also narrators *of* their own story.

As their roles shift, the reaction from the gang members standing guard with their guns initially confirms but also shatters stereotypes about young underprivileged males. Inebriated and with their pockets full of money from their robbery, the armed youth tell Michael something that unexpectedly points to the potential of artivism to trigger change. Emphatically, they reiterate that Michael should consider himself lucky for holding a camera instead of a gun. In just over a minute of footage (00:43:11–00:44:30), the masked adolescent who behaves as the leader of the gang repeats four times to Michael: "Thank God for this opportunity and embrace it." In contrast, half-jokingly, he laughs at the "craziness" of their criminal persona while pointing at one of his peers holding a handgun. Throughout the conversation, they blame their criminal acts on lack of employment opportunities, and they admit that easy money from robberies and drug trafficking "goes" as quickly as it "comes." They all consume drugs to withstand the brutal nature of their life in crime and the trauma from their internment at the FEBEM. As the camera makes these youth visible and provides them with a platform from which they can talk about themselves, a transformation has no doubt occurred, even if only momentarily.

While mostly absent from the daily work of Quixote-inspired organizations, the sense of immediate danger as Michael approaches a group of potentially violent offenders helps nuance the perceived benefits of renaming, visibility, and the porousness of identity for the underprivileged. Initially, the masked youth brag about robbing a store and go on record with a confession of their crime, a reckless act of agency that could potentially land them in prison (conveniently, of course, they cover their faces.) Michael himself risks his life in order to capture with his modest camera the most marginalized of casts, a group of intoxicated, confessed teen criminals in a poverty-ridden part of town. Counterintuitively, nonetheless, the urge to tell their story in their own words is for the underrepresented more powerful than fear itself or simple caution. Instead of avoiding the spotlight after committing a crime, the youth actually thrive in front of the camera, metamorphosing in front of our eyes from armed criminals into youth who want to be seen and heard. After admitting to their robbery and drug consumption, they mutate into self-consciously performative subjects who, as they state repeatedly, would rather hold a camera than a gun. With fair access to gainful employment and education, they claim, they would quit their life in crime, for breaking the law will inevitably get them jailed or killed before they turn thirty.

Despite the youth's hopeful statements, however, the raw, unedited, and unpolished aesthetics of a handheld camera shooting a poorly lit scene in the middle of the night betrays the obstinate and ugly nature of reality for the underprivileged. We cannot naïvely assume that this moment of transformation alone had any significant effect on the long-term prospects of the four young individuals that converse with Michael during this scene. Although I can only speculate, most of them will likely be either dead or in prison by now, and Michael's short experiment will have had hardly any impact on their lives. Stored in some CD-ROM, with editing and sound of arguable quality at best, the film itself has by now likely faded into oblivion, for it was never distributed to commercial cinemas, and it is not even posted on the Projeto's own YouTube channel.

Despite the precariousness of its transformative experiences, this project sheds new light on how a different point of view can trigger transformation in Quixote-inspired activism. At least for Michael and other Projeto Quixote participants, including the film's viewers, these fleeting moments in which a new olhar shifts the narratorial point of view from mainstream media to the eyes of the underprivileged may turn out to be life-changing experiences. When given the opportunity to talk, the Other, thirsty for recognition and eager to communicate, proudly takes center stage, for chances to share their story only seldom materialize. Whether through a film, play, or any other form of artistic expression, the spectacle of performance serves the underrepresented as a particularly powerful point of entry into public discourse (Vargas 192). Quixote-inspired activist projects begin with a mutation that turns the invisible and the silenced into uncommon, remarkable subjects who occupy new locations from which to tell previously unheard narratives. In Cervantes' book, in rather strident ways, the obscure hidalgo Quijano transforms himself by the power of just words and acting into an eye-catching knight-errant, even if frequently ridiculed and defeated. In *Exiles from the World*, a modest handheld camera changes the life course of project participants, all former FEBEM interns. By telling and performing stories from the margins, this Quixote-inspired olhar transculturates the Spanish classic into a dazzling exercise in performing visibility. The viewer marvels not only at who we see on screen (intoxicated youth with serious weaponry in their hands who have just committed an armed robbery) but also at the eyes through which we see them (those of another FEBEM convict who holds the camera and films the improvised conversation). Transforming the extreme Other—the excluded, the violent, the outcast—into narrators as well as subjects of unheard stories, *Exilados* radically alters preconceived roles in the social narrative. By shifting the point of view, we the audience hear marginalized, intoxicated, and traumatized individuals freely confess that they would prefer a different life story for themselves stripped of guns and violence. Further along in his artivist process of transformation, Michael uses his legal name and image on camera in contrast to the covered and anonymous robbers. Camera in hand, he stands as a consumed performative activist whose liberation from a life of crime has only just begun.

This last, revealing example and the many others discussed throughout this chapter confirm the inadequacy of previous definitions of performative activism as mere public shows of protest. A revised formulation of the concept must reflect the everyday practice that seeks social change through the rescripting and enacting of new individual and collective roles. As documented in *Exilados do Mundão*, performative activism roots itself firmly in its community of origin. Anchored in its neighborhoods, working closely with its inhabitants, it promotes cultural activities that seek change door-to-door, one person at a time, street by street. In doing so, cultural nonprofits and artivists practice the "deliberate and ongoing attempt to reclaim [the] physical and psychological space" of the excluded and the marginalized that mainstream society typically ignores, vilifies, or attempts to eradicate (Neate and Platt 163). In community activism, interventions may unfold in highly volatile contexts, such as the marginal area where Michael encountered the young, intoxicated criminals in the middle of the night. It is precisely in those unrehearsed, one-of-a-kind moments when Dr. Lescher's premise that *Don Quixote* represents above all a new perspective or olhar gets tested in the crudest of ways, for its consequences can never be fully anticipated or controlled.

Beyond the mere public expression of protest, thus, Brazilian Quixote-inspired performative activism repurposes or even cannibalizes culture (in this case, classic culture typically associated with elite audiences) to deploy a new olhar and new forms of storytelling amid the most marginalized environments. In its pursuit of recycling and transformation of not just the underrepresented but of society as a whole, performative activism shares in community-based contexts the same four attributes that I listed in my previous re-definition of transculturation in Chapter 1. Across the Americas and particularly in Brazil, after all, *Don Quixote*'s adaptations and its activist applications prove inextricably linked though a common transcultural experience. Again, I use Michael's example to illustrate the four main features that I observed in the activist practice of Quixote-inspired nonprofits.

At the community level, performative activism engages in complex negotiations of multiple and at times conflicting identities and interests within a variety of social contexts, including institutions, families, and the streets. In Michael's particular case, he had to first gain acceptance into the documentary project, discuss its goals and methods with the Projeto staff, and then carry out the assignment by, as per his own choice, approaching a group of intoxicated teen robbers. Secondly, performative activism sets wide-ranging social justice goals for itself, but prescribes no specific end result. In the *Exilados* scene, Michael did not request or impose any specific project goals on the masked youth, and he could certainly not have predicted the actual outcome of the encounter. In the end, out of endless other possibilities, the teens nonetheless arrived on their own at the conclusion that they would rather hold a camera than a gun. Thirdly, and as an implicit consequence of the lack of a concrete new social paradigm, performative activism functions as intrinsically self-reflexive and self-aware. It emphasizes the *process*, rather than specific outcomes, by which the rescripting and performing of personal and collective identities can lead to change. In the case of *Exilados do Mundão*, most of the film discusses the methodology of the project itself (for instance, how to use a camera to capture that new olhar), while concrete and measurable goals are hardly, if ever, mentioned.

Finally, performative activism promotes a concept of agency that fosters communication across all populations and social strata and that seeks to create an open-ended impact on interpersonal relations and collective perceptions. This complex process of reimagining identities and social interactions can happen via diverse forms of expression, including visual, embodied, and sonic, as well as through various means of dissemination, such as onstage, in the street, onscreen, printed, or online. For instance, the *Exilados* project starts as an oral appropriation of a literary classic, *Don Quixote*, then turns into a filmic experiment that can be shared through a number of platforms (online or onscreen). The four features that I identified in performative activism converge in one common goal: the use of writing, artistic production, and performance for enacting a new collective narrative in which roles are reimagined and social relations unfold in more inclusive and equitable ways.

Typically spearheaded by highly educated artists and professionals, performative activism may be criticized for being elite-driven and idealistic, particularly in our Cervantes-based case study. After all, the underprivileged might not have the time or the urge to interpret and perform a seventeenth-century classic such as *Don Quixote* when they must in fact meet much more pressing needs, such as putting food on the table and protecting themselves from domestic, street, and/or institutional violence. From this perspective, performative activism might be regarded by some skeptics as a somewhat futile exercise in self-indulgence by a group of educated activists who administer theater and art-based workshops to the underserved because they lack the means or influence to provide what the excluded *really* need, such as jobs and financial assistance. Even if we accept that performative activism can ignite personal transformation on and off stage, the individual commitment to role-playing and artistic production may not necessarily translate into structural change at the community or, much less, the national or transnational levels. Moreover, the assessment of performative activism's impact on both the individual and the larger society proves a near-impossible task, for success in rescripting narratives and facilitating protagonist roles for the underrepresented remains a largely intangible outcome. In my view, these are all hard but valid questions about the expediency of performative activism to effect meaningful change that nonprofits would benefit from asking themselves as a potentially fruitful self-reflective and self-critical exercise. And yet, this is far from a complete picture of the true potential of performative activism to better the lives of its practitioners.

For Quixote-inspired organizations, in fact, Cervantes' classic confirms the power of performance to effect change in ways that may be less quantifiable and tangible than qualitative and humanistic. In the process of triggering individual and collective change, the *how* and not the what becomes itself a site of intervention both in the novel and in contemporary Brazilian activism. As the paradigm that fuels the work of Quixote-inspired nonprofits, the novel itself offers plenty of evidence of how performance can initiate deep transformation. Within the revolutionary space of discursive and artistic expression, change is first effected from within, as when Quijano decides to become Don Quixote or anyone he wishes, including the Twelve Peers of France and the nine Paragons of Fame. Furthermore, broader collective change can ensue through a chain reaction of individual transformations, as demonstrated by Sancho and the many otherwise unremarkable characters (among them Sansón Carrasco or the duke and duchess) who embrace Don Quixote's theatricality to the point of radically altering and even risking their own lives. Kindled by Quijano/Quixote, performative activism spreads like fire through numerous characters in the book, who voluntarily transform themselves by rewriting and enacting new roles for themselves. More remarkably yet, the potential of performance for transformation can be documented in the ongoing and fervent consumption of everything *Don Quixote* through today, from plays to paintings, sculptures, films, comics, business labels, and other appropriations.

Four hundred years later, a handful of Quixote-inspired theater companies and nonprofits across the Americas and particularly in Brazil, together with their audiences and project participants, have been touched by the contagious urge to rename themselves and their world. In theaters across the Americas and on the social stage, in the streets and at home, they continue to rescript and perform new roles for themselves. In doing so, these budding groups of activists strive to effect social change by breathing new life into Cervantes' fictional character through the re-enactment of his radical performative proposal. Peterson, Valéria, Michael, Andreia, Telma, Auro, Washington, Hélio, Sandro, Márcio, and thousands upon thousands of audience members and participants in Quixote-inspired artivism have had at least a taste of Cervantes' extraordinary recipe for transformation. Alive and well, *Don Quixote* has become today an action verb, a symbol for *living* literature, a performance of new forms of citizenship on the everyday stage.

CONCLUSION

Don Quixote Lives On

Performative Activism in the Americas

After the worldwide celebrations of *Don Quixote*'s four-hundredth anniversary in 2005 and 2015, Cervantes' classic continues to thrive outside institutionally sanctioned environments in activist practices across the Americas, from Spanish-speaking countries to the United States or Brazil. What started for me as somewhat of a casual encounter with the Projeto Quixote in São Paulo turned into a book project that has uncovered a consistent pattern of activism that, while statistically insufficient, transculturates *Don Quixote* through numerous projects across the American hemisphere in innovative, multilingual, and yet strikingly similar ways. Unrelated to each other, these initiatives share several key features that point to a form of cultural activism inspired by *Don Quixote* that employs literature, art, and theater for social betterment. At the street level, striding along centers of cultural authority as well as the margins of society, *Don Quixote* inspires communities of practitioners for whom art and performance can enable particularly the underrepresented to rescript a protagonist role in their life story.[1] The hidalgo Quijano's creation of the knight-errant Don Quixote models the revolutionary concept that acting can rehearse and enact a direct intervention into the social imaginary. For activists across the Americas, theatrical practice can democratize access to the creation of collective narratives and ultimately alter the social stage. In this conclusion, I sum up the main features of Quixote-inspired activism highlighted throughout this book. Then I discuss the main challenges faced in general by cultural activism and, in particular, by the nonprofits analyzed here: the purported crisis of the humanities in the age of mass and instant communication and the lack of assessment tools and data collection. At the same time that I point out these potential shortcomings, however, I also offer some reflections that could help alleviate legitimate concerns about the effectiveness of performative activism. And finally, I ponder the future of Quixote-inspired activism by briefly examining three powerful examples that took place recently in three countries: Cape Verde, Brazil, and the United States.

While deeply idealistic and even arguably naïve, the exercise in artistic freedom that Cervantes' novel inspires in its contemporary practitioners does not rely on madness. For Quixote-inspired activists, Alonso Quijano did not lose his mind but intentionally decided to script and act out a new role for himself. He based his knight-errant on chivalric heroes that he could never replicate in the "real" world and that at his age and in the Spain of his time seemed not just ill fitting but even ridiculous. However, when applied to deeply marginalized communities, the Quixote life project materializes in less comical terms; it unfolds rather as a radical attempt at imagining and performing a better society. The initiatives I discussed here reject mainstream portrayals of underprivileged youth as either victims or monsters who elicit nothing but pity or fear. By performing new societal roles for themselves, the underserved attempt to effect social change from within. For these activists, "another story" is possible, as the Projeto Quixote's motto states in a clear manifestation of the radically discursive nature of their enterprise. But how do these projects attempt to modify the social narrative about and by the Others (the marginalized, the ignored)? In order to develop awareness of the power of performance for individual and collective transformation, Quixote-inspired activism heavily relies on metatheater and self-awareness, on the process of creating and staging a new story, particularly around issues of marginality. For social roles to change, they argue, and especially to modify a social stage that breeds exclusion and inequality, activists and participants must first master the art of theater and performance. In this regard, once again, the hidalgo and obsessive reader Alonso Quijano, rather than Don Quixote the warrior, emerges as a hero of reading and acting who lives his life as if it were a book. In his ability to reimagine, rewrite and enact a new world, the reader turned author, director, and actor of his own story radically transforms his life and the world around him.

In the Americas, *Don Quixote*'s community-engaged transculturation revolves around the notion of performative activism. In a perfect conflation of the message and the medium, the goal of personal and collective transformation that articulates Brazilian social justice activism since at least Paulo Freire is embodied by the ever-evolving figure (in the book as well as in the way it is reappropriated over time) of Don Quixote. This symbiotic relation between message and medium both triggers and results from a process of transculturation, of cultural transformation, that adapts a seventeenth-century Spanish-language novel into a variety of activist theatrical and artistic practices in twenty-first century Brazil and the Americas. Unlike nation-building and academic projects, generally conceived and implemented by elites in institutional spaces, transcultural and activist transformation at the community level is typically initiated by educated activists but then potentially embraced and practiced by diverse members of society, among them the underprivileged and underrepresented. Although focused on performative activism, these organizations also recognize the project participants' material needs as well as the potential benefits of artistically intervening in underserved urban spaces.

Out of this whirlwind of cultural, individual, and collective recycling of people, preconceptions, objects, and spaces, three concurrent tactics channel the urge for change into practice: (re)naming, increasing visibility, and destabilizing fixed identity and social categories. Quixote-inspired projects in Brazil mindfully walk a thin line between the restoration of excluded youths' legal identities and rightful place in society and the preservation of their typically self-chosen street names, for both serve important purposes. While legal identities may facilitate the youths' rematriamento into their families, schools, and governmental programs, street names can also protect them from abusive families and/or institutions and may feel empowering, as they are often self-given. In general, nonetheless, Quixote-inspired nonprofits seek the legal integration of children and youth into society through the recovery of their institutional identities and the full recognition of the rights and obligations that come with it.[2] Connected to the issue of naming, the excluded and the underrepresented can gain a sense of heightened visibility on the social stage through art and performance. Rather than being seen as potential threats, through artistic and theatrical expression the marginalized may garner their audience's appreciation. In these moments of exchange between producers and consumers of culture, perceptions alter, and barriers break down. It is through this kind of transformative exercise that the rescripting and acting of new roles, particularly for the excluded and the invisible, may by extension transform society at large for the betterment of all. When audiences appreciate and possibly participate in a performance, they might also embark themselves on a journey of self-transformation that can lead to a less prejudiced, more egalitarian mindset. The ultimate objective is to transform acts of oppression, whether large or small, systemic or individual, into moments of liberation. Together, these tactics suggest a practice of cultural citizenship that goes beyond the affirmation of any one ethnic, racial, or class group and focuses instead on the artivist methods by which a more connected, equal society can be built.

Cutting across racial, ethnic, gender, religious, and class lines, performative activism relies on words and acting to transform society without prescribing a preconceived end product or even a uniform formula for change. Instead, and through a close and unbiased collaboration between adults and children, the college educated and the streetwise, the documented, the undocumented, and the ex-convict, these projects all propose a self-conscious theatrical practice that rescripts social relations via what Paulo Freire described as the powerful combination of ethics and aesthetics. For Freire and artivism in general, culture and art have a role to play in the advancement of a more ethical society, for equality cannot be achieved just by tending to material needs; artistic, performative, and literary expression remain an inalienable right for all. In response to this demand for new storytelling, particularly among the underrepresented, *Don Quixote* lives on four centuries after its original publication in streets around the world and in community spaces. Contrary to the perception that, in today's society, literature and the humanities are irrelevant in public discourse, *Don Quixote*'s practitioners now apply Cervantes' story to the betterment of society more frequently and deliberately than ever before.

In this regard, this book functions as a platform for a budding discussion on the merits of practicing literature and studying the humanities in action. In an era of instant communication and mass consumption, many within and outside academia have proclaimed the crisis of the humanities and forecast its eventual but certain demise. In the United States alone, both federal and state governments have slashed funding for higher education and academic research, particularly in the humanities and social sciences, and Brazil has suffered even more stringent cuts since 2014. In the United States, major reports commissioned in 2013 by the American Academy of Arts and Sciences (*The Heart of the Matter*) and Harvard University (*The Teaching of the Arts and Humanities at Harvard College*), together with renowned academics such as Stanley Fish ("The Crisis of the Humanities" and "Crisis of the Humanities II"), have sounded the alarm for the decrease in humanities majors and the elimination of entire humanistic and art programs in a handful of schools and universities. However, the crisis of the humanities might not be as severe or gloomy as reported, and it certainly offers some bright spots and new opportunities. While some scholars and administrators have contextualized university enrollment data in more nuanced and less ominous terms,[3] others proclaim that the future of the humanities belongs both inside and outside the often-elitist walls of university campuses. Significantly, Lynn Pasquerella, a philosopher and current president of the American Association of Colleges and Universities, joins advocates of community-based learning and scholarship in proposing a humanities practice that is "much more than [a] traditional extension of scholarship" in order to attract "practitioners beyond the academy" through a variety of community engagement projects (3).

Thanks to the daily work of activists such as the ones discussed in this study, the humanities and literature in particular may well be evolving in exciting directions in the present moment. At the street level, contemporary transculturations of Cervantes' classic by community theaters and organizations in Brazil and across the Americas offer a much-needed new perspective on the activist role of the humanities, one that literary studies in general and Cervantes scholarship in particular tend to sideline, if not ignore. Tellingly, previous formulations of transculturation and performative activism, both critical concepts in the humanistic study of cultural relations and performance, painfully ignore community perspectives in favor of either elitist nation-building projects or mass movements of public protest. While some question the relevance of the humanities, I would submit that the time has arrived for humanistic and literary researchers to significantly broaden our methodological scope in order to examine and participate in applied, community-based appropriations of literary and cultural works. In my view, a higher number of our research and course projects should leave the elitist space of academic libraries, museums, and classrooms in order to study and amplify at the street level, alongside community organizations and residents, the potential social impact of humanistic initiatives (Miñana, "Making Change Happen").

The question of the "real" impact of performative activism, Quixote-inspired or otherwise, points to another of the challenges facing cultural nonprofits today beyond, of course, perennial budget shortages. In the contemporary neoliberal context, quantifying outcomes and assessing return on investment has taken over most aspects of social work, including healthcare, education, and philanthropy. From a humanistic point of view, the argument could be made that the benefits of cultural activism cannot be measured. From a contrarian point of view, however, others may claim that the lack of quantifiable outcomes and assessment only confirms the futility of art-based interventions to effect "real" change. As is most often the case, the truth likely lies somewhere in the middle. While in some ways cultural activism may produce intangible benefits, from a boost to self-confidence to joy and calm amid the pressures of the everyday, nonprofits must still be accountable for the expenditure of their financial and human capital. The largest of the Quixote nonprofits, the Projeto Quixote, publishes on its website annual data ("Resultados") on the number of children and families attended to and the number of services provided, plus examples of testimonials and direct quotes from project participants. Their manifold publications, workshops, and scholarship review their methodologies as well as some of their successes and challenges through a variety of case studies and data gathering. Furthermore, they are audited every fiscal year, and the resulting financial report is posted on their website. More importantly, however, deep assessment of their outcomes and rates of success, currently lacking to a great extent beyond testimonials and the two films discussed in Chapter 6, could help the organization refine their goals and effectiveness. With such grand and vague goals as "transformation" or producing "another story," innovative ways of at least documenting, if not quantifying, the process of change could go a long way to help hone effective methods and denounce structures of inequality or even simply identify cracks in the system. In this book, built around the literary analysis of *Don Quixote* in the context of contemporary performative activism, I limited myself mostly to testimonials, participant observations, and critical discourse analysis of texts such as scripts, performances, protest signs, promotional materials, and media products. However, for future studies, interdisciplinary teams and university-NGO partnerships appear to me as the most promising means of designing and deploying mixed research methods, both quantitative and qualitative, with a long-term outlook. Sustained over a period of time, research partnerships could facilitate recurring engagement with project participants, including individuals, families, and institutions. A network of program alumni could be developed more formally, which in turn would extend the support system offered by these nonprofits to its graduates well beyond the completion of a given program. Just as importantly, current active participants in Quixote-inspired activism could be connected with alumni of these programs for the benefit of all. Once again, the Projeto Quixote modeled such research agreements through projects like *Exilados do Mundão*, with participation from Brazilian and Canadian universities (the Projeto Quixote itself grew out of the Federal University of São Paulo). Nonetheless, more permanent and broader partnerships are needed.

After the decade between 2005 and 2015 of Cervantes' worldwide celebrations, Quixote-inspired performative activism continues to evolve in ways that are remarkably consistent, but once again only across an admittedly limited sample of unrelated initiatives. In surprisingly cohesive ways, several of the performative activists discussed in this book and others who have more recently started embedding *Don Quixote* in their projects are transitioning into a model in which adaptations of Cervantes' classic are still facilitated by cultural activists but increasingly written and performed mainly by children and youth themselves. If Quixote-inspired performative activism aims to see reality through a different olhar and demands a protagonist role for those on the margins, this progression seems only logical. As an early example, Valéria di Pietro's 2002 *Num lugar de la Mancha* play performed by FEBEM interns evolved over a period of only a few years into the Instituto Religare, where Peterson Xavier and others wrote, produced, and performed their own plays. In a similar move, Márcio Meirelles and Andreia de Almeida, the creative forces behind the plays *Um tal de Dom Quixote* and *Quixotes*, respectively, have also undertaken projects in Cape Verde and São Paulo in which young participants took the lead in the writing, production, and performance of their own adaptations of *Don Quixote*. In these two cases, participants did not read Cervantes' text in a structured and sustained way as part of the development of their projects. In a third and last example out of Brooklyn, New York, however, children of Latin American migrants wrote an original, bilingual musical play adapted from Cervantes' classic via their own careful reading and translation of a selection of episodes from the original Spanish-language novel.

In 2014, Márcio Meirelles participated with young theater practitioners in Brasil, Portugal, and Cape Verde in a tri-national project called K-Cena, which when read out loud sounds in Portuguese like "What a stage" or "What a scene." For several weeks, Meirelles worked with around sixteen young actors in Mindelo, Cape Verde, a small city that the playwright himself describes as having "80 mil habitantes e 18 grupos de teatro" (eighty thousand inhabitants and eighteen theater ensembles; L. Neves E3). With Meirelles' guidance, the group collectively wrote *Em defesa das causas perdidas—Uma carta para Dom Quixote* (*In Defense of Lost Causes—A Letter for Don Quixote*), which Meirelles himself describes as a sort of manifesto or what he calls "documentary theater" (*teatro documental*; L. Neves E2). Blending adaptations of *Don Quixote* and other cultural references (Portuguese-language literature, Cape Verdean music, and even a political speech by the country's prime minister), *Em defesa* raises issues of inequality, racism, and other social justice-oriented topics that directly concern project participants. The play-letter concludes with "Discurso 7, Dom Quixote" (Speech 7, Don Quixote), in which female actor Deka Saimor elaborates on the social implications of Cervantes' hero. The echoes of the performative interpretations of *Don Quixote* illustrated throughout this book with unrelated examples from Brazil, Mexico, Colombia, and the United States are remarkably, almost uncannily obvious:

> isto aqui é um palco
> isto aqui é teatro
> sou deka
> sou atriz . . . como atriz tenho um papel político
> lido com o poder
> o poder de representar
> representar todos
> dar voz a quem não tem
> e questionar a voz de quem tem . . . qual é o nosso papel?
> fazer todos os papéis
> para que o mundo se reconheça
> e perceba que pode mudar
> . . . como atriz também sou um dom quixote.

> *this here is a stage*
> *this here is theater*
> *i am deka*
> *i am an actress . . . as an actress, i have a political role*
> *i deal with power*
> *the power to represent*
> *represent everyone*
> *give voice to those who don't have it*
> *and question the voice of those who have it . . . what is our role?*
> *to perform all roles*
> *so that the world recognizes itself* [*in our performance*]
> *and realizes that it can change*
> *. . . as an actress, i am, too, don quixote.* (Meirelles et al. 30)

Saimor's reading of the Spanish-language icon is profoundly metatheatrical and discursive, rather than merely romanticized and chivalric, for it centers on giving voice through acting to those who do not have it. The fighter for social justice who literally takes center stage wields no weapons but rather self-identifies as an actress with a political role and a clear mission: "to perform all roles / so that the world recognizes itself / and . . . can change." Change here springs from performance, and in that transformative social function, the artist, the actress, the artivist is, "too, Don Quixote."

While Andreia de Almeida continues to perform her *Quixotes* occasionally, her Quixote, Espaço Comunitário (QEC) nonprofit encourages young participants to appropriate *Don Quixote* with minimal supervision from educated adults. In July 2015, for instance, I visited an exhibit of paintings and drawings by QEC participants, complemented with dances, essays, and poems based on selections from *Don Quixote* discussed in small groups. In a 2018 singing workshop, students wrote the lyrics and composed a song entitled "Que xote é esse" (a wordplay between *Quixote* and *Que xote*, *xote* being a traditional Northeastern dance adapted from the European polka), which was featured in a video by Beel Films published on Facebook on July 26, 2018. In this song, performed by a choir of male and female voices with just an acoustic guitar accompaniment, the youth infuse the most quixotic of scenes, the knight's tilting at windmills, with their own daily life struggles: "O meu moinho eu vou derrotar / E os meus sonhos realizar" (I'm going to defeat my windmill / And make my dreams come true), they sing with conviction. The windmills or giants they confront embody different manifestations of contemporary teen angst: "me deixar levar . . . ficar sozinho . . . o medo do fracasso" (to not stand up for myself . . . to be alone . . . fear of failure). How do Brazilian youth in a Quixote-based cultural project, thus, fight back against the real giants or windmills that threaten their happiness? Joyously, they sing: "Eu os enfrento atuando, dançando, pulando, brincando . . . Eu os enfrento escrevendo, abraçando, criando, tocando" (I face [my windmills] performing, dancing, jumping, playing . . . I face them writing, hugging, creating, playing music). The arsenal with which to combat their personal and social windmills/giants consists of merely artistic and performative weapons. Rather than the belligerent knight-errant, thus, it is the artist behind Don Quixote who models positive and resolute change for the youth who want to defeat their windmills and right their wrongs. Toward the end of the song, a young man and woman stare into the camera and recite their final words of Quixote-inspired wisdom in a perfect conflation between theater and life: "Os moinhos do palco / são os mesmos moinho da vida" (The windmills on stage are the same windmills [that we face] in real life). With this short sentence, the essence of Quixote-inspired performative activism springs to life, for theater offers itself as the key with which to unlock and unleash personal and social transformation in the everyday. If these youth face "the same windmills" on stage and in "real life," then theater becomes an ideal mechanism to rehearse and enact change, as Quijano/Don Quixote demonstrates with his self-transformation and deliberate performance in the fields of La Mancha.

In Brooklyn, New York, Stephen Haff's Still Waters in a Storm non-profit organizes co-curricular activities for about twenty local children (as many as one hundred may be waitlisted at a given time), irresponsibly described in some media outlets as either children of undocumented migrants or undocumented themselves (Courchay 4). A former teacher, Haff introduces his students, ranging from five to eighteen years old, to the most traditional form of the humanities: the study of Latin and the collective reading, translation, and interpretation of classics such as John Milton's *Paradise Lost* and *Don Quixote*. Since 2016, three times a week the group works on adapting the original Spanish-language classic into a bilingual (mostly English-language) musical play entitled *The Serialized Traveling Adventures of Kid Quixote*, with the help of professional composer Kim Sherman (Luiselli 3). I learned recently from Haff himself that a book on the project, titled *Kid Quixotes: A Group of Students, Their Teacher, and the One-Room School where Everything Is Possible*, will be published in April 2020. With a growing fan base, the project has hosted a number of celebrities such as Zadie Smith, Michael Ondaatje, Valeria Luiselli, Richard Price, and Monica Lewinsky; other famous artists and writers, including Joshua Bell and Salman Rushdie, have supported the organization. Not surprisingly, as this seems a recurring theme with Quixote-inspired activists, Haff started his career in theater and cites Augusto Boal as one of his two chief models (the other is Canadian social justice playwright George F. Walker). Before founding Still Waters in a Storm, Haff formed a group with inner-city youth, the Real People Theater, which toured Europe and Canada performing their own contemporary adaptations of Shakespeare (Goldman 4). As Haff himself states, the Quixote project culminates his "over twenty years of involvement in theater and as an activist educator" (5).

Often, class sessions begin with Haff and the students taking turns reading passages aloud in the original Spanish; then, much like in the Brazilian projects, the text is transculturated into the project participants' bilingual and bicultural realities through various forms of art (drawing, writing, composing, and performing). In a personal interview, Haff explained to me that his Quixote-inspired activism aims to open a space for children whose story is typically told by others (journalists, politicians, social workers, teachers) to reclaim their own narrative and share it with the larger public. "When you take control of your story," he concluded, "you take control of your life." Rather than a condescending view, Haff asserts, what develops when audiences see and hear these children perform is sincere admiration for their intelligence and artistic talent.

In a revealing statement about the challenge of transculturating Cervantes' classic, Stephen Haff explains that Don Quixote's vision of reality, with giants and windmills colliding in his mind, produces "two worlds in one," which then begs the question for the translators of the work: "How do you make two worlds into one?" (Courchay 9). In many ways, this question summarizes the challenge of transculturation as a whole, whether applied to nation-building or social justice contexts at the community level. Through art and performance, Still Waters students adapt the duality of Don Quixote's worldview into their own bilingual and bicultural realities as children of Spanish-speaking migrants, some of whom remain under constant threat of deportation, particularly in the Trump era.

FIGURE CONCLUSION. Sarah as Don Quixote with Rocinante and the book (Still Waters in a Storm, Brooklyn, NY). Photograph by Tom Schaefer

(Irremediably, many conversations among the children themselves center on President Donald Trump's aggressive antimigrant policies.) Moreover, when we become aware of the multiplicity of our reality in the process of fusing two worlds together, Haff explains, "Ultimately what you're doing is putting yourself into the story" (Courchay 9). By intertwining the kids' circumstances with Don Quixote's story, the play offers itself as a bilingual (mostly English-language) statement of intent by children who, like at-risk youth in Brazil, take a protagonist role in not merely a theatrical project but a social experiment, as well. The two worlds in today's America that collide in President Trump's political agenda, the Anglo and Latinx cultures, produce a multilingual reality of mutual respect in the *Kid Quixote* version.

The play includes five scenes adapted from several chapters of the novel's first volume. Inspired by the adventures in which Don Quixote helps Andrés (I.4), Marcela (I.10–14), and the galley salves (I.22) and the one in which farmer Pedro Alonso assists a fallen Don Quixote (I.5), the children and youth crafted their adaptation around the notion of helping others. Collectively, the children wrote the lyrics and, under Kim Sherman's guidance, contributed to the score of several songs, including one titled "The Rescuing Song." Significantly, in reference to migrants who in some cases crossed the border through the desert (the song mentions the "burning, burning desert light"), the broad notion of "helping" others becomes the specific action of "rescuing."[4] Together, project participants sing "por favor entiéndanme" (please understand me), for "we're not going to steal your gold" or take "your throne." Debunking the false accusation that migrants represent a threat to the country's economy, the "Can we help?" chorus further asserts the socially proactive and beneficial role that these children in particular, and migrants in general, exercise in their host country. At the most fundamental level, they want a chance to live their childhood ("Somos niños, no nos ven? / Déjanos ser feliz"; [We're children, can't you see? Let us be happy]) and be heard. Toward the end of the song, they forcefully sing their most urgent plea: "Responsible grown-ups, pay attention to me!"

Upon the children's own request, and in a decision fully consequent with their urge to be heard ("pay attention to me!"), the group started corresponding through another nonprofit with undocumented minors who were recently brought into the United States by their parents, then separated from them by US authorities, and finally taken to detention centers all over the country. In their adaptation of the galley slaves scene, in which Don Quixote frees chained prisoners on their way to serving their sentence in the galleys, members of the cast interrupt the action and read out loud quotes from a small sample of the thousands of voiceless and invisible children who are separated from their parents and incarcerated in the United States today (I write this in May 2019). Children whose words are quoted in the performance are identified by their first name. Once again, tactics such as naming, visibility, and the destabilization of social roles (the "criminals" here are children forcibly separated from their parents and incarcerated) conflate around the act of performing itself. Through the contemporary performance of a *Don Quixote* adaptation, the liberation of the oppressed, whether incarcerated undocumented children or the often-stigmatized children of migrants in Brooklyn, New York, is not only a discursive mission but also one that can effectively win hearts and minds as a first step toward true transformation.

Although the guidance of educated activists such as Meirelles, de Almeida, and Haff should not be understated, it is significant that the young protagonists in these projects, most of them from underserved and underprivileged backgrounds, appropriate *Don Quixote* in ways strikingly consistent with the many Quixote-inspired cultural programs across the American hemisphere that I examine in this book. This could anecdotally be taken as yet further confirmation that, at least since the late 1990s, a new performative reading of Cervantes' classic has emerged with particular strength in the realm of youth community activism. Expanding on previous understandings of performative activism, these projects do not only participate in public discourse by staging social justice-oriented plays, but more importantly they also submit that renaming, rescripting, and performing new individual roles, especially among the underprivileged, can lead to the deep transformation of our collective imaginary. Through the painstaking work of creating and performing powerful theatrical experiences, direct interventions into the lives of people in vulnerable as well as privileged communities can occur. Another story is possible if we gather the courage and acquire the skills to rewrite and perform a new social narrative, as Alonso Quijano did when he transformed himself into the timeless Don Quixote. Like so many characters within the book itself, twenty-first-century urban *quixotinhos* take on Quijano's challenge to enact a different script for themselves in order to transform society as a whole. In a seemingly endless cycle of social justice cultural activism, Cervantes' four-hundred-year-old character endures today in the actions of those performers who, like Quijano himself, continue living Quixote.

NOTES

INTRODUCTION

1. Throughout this book, I employ the phrase *Quixote-inspired* activism to refer to any socially minded artistic project that finds direct and explicit inspiration in Miguel de Cervantes' *Don Quixote* but freely adapts the book according to its own activist purposes and aesthetic sensibilities. Quotes from *Don Quixote* come from Edith Grossman's 2003 translation, universally considered today the standard English-language version of Cervantes' masterpiece. All translations from Portuguese are mine unless otherwise noted.
2. Diana Taylor favors the use of *performatic* as an adjective for *performance* in everyday life, for in Austin's definition *performative* refers only to actions done with words within sanctioned, conventional contexts such as a courtroom or a church (*Performance* 120). Though Taylor's point is well taken, I still employ *performative* in my study in order to limit, to the extent possible, the use of neologisms such as *performatic*.
3. In my definition, performative activism constitutes a form of "artivism," for theatrical practices and performance in general constitute artistic expressions. Within artivist practices, performative activism specifically centers on the potential of rescripting and acting individual roles that defy stereotyping and oppressive language (racist, sexist, etc.) to promote individual and social change.
4. I use *tactic* as defined by Michel de Certeau: a form of resistance that, without "spatial or institutional localization . . . belongs to the other" (xix). De Certeau makes a useful distinction between strategies and tactics. Strategies determine what is "proper" and emanate from "a subject of will and power (a proprietor, an enterprise, a city, a scientific institution)." In contrast, *tactics*

are deployed, for instance, by a consumer deciding at the supermarket, on the wing, what to buy. For "the other," what counts is "the decision itself, the act and manner in which [an] opportunity is 'seized'" (xix).

CHAPTER 1

1. The late president of Venezuela, Hugo Chávez, exhumed Bolívar's presumed remains for DNA testing in 2010. The study certified the mixed racial configuration of the individual whose remains were tested ("Informe forense").
2. Outside of Latin America, the debate over the effects of transculturation on the ability of former colonies to further their own distinctive cultural identity also oscillates between embracing the redeeming effects of hybridism and exposing its inherent contradictions. On the one hand, and along the lines of Quijano, Trigo, and Beverley, Phyllis Peres adopts a cautionary attitude toward hybridity's presumedly liberating effects from colonial oppression in the case of another former Portuguese colony, Angola. Applying Ella Shohat's "Notes on the Post-Colonial" to the African country, Peres affirms that imperial powers "justified colonialism itself as a hybridizing mission" to civilize barbaric indigenous cultures through European intervention (14). For proponents of transculturation, in contrast, the meshing of cultures significantly alleviates the effects of coloniality on the oppressed. Such an optimistic outlook most notably characterizes Homi Bhabha's theorization of the location of culture in the "postcolonial" moment. In Bhabha's view, hybridity (roughly an English-language equivalent to mestizaje) may reverse the negative effects of colonialism by opening up a third space, neither that of the colonizer nor the colonized, where culture might in fact "elude the politics of polarity" (114; see also 39).
3. As it often happens with Brazilian Quixote-inspired activism, rather unexpected overlaps and common threads connect otherwise unrelated initiatives. Sponsored by the Tetra Pak Foundation, a project called Cultura Ambiental nas Escolas (Environmental culture in schools) commissioned in 1998 a film entitled *Quixote reciclado* (*Recycled Quixote*). Directed by Philippe Henry, by the end of 2018 the film had been viewed forty thousand times on YouTube and has been utilized in classrooms across the country. In Henry's movie, Don Quixote fights the monsters of consumerism and waste to preserve nature through recycling and the transformation of trash into new products. After fifty-one minutes of a rather extravagant plot only loosely based on Cervantes' story, the movie ends with the following statement projected against a background of recyclable waste: "Nos livros e na natureza, tudo se transforma. Isso também pode ser verdade na vida real" (In books and in nature, everything transforms itself. This can also happen in real life). As in

the Cooperaacs project, Henry likens the recycling of used products to social and personal change. Transformed by books, the movie states at the end, Don Quixote embodies in his heroic, literary persona the positive impact of waste recycling on nature.
4. Since the early 2000s, Walter Mignolo and a number of other Latin American, North American, and European theorists have employed the term *decoloniality* to describe a particular form of transculturation. Heavy on theoretical jargon, decoloniality refers to "variegated enunciations springing from global-local histories entangled with the local imperial history of Euro-American modernity, postmodernity, and altermodernity" (Mignolo and Vázquez 1). At the risk of over-simplifying a theory that remains somewhat unwilling to simplify itself, decoloniality seems to focus on cultural projects that open up spaces outside or against the colonial mindset. In this sense, this theory limits its scope to transcultural works that would qualify as properly decolonial. Instead, I opt to employ and revise the concept of transculturation, which in my view more neutrally captures the process by which two or more cultures interact in a (neo)colonial context.
5. In an effort to make sense out of this terminological maze and bring some conceptual coherence to the field, Richard Rogers lists four types of cultural appropriation: exchange, domination, exploitation, and transculturation, which he describes as hybrid forms facilitated by transnational capitalism and its globalizing effects (477). In the end, however, Rogers documents the confusion more than resolves it. Besides the questionable linking of transcultural phenomena to the effects of neoliberal globalization (transculturation has existed since well before our time), Rogers admits that all forms of appropriation, even those that occur under domination and exploitation, exhibit different degrees of transcultural or reciprocal influence.

CHAPTER 2

1. In his nearly one thousand-page edited volume, Luis Quiroz provides citations and excerpts attesting to the direct influence of Cervantes, and specifically of *Don Quixote*, in Bolivian literature and art. Extrapolated to the whole of Latin America, the same study would likely require many volumes of several thousand pages each.
2. Contradictory transcultural practices also abound in nation-building efforts across Latin America beyond the case of Don Quixote. We find one particularly revealing example at the beginning of what is widely regarded as the foundational text of Argentinian national identity: Domingo Faustino Sarmiento's *Facundo, o civilización y barbarie en las pampas argentinas* (Fa-

cundo: *Civilization and Barbarism*), published in 1845. In the first few pages of his book, Sarmiento relies on European citations, sources, and attributions to legitimize his nation-building scheme, which he describes as a "civilizing" process in opposition to the "barbaric" nature of the (in any event already decimated) indigenous population. Shockingly, however, upon close examination the Western intellectual references utilized by Sarmiento to buttress his modernizing project prove mostly erroneous, when not overtly fabricated. As Idelber Avelar explains, Facundo's "civilizing gesture is from the beginning contaminated by a savage, barbaric relationship with its sources" (251–52). Transculturation here again falls into the most fundamental of contradictions. It openly rests Argentinian idiosyncrasy on the superiority of European civilization over indigenous barbarism, yet it does so by ravaging the very Western sources upon which it claims to stand.

3. In 1928, Paulo Menotti del Picchia published the dramatic poem "O amor de Dulcinéia" ("Dulcinea's Love"). Del Picchia participated with Oswald de Andrade and others in the Week of Modern Art in São Paulo in February 1922, which formally consolidated the Modernist movement in Brazil. However, while de Andrade proposed in his "Manifesto Antropófago" a return to the primitive by way of the European avant-garde, in 1924 del Picchia co-founded the more conservative and radically nationalist Movimento Verde-Amarelo (Green-yellow movement, in reference to the colors of the Brazilian flag). Despite del Picchia's ultra-nationalism, the unquestionable originality of "O amor de Dulcinéia" has little to do with nation-building efforts such as the ones discussed here. In del Picchia's poem, the roles of Cervantes' protagonist pair are reversed: Sancho behaves as an idealist, sees giants instead of windmills, and dies at the end; Don Quixote, in contrast, talks like "a bourgeois" (Mancing 57).

4. For a literal but detailed look at Monteiro Lobato's adaptation of Cervantes' text, see Cabral and Brocchetto Ramos. Maria Augusta da Costa Vieira analyzes other twentieth-century characters modeled after Don Quixote, such as Colonel Vitorino Carneiro da Cunha in José Lins do Rêgo's *Fogo morto* (1943) ("Tipología quijotesca" 5).

5. The most famous Brazilian illustrations for *Don Quixote* also come in the second half of the twentieth century from the political left. In 1956, Candido Portinari, who ran for office twice as a member of the Brazilian Communist Party, completed twenty-two illustrations of Cervantes' classic for an edition that was never published due to financial limitations. In 1973, however, his twenty-one drawings (one was stolen in Paris) came out in book format with accompanying poems by Carlos Drummond de Andrade. A poet and essayist, Drummond de Andrade self-identified with Don Quixote through his own concept of "gauchismo" (from the French *gauche*, left), a reference to off-center people who inhabit the margins of society (Navarro Flores 311, 314).

6. García's version has shared some of Don Quixote's own theatrical success, for several other companies across the Americas have staged his play. La Can-

delaria has performed *El Quijote* at least in Colombia, Mexico, Peru, Brazil, and some fifteen other countries, and Repertorio Español has also staged it in New York (dir. Jorge Alí Triana, 2006) and at the Milagro Theater in Portland, Oregon (dir. Olga Sánchez, 2010), among other locations. These companies have embraced and even amplified the metatheatrical aspects of García's version. While much of the text already revolves around the theme of acting, in the Repertorio Español performance, several actors take turns playing Don Quixote as well as other characters in an overt exposé of the discursive, mutable nature of both theater and identity (Gascón 101). If on stage any character can become anyone he or she wishes, as the Repertorio Español implicitly asserts, theater can then function as an instrument of liberation from predetermined social roles.

CHAPTER 3

1. Several of Cervantes' works, and particularly his interludes and plays published in 1615, reflect on the Baroque "all the world's a stage" commonplace. Most pointedly, *El rufián dichoso (The Fortunate Ruffian)* and *Pedro de Urdemalas (Pedro, The Great Pretender)* directly engage the notion of individual and collective transformation through performance that Brazilian activism so dearly embraces in its appropriation of *Don Quixote*. For a commentary on this topic in *El rufián*, see Miñana, "'Veréis el monstruo.'" Similarly, *Pedro de Urdemalas* features a protagonist in constant metamorphosis, a self-described "Proteo... segundo" (v. 2675, *El rufián dichoso* 371; "second Proteus," *Pedro, the Great Pretender* 103) who seeks social advancement by joining a theater troupe that performs before the Spanish royalty (vv. 3044–45, *El rufián dichoso* 386; *Pedro, the Great Pretender* 114). William Egginton's *How the World Became a Stage* offers a broader discussion of theatricality as "the central cultural practice" that brings about the modern world in the sixteenth and seventeenth centuries (2).
2. In *The Man Who Invented Fiction*, William Egginton alleges that *Don Quixote*'s revolutionary fictional language builds on Cervantes' own tumultuous biography. The perspectivism, the ambiguity, and the irresoluble tension between opposites (reality and fiction, idealism and pragmatism, etc.) that inaugurate literary modernity are Cervantes' response to his own life of service, honor, disappointment, imprisonment, and destitution. However, the connection between writing and social mobility that concerns Greenblatt and particularly Brazilian activists does not feature prominently in Egginton's definition of Cervantes' "modern world."
3. An earlier application of Freire's theories within a marginalized young community foretells the goals and methodologies that Brazilian Quixote-based initiatives later on adopted. Founded by and for at-risk youth in 1989, the Te-

atro Trono company in La Paz, Bolivia, regarded Freire's concept of (re)naming as a precondition for change. The group grew out of a rehabilitation center in La Paz popularly known as the *trono* (throne). *Trono* comes from both the verb *tronar* (slang for wasting your life) and the rather preposterous notion that recovering patients live at the center like kings, for care is provided at no cost to them. Protesting such a misguided notion, a handful of former interns founded the group Teatro Trono, which within only a few years grew into an independent professional company that organized performances, film series, and exhibitions. Over time, they also established a neighborhood library, a magazine collection, and a playground. Against social stigmatization, the artists named their company Teatro Trono to clearly identify the rehabilitation center as their ideological and artistic center of gravity, thus reappropriating a derogatory term into a tool for liberation. As the Teatro Trono founders write, "el niño es el único rey en el mundo de la imaginación y la fantasía. Le pusimos Trono (a la compañía) para ser reyes de ese mundo" (children rule the kingdom of imagination and fantasy. We named [the company] Trono [Throne] in order to become kings of that world; Nogales Bazán et al. 12). Instead of beneficiaries of a presumedly magnanimous system, the new "kings" at Teatro Trono reign over a land of fantasy where naming and performing purposefully transform oppression into a child's kingdom.

4. Boal's assertive insertion of the classics into contemporary political debates has been replicated across continents. During the 1980s, to give but one illustrative example, Neil Cameron, an Australian proponent of community and popular theater in the English-speaking world, staged in Glasgow, Scotland, an adaptation of Émile Zola's *Germinal* (1885), a novel that chronicles the tragic struggles of nineteenth-century French coal miners. Cameron's version of *Germinal* explicitly offered moral and ideological backing to Scottish miners who opposed Prime Minister Margaret Thatcher's neoliberal policies (Cameron 67).

5. While Boal's basic tenets undergird the theatrical practice of Márcio Meirelles, Valéria di Pietro, and Telma Dias, they do not strictly follow any one of his unique dramatic categories (forum theater, invisible theater, legislative theater, and the like). Similarly, unadvertised and free-of-charge street performances of Andreia de Almeida's *Quixotes* by Circo Navegador evoke Augusto Boal's invisible theater, which when enacted in public spaces captures "the attention of people who do not know they are watching a planned performance" (Cohen-Cruz and Schutzman 237). Unlike Boal, however, de Almeida renders her dramatic artifice immediately visible by staging such a simultaneously familiar yet foreign (both geographically and historically) narrative as *Don Quixote*. In contrast to Boal's "invisible" performance, de Almeida remains faithful to her Italian training in Eugenio Barba's theater anthropology, which shares the Freirean ideal of art's liberatory power but cultivates it through the self-conscious exposure of its own theatricality.

6. This is not of course an exclusive trait of Quixote-inspired projects. For decades, theater has been deployed for therapeutic as well as progressive purposes in acutely marginalized contexts, including prisons and mental-health institutions. Theatrical initiatives such as Diana Conrad's in Alberta, Canada (Conrad 139), the Medea Project's in California ("About the Medea Project"), and Neil Cameron's in Melbourne, Australia (Cameron 131), stage performances with incarcerated youth, female inmates, and mentally ill children, respectively. As a testament to their inherent value and life-changing potential, some of these theatrical projects have become the subject of feature films and extensive journalistic reports. To offer but two examples, the Taviani brothers' film *Caesar Must Die* (2012) documents inmates' staging of Shakespeare's *Julius Caesar* at Rome's Rebibbia prison, while NPR's *This American Life* (episode 218, "Act V"; 9 August 2002) narrates for its listeners a production of *Hamlet* at the Missouri Eastern Correctional Center (see Kozusko 245).
7. Riddled with human-rights violations, the FEBEM closed down in late 2006 and was re-founded as Fundação CASA, or Home Foundation, in early 2007.
8. The Bando modeled itself after Abdias do Nascimento's Teatro Experimental do Negro (Black Experimental Theater), established in Rio de Janeiro in 1944. Originally, the company started as a theater workshop promoted by a cultural nonprofit and percussion group of national fame called Banda Olodum, which in turn emerged from a Carnival group of the same name founded in 1979 (Uzel 13–14, 23–30).
9. The first black Sancho, however, was the legendary Grande Otelo, stage name of Sebastião Bernardes de Souza Prata. Grande Otelo performed the squire in Flávio Rangel and Paulo Ponte's adaptation of Dale Wasserman's *Man of La Mancha*, premiered to great success in the 1972–1973 season in São Paulo (Cabral 228).

CHAPTER 4

1. I want to thank Robert Bayliss for underscoring in a personal conversation that took place in 2012 the fact that these Brazilian plays could well amount to a third and novel interpretation of *Don Quixote*, different from the two traditional approaches described here.
2. What follows is an extreme over-simplification of the thousands of visual, literary, musical, and scholarly adaptations of *Don Quixote* that could be grouped under these two broad interpretations of Cervantes' masterpiece. Each individual example would surely come with its own nuances and idiosyncrasies, so I admittedly choose to reduce the rich complexity of these perspectives on *Don Quixote* to their lowest common denominator. For more information on the Romantic approach, besides the studies cited here, see

A. G. Lo Ré's detailed and somewhat extravagant interpretation of "The Three Deaths of Don Quixote: Comments in Favor of the Romantic Critical Approach." For more on the satirical reading, see James Iffland's work on laughter and *Don Quixote*, including his 2003 review article "Laughter Tamed," and José Antonio Maravall's classic *Utopia and Counterutopia in the Quixote*.

3. In a 1958 article, Oscar Mandel identifies these two traditions as hard (the satirical) and soft (the Romantic) readings. In an unpublished Ph.D. dissertation from 2013, Mark D. McGraw fails to cite Mandel but concludes that it is the soft (Romantic) reading "that connects us personally to the knight" (274). As I document in this book, however, in my Brazilian examples it is the performative actions of the actor/hidalgo Quijano, rather than the actions of Don Quixote himself, that trigger a deep connection with the audience, and particularly with underprivileged audiences, as they endeavor to change their role in the social narrative.

4. So successful has Cervantes proven in this regard, as reviewed in Chapter 2, that nationalists in Spain, across Latin America, and even in Brazil have adopted the old, ineffectual warrior as an icon that epically embodies their respective ideas of nationhood (Britt Arredondo; Riera). This counterintuitive political endorsement can only be explained through the erasure of the mundane hidalgo that results, in Eric Ziolkowski's expression, in the "sanctification of Don Quixote" as a hero who despite his many flaws exhibits an indomitable idealism. Every time the knight falls, he proudly stands up again; where others find only comfort and conformity, he sacrifices himself for the common good—and his much-desired fame.

5. In Sandoval-Sánchez and Saporta Sternbach's view, "border hybrid identity formation," a concept that could be applied to the Brazilian transculturations of *Don Quixote* as well, results from the interaction between subject (self), location (context), and agency as means of self-representation (33). These three concepts are also integral to Cervantes' dual protagonist. He features a complex self, Alonso Quijano, who becomes Don Quixote to escape his social location, that of an irrelevant hidalgo, as well as his forgettable hometown in La Mancha, then an impoverished central region of meager political and economic influence. Most importantly, he boasts a transformative sense of agency, for he renames himself and tenaciously performs the fictitious knight-errant Don Quixote of La Mancha until he falls fatally ill. Only on his deathbed does Quijano renounce the "madness" of his self-created identity.

6. The original titles of parts I and II of the novel also denote a similar effort to diminish the hidalgo's role in his radical self-transformation. Following common practice at the time, the titles may not have been written directly by Cervantes himself but by his editor; we simply do not know. Nonetheless, the published titles further illustrate and reinforce the obliteration of the ordinary, obscure hidalgo Quijano who breathes life into the knight-errant. Part I, *El ingenioso hidalgo don Quijote de la Mancha* (1605), presents a contra-

diction in terms, since the *ingenioso hidalgo* (ingenious hidalgo) cannot *be* but can only *act* as the knight-errant *(caballero)* Don Quixote. In other words, an hidalgo cannot be a *Don,* a *caballero,* or a knight. Paradoxically, the title of Cervantes' first volume fails to thoroughly erase the theatrical nature of an hidalgo whose obsessive reading habits transform him into a performer of knight errantry. In part II, the process of the hidalgo's eradication comes full circle. *El ingenioso caballero don Quijote de la Mancha* (1615) still emphasizes the character's "ingenious" nature, but it coherently refers to Don Quixote as *caballero*; the hidalgo has disappeared altogether. His transformative process now complete, Alonso Quijano fades into the background, and for the greater part of the story only his more flamboyant self remains fully visible.

7. A handful of moralistic critics through the mid-twentieth century, of negligible influence in contemporary readings of the novel, regarded Quijano's conversion as his ultimate embrace of the Christian faith over his previously blind adherence to chivalric principles (Friedman, "Executing the Will" 121; Canavaggio, *Don Quijote* 193–95, 282–83).

8. In a commentary that could apply to *Don Quixote*'s ending, George Yúdice connects the self-management of one's public image with the anxiety over literary authorship. In his joint reading of Michel Foucault's performative ethics and Mikhail Bakhtin's polyphonic narratives, Yúdice defines cultural agency as the skillful performance of social norms passed down through historical traditions and literary voices (3). From this point of view, the control over one's life narrative becomes a deeply political issue that plays out not only in the social but also in the literary and theatrical arenas. When Yúdice recognizes "performativity as the fundamental logic of social life today" (28), he acknowledges a strategy that Quijano fully exploits by acting as Don Quixote. The hidalgo brilliantly stitches together an amalgam of past literary voices (chivalric, bucolic, folk) to create the knight-errant. Frequently mocked and beaten up as a failed military hero, his greatest success is literary and performative, for his story continues to be read, told, and performed in and out of the book.

9. Facing death, Don Quixote relativizes the concept of truth as highly subjective and born out of play: "É da brincadeira que aflora a verdade, a nossa verdade!" (It is from banter that truth emerges, one's own truth!; 12). Even in his final moments, Don Quixote defends the value of playing and acting as a gateway into personal truth.

CHAPTER 5

1. As di Pietro told me in personal conversations, she learned from Paulo Freire's *Pedagogy of the Oppressed* that the betterment of society as a whole depends on

the oppressed as much as the oppressor, for transformation must originate in each of us and reach everyone. Frequently, in fact, the roles of oppressor and oppressed are interchangeable and often overlap. For instance, an oppressed worker at a factory may act as an oppressor in the domestic sphere.

2. One recent example shows the risks involved in the activist performance of oppression. In order to spark a conversation about street-connected populations, college-student activists across the United States have staged in recent years performative protests such as sleeping in tents outside of their dorms and dressing in worn-out, dirty clothes. Though well-intentioned, this effort has been criticized for its stereotyping and lack of understanding of the root causes of the problem. At the University of Massachusetts in Amherst, Timothy Scalona, a student who himself experienced poverty and homelessness, found his peers' performative activism trivializing, if not outright offensive. In a column published in the *University Wire* on November 29, 2017, Scalona complains that, "When a student acts out the suffering of homelessness from the comfort of their own privilege, it makes the situation out to be almost a tourist attraction" (Scalona).

3. Numerous scholars of globalization and ethnic studies have defined cultural citizenship as a resistance tactic for marginalized minorities, such as Afro-Brazilians, to preserve their cultural and legal rights. According to Toby Miller, cultural citizenship "concerns the maintenance and development of cultural lineage through education, custom, language, and religion and the positive acknowledgment of difference in and by the mainstream" (2). In the United States, this notion is best illustrated by the efforts of minorities, particularly Latinxs, to be recognized as citizens with full rights and responsibilities in an Anglo-dominant society that perpetually regards them as foreign. As William V. Flores explains in ways seemingly applicable to the youth activist groups I discuss here, Latinxs in the United States exercise cultural citizenship by claiming "space in society [and] rights [through] self-definition, affirmation, and empowerment" (262). However, performative activism exercises cultural citizenship in ways that may include but may also go beyond minority groups' "cultural lineage" and "self-definition," as I document in this and the next chapters.

4. The contrast between fantasy and reality constitutes a most Cervantine of themes, for in Don Quixote's world windmills appear as giants, and knightly codes of conduct crash head-on against quotidian life. More pointedly, though, Cervantes' Spain also oscillated painfully between the illusion of greatness as one of the largest empires in history and, on the other extreme, the harsh realities of its broken social fabric, plagued by poverty and inequality. In this regard, the parallels between contemporary Brazil and Cervantes' times prove significant.

5. As Cristina Beltrán has persuasively argued, characterizing a group of people

or even a whole nation as a "sleeping giant" suggests both their passivity and their uniformity, two premises that are equally inaccurate in Brazil. Yet, the allure of an awakening giant represents for a diversity of people "the long-standing desire to be seen as a vital inescapable part of the . . . political landscape, a demographic powerhouse that has earned its right to both representation and recognition" (5).

6. Somewhat of a visual precedent to the Johnnie Walker campaign, an iconic 2009 cover of the *The Economist* captured Brazil's spectacular rise on the world's economic and geopolitical stage with the digitally manipulated image of Rio de Janeiro's famous Corcovado (the Christ the Redeemer statue) taking off like a rocket. A figuratively and literally towering symbol that physically presides over the city, in this image the gigantic statue ascends to the summit of global popularity, sanctioned by one of the most prestigious economic journals in the world.

7. For the purpose of this study, I find an immediate precedent to the protestos' discursive strategies in artivist and particularly filmic efforts to keep Brazil's dramatic income and social inequality in the public eye, especially as it affects children and youth. Although a constant for the last several decades, the denunciation of poverty and its impact on society's most vulnerable individuals (children, adolescents, women, and prison inmates) experienced a strong cultural revival in the late twentieth century and first decade of the twenty-first. In 1965, Glauber Rocha theorized an "aesthetics of hunger" that revolutionized Brazilian cinema by featuring the marginalized and poor as protagonists of sober cinematic exposés of the profound inequalities that plague Brazilian society to this day. Updating for a contemporary audience the aesthetics of hunger, a number of extremely successful films in the early aughts, such as *Cidade de Deus* (*City of God*, by Fernando Meirelles and Kátia Lund, 2002) and *Ônibus 174* (*Bus 174*, by José Padilha, 2002), showcased from a variety of points of view and styles the lives of underprivileged youth caught in a spiral of violence (Chan and Vitali). While divergent in their approach to treating poverty and marginalization, these movies share with Quixote-inspired activism a keen awareness of the discursive and performative nature of activism. Not only do these films shine a spotlight on marginalized youth, elevating them from a secondary to a protagonist role, but they also do so by experimenting with new forms of storytelling (*City of God*) or by explicitly challenging media and public portrayals of at-risk children as either criminals or victims (*Bus 174*).

8. The feeling of anger and despair lingered among particularly the right and Evangelicals. Ultimately, it fueled the 2018 election of Jair Bolsonaro, a far-right candidate and self-confessed nostalgic of the dictatorship period, as the country's new president.

9. Brazilian demonstrators proved keenly aware of the complementary role of social media during the protests. Significantly, handwritten signs held by

young demonstrators in marches throughout the country proudly proclaimed "Saímos do FB" (We left [or got out of] Facebook). In contrast to the comfort of simply "liking" or circulating a post on Facebook, a form of participation that some term *slacktivism*, Brazilian youth left virtual sites in order to take an active role in the street protests (Farias and Alves 162). As with Facebook, the Brazilian Autumn clearly established Twitter's role as a conduit for disseminating information that amplified rather than replaced what was happening in the streets. Out of more than eighty-five thousand images related to the marches shared during June 15 and July 18 of 2013 on Twitter, pictures of handwritten signs carried in the streets greatly outnumbered digital images (such as posters and memes) in frequency and popularity (Gomes Goveia 14). While youth were leaving Facebook for the streets, the most popular pictures shared on Twitter featured the collective handwriting of the national story carried out by street protestors through homemade signs.

10. Vital to the dissemination of these alternative Brazilian stories, signs, banners, and placards serve at least three different purposes. First, they thread a "narrativa do acontecimento" (narrative of the event) that provides information about the event, its causes, goals, and participants (Sena 107). Second, because demonstrations by necessity seek change, the narratives articulated through chants and signs ultimately aim to persuade fellow citizens and government of the legitimacy of their purpose (108). For this reason, signs represent "atos políticos e éticos" (political and ethical actions) that articulate a "política de representação," or "politics of representation," divergent from the narrative sanctioned by the elites (Chagas 45). Third, if the aim of this bottom-up politics of representation is to further social change and "do things" with words, signs and banners are intrinsically performative in an Austin- or Freire-like manner, for they "dizem fazendo" (literally, talk by doing, or get things done through language) (M. Neves 10, 13).

11. Starting in the 1990s, progressive organizations successfully manipulated corporate advertisements through low-cost counter campaigns launched online. Famously, computer-animated polar bears in the groundbreaking Coca-Cola commercials that began airing in 1993 were used in a 2000 web-based campaign developed by Adbusters and Greenpeace to issue a dramatic cry against global warming (Bennett 21). In the Adbuster version, frightened polar bears sat on melting ice floes, as the HFCs used in the cooling and bottling process of Coca-Cola are thought to contribute to the greenhouse effect. With a great dose of imagination and in a relatively inexpensive way, environmentalists repurposed Coca-Cola's global marketing strategy to effectively illustrate the devastating effects of climate change.

12. In yet another twist on popular culture, the Guy Fawkes masks used by the transnational hackers Anonymous, a fiercely anti-neoliberal organization, became hugely popular both online and in the streets. The mask features a

defiantly smiley, somewhat abstracted white face with an elaborate moustache reminiscent of the seventeenth-century historical Guy Fawkes, an English Catholic who tried to assassinate King James I in 1605, upon whom Alan Moore and David Lloyd created their *V for Vendetta* comic book in 1982. Further popularized by James McTeigue's 2005 movie, *V for Vendetta* portrays an anonymous citizen wearing a Guy Fawkes mask as he single-handedly takes on a totalitarian government in the likeness of George Orwell's "Big Brother" of *1984*. In a humorous yet dramatic variation, the *V for Vendetta* in the comic book was translated in Brazil into *V for Vinegar*. Due to its usefulness in lessening the effects of tear gas, vinegar became popular among demonstrators to counter police aggression. During the early days of the protests, in fact, the São Paulo police (in)famously detained several people accused of vinegar possession. Needless to say, when this became public many half-jokingly labeled the protests the "vinegar revolution."

13. As hundreds of thousands of handwritten signs and banners narrated another (national) story, to paraphrase the Projeto Quixote's "Uma outra história" motto, the cunning reappropriation of commercial and popular-culture discourse coexisted with individualized messages relaying personal stories at times humorous but often dramatic. The examples are countless, but a representative case can be found in the research of Ercio Sena in the city of Belo Horizonte, the country's third-largest metropolitan area by population. For over two hours, Sena counted and catalogued from the same vantage point the signs that dotted the June 26 demonstration in the capital of Minas Gerais, attended by around sixty thousand individuals, according to police estimates. Taking place toward the end of the two-week period that would later prove the peak of the Brazilian Autumn, this demonstration was less well attended than previous ones, and the author recognizes that the use of signs had decreased as well. Nonetheless, he provides telling examples of how some demonstrators used signs to "tornar visível o drama pessoal e, portanto, de dar-lhe importância pública" (make dramatic personal stories visible and, thus, give them public relevance; 110). For instance, one demonstrator marched "Por você Paloma que esperou por uma cirurgia por 13 anos" (For you, Paloma, because you waited thirteen years for a surgery), and another "Por você minha mãe que trabalhou por 40 anos sem direito a aposentadoria" (For you, mom, because you worked for forty years but have no right to a pension). Via both clever appropriations of commercial slogans and the public voicing of personal narratives, the people's demands grew over two weeks in June from a localized rumor to a national clamor that politicians could no longer ignore.

14. In *The Expediency of Culture*, George Yúdice embraces cultural activism but warns against its use as an expedient tool to generate revenue, jobs, and services in marginalized communities, which to varying degrees may unwillingly

replace due government action. As Yúdice explains, cultural activism may in fact relieve government and capital from their obligation to provide adequate services and job opportunities for its citizens, particularly those in underprivileged communities (12–13, 25). To avoid this overextension of the expediency of culture, cultural nonprofits should continue to advocate that government as well as companies fulfill their obligations toward underserved citizens and workers.

15. Although GCA has expanded its activities to some twenty favelas in the city, and subsequently to other cities in the country, including São Paulo, it always does so by relinquishing control of its day-to-day operations to local residents. GCA believes that the particular idiosyncrasy and autonomy of each favela community must be respected. In the film, Anderson explicitly refuses to grow GCA through a franchise-like model as if it were a sort of cultural McDonald's.

16. Still, many favela residents associated with drug trafficking appear in the documentary with their heads covered. Even some of the performers in AfroReggae concerts, who sign a pledge not to use or deal drugs as a pre-requisite to join the organization, use ski masks on stage, likely to symbolize the favela's collective identity and to protest against violence.

17. Often, the leap from the local to the global occurs through foreign foundations, multinational companies, and other artistic projects such as documentary films that afford highly localized community organizations a chance to achieve some level of visibility abroad. However, even with the best intentions, outside producers and directors, such as those of *Favela Rising*, may inadvertently reinforce stereotypes by oversimplifying complex issues into one audience-friendly, Hollywoodesque linear story of personal success (Pueo Wood 87). *Favela Rising*'s emphasis on Anderson Sá's story of individual triumph over adversity has in fact been widely criticized for underestimating the deeper structural issues that afflict favela residents (Larkins; Cala Buendía 105). To this effect, Juan Poblete offers a warning that echoes George Yúdice's cautionary words on the expediency of culture: That in the present time of mass media and entertainment, "cultural consumption may be the shape that [indirect] control takes in neoliberal global times" (252). In other words, foreign and transnational initiatives such as *Favela Rising* may serve to regulate, control, and facilitate the consumption of AfroReggae's community activism for global audiences, while failing to provide an accurate depiction of Brazil's structural and systemic challenges.

18. Logically, AfroReggae is not the only phenomenon to emerge from favela dwellers' resilience and creative talent. In another example of the eagerness with which mainstream audiences embrace cultural production from the margins, São Paulo-based writer Ferréz spearheads a highly successful new genre called "literatura marginal" (marginal literature). His first novel

Capão pecado (1999), which takes place in the Capão Redondo favela in the *periferia* of São Paulo, likely remains his paramount and best-selling achievement. Overlapping with CGA's artivist objectives, Ferréz and other authors of marginal literature aim "to inspire self-esteem in marginalized youth, to inspire them to write" (Maddox 468). In the same *periferia* neighborhood of Capão Redondo, Sérgio Vaz started in 2001 the Sarau de Cooperifa ("Cooperifa" stands for Cooperativa Cultural da Periferia). The *sarau* is a jam session of poetry and spoken word held every Thursday evening in a local bar and regularly attended by around three hundred residents. With meager if any support, the Sarau de Cooperifa expanded activities to film festivals, exhibits, and other cultural campaigns and served as a model for the proliferation of dozens of similar *saraus* all over São Paulo and Belo Horizonte, the capital of the neighboring state of Minas Gerais (Tennina; Kiefer). Thus, through literary and other artistic interventions, underserved communities transform themselves into spaces of creativity and self-worth rather than merely of crime or despair. As they transition back and forth between the production and consumption of culture, residents in underprivileged urban neighborhoods take control of their own narratives.

CHAPTER 6

1. In Chapter 1 I already commented extensively on Cooperaacs' Quixote project, also in São Paulo, and make passing references throughout the book to Quixote-inspired efforts across the country with a relatively lesser social justice footprint. Such initiatives would include projects carried out by public or private schools, independent theater companies, neighborhood samba schools and carnival associations, foundations (Philippe Henry's film on the recycled Quixote comes to mind), and a handful of online sites (Facebook pages, blogs, and the like).
2. After di Pietro's retirement, the Religare reopened its doors in January 2017 in a new space in the Jardim Helena neighborhood, the city's most northeastern neighborhood, with a broader scope of activities for local residents of all ages and a seemingly decreased emphasis on the "cultural and social recycling" of underserved youth. While di Pietro is still quoted as the inspiration behind the project on the Instituto's Facebook page, I could not find any visual or written references to *Don Quixote* in this new iteration of the cultural nonprofit.
3. Funding sources vary by organization. Officially designated as Ponto de Cultura (Cultural point) by the Ministry of Culture, Instituto Religare was funded through federal and state contributions. QEC offers free workshops thanks to the support of a long-established nonprofit, FUNSAI (Fundação

Nossa Senhora Auxiliadora do Ipiranga), which funds its activities mostly through private donations. Lastly, the Projeto Quixote used to receive substantial funds (up to two thirds of their budget) from the state and city of São Paulo, but since the 2014 crisis they have had to raise more money through donations and by rendering services such as graffiti or workshops for other educators and renting out a large conference room in their headquarters called Espaço Quixote, which seats up to one hundred people.

4. Personal change is certainly not a foregone conclusion in theatrical activism, however. In 2017, Julio Vélez Sainz reached out to Peterson Xavier via Facebook and learned that the actor who played Sancho, André Luís Pereira, had been arrested in 2013 in relation to a deadly shooting (Vélez Sainz 23).

5. Cognizant of the importance of names, Quixote-inspired organizations openly discuss with project participants the implications of self-identification and (re)naming. In her theater and art-based workshops, Andreia de Almeida, the creative force behind Circo Navegador's *Quixotes* and the Quixote Espaço Comunitário, always asks children and youth who participate in her projects to introduce themselves by saying their names out loud. For the last two decades or so, she has been working first with favela youth in her native Santo André and later with local residents in the Quixote Espaço Comunitário, which she founded in 2008 in the São Paulo neighborhood of Ipiranga. Typically, participants use only their street names or nicknames when they first identify themselves. Then de Almeida has them physically take a leap forward and, when they land, recite their actual legal name, which in Brazil often includes two proper names plus two last names (one comes from the father and the other from the mother). In personal conversations, de Almeida explained to me that this exercise develops in participants an awareness of their identity as individuals entitled by law to both rights and responsibilities even (and particularly) if they live in government-forgotten marginal neighborhoods or in the streets.

6. As discussed in Chapters 3 and 4, Quijano's very creation of Don Quixote violates the three most fundamental norms of his time: biological (he is born old outside the natural order), social (he calls himself "Don," a privilege denied to hidalgos), and religious (he creates his own persona through a literary word that seemingly parodies the biblical Genesis). Such radically subversive performance undeniably breaches every "law instituted by God [and] by society," which according to Michel Foucault constitutes the defining feature of monstrosity, the most extreme form of otherness and a grave threat to mainstream society (*Abnormal* 64).

7. Several scholars have in fact criticized the notion of cultural citizenship as too reliant on its symbolic potential. In her study of young Latinas in marginalized areas of Chicago, Jillian Báez rightly points out that most frequently the symbolic and material aspects of citizenship function as two sides of the

same coin. Each individual's social standing determines what needs feel the most pressing to him or her at any given time. Typically, Báez explains, the symbolic concerns mostly "documented and upwardly mobile" individuals, while "material forms of citizenship are far more pressing to more marginalized and vulnerable ... communities" (269). In the case of Brazil, the main challenge for underprivileged children and youth is not their legal status, for most are Brazilian-born citizens, but rather their access to the legitimate benefits and legal protections constitutionally afforded to them as minors.

CONCLUSION

1. There exist a number of less explicitly activist but equally significant efforts to insert *Don Quixote* into community-based contexts through art and theater. Among many others, three worthy annual events along the American hemisphere warrant mention: the extraordinary Festival Internacional Cervantino in Guanajuato, México, now in its forty-seventh edition; the Festival Cervantino in Azul, Argentina, which began in 2008; and the El Quixote Festival, founded by Puerto Rican artist Rafael A. Osuba, which has organized bilingual cultural activities across the state of North Carolina since 2015.
2. In cases such as the Zapatista rebellion against the Mexican government, on the contrary, the performative activism led by Quixote-inspired Subcomandante Marcos builds on the rejection of institutional identities. For protection and as a denunciation of the *mal gobierno* or "evil government," Zapatistas typically use ski masks or bandanas to cover their faces and give themselves names different from their legal identity. Although Marcos' "real" identity is thought to be Rafael Guillén Vicente, he, like Don Quixote, practices name changing as a resistance tactic. In 2006 he referred to himself as Delegate Zero rather than Marcos, and in 2014 he permanently changed his name again to Galeano in honor of a fallen *compañero*. Outside mainstream society, Zapatistas aim to (re)create a world different from the one shaped by centuries of colonization and nowadays dominated by neoliberalism. They are mapping a new geography by renaming towns and regions with titles as poetic as "Torbellino de nuestras palabras" or "Whirlwind of our words," as well as producing new structures of governance such as the Juntas del Buen Gobierno (Good government juntas). Above and beyond the "another story" proclaimed by the Projeto Quixote, Zapatistas pursue a more sweeping and radical goal: "another world is possible." Not by chance, obviously, this is the motto of the Zapatista-inspired World Social Forum, an anti-neoliberal alternative to the Davos World Economic Forum in Switzerland that is regularly convened in Brazil.

3. Christopher Newfield, for instance, employs hard data to document the economic benefits of humanities courses to the higher-education institutions that offer them. Other scholars point out two significant flaws in the most alarmist reports. First, starting in the 1970s, the increasing access of female students to fields other than the humanities, education, and nursing is a positive root cause of the perceived decline in our majors. Second, interdisciplinary and new humanistic programs such as Gender or Ethnic Studies, as well as double majors, are not typically counted in most reports (Cooper and Marx; Reisz; B. Schmidt).
4. This altruistic concept also underlies initiatives concurrent to the translation project. In a short video published on Vimeo, fourteen project participants state, looking directly into the camera, "I am Don Quixote, and I want to rescue," and then each child finishes the sentence with at times rather deep if brief thoughts, including "my childhood," "all migrants," "little girls," "myself," and "each other" (Still Waters, "I Am Don Quixote").

WORKS CITED

Abel, Lionel. *Metatheatre: A New View of Dramatic Form*. 1963. Literary Licensing, 2012.
"About the Medea Project." *The Medea Project: Theater for Incarcerated Women*, home page, themedeaproject.weebly.com. Accessed 6 October 2018.
Abril Sánchez, Jorge. "El Quijote. Directed by Olga Sánchez (Portland, Oregon, 9 May 2010)." *Comedia Performance*, vol. 9, no. 1, 2012, pp. 228–34.
Adomaitis, Kasparas. "The World's Largest Cities Are the Most Unequal." *Euromonitor International*, 5 March 2013, blog.euromonitor.com/2013/03/the-worlds-largest-cities-are-the-most-unequal.html.
AfroReggae, Grupo Cultural. "Grupo Cultural AfroReggae." www.afroreggae.org.
Albuquerque, Severino J., and Kathryn Bishop-Sanchez. *Performing Brazil: Essays on Culture, Identity, and the Performing Arts*. U of Wisconsin P, 2015.
Allen, John Jay. *Don Quixote: Hero or Fool. Remixed*. Juan de la Cuesta, 2008.
Álvarez, Sonia, Evelina Dagnino, and Arturo Escobar. "The Cultural and the Political in Latin American Social Movements." Introduction. *Cultures of Politics/Politics of Cultures: Re-visioning Latin American Social Movements*, edited by Álvarez, Dagnino, and Escobar, Westview Press, 1998, pp. 1–32.
Amado, Janaína. "The Brazilian Quijote: Truth and Fabrication in Oral History." *Luso-Brazilian Review*, vol. 35, no. 1, Summer 1998, pp. 1–9.
Aparicio, Frances R., and Susan Chávez-Silverman. *Tropicalizations: Transcultural Representations of Latinidad*. UP of New England, 1997.
Ardila, J. A. G. "Las adaptaciones teatrales del *Quijote* en Inglaterra (del siglo XVII al XIX)." *Anales Cervantinos*, vol. 41, 2009, pp. 239–50.
Ariza, Patricia. "Una utopía para el nuevo milenio." *Teatro la candelaria. El Quijote*, Teatro Segura, 2005, pp. 15–17.
Arruda, Agnes de Sousa, and Hércules Silva Moreira. "Das ruas para a web e vice-versa: Os cartazes de protesto como folkcomunicação no mundo real e no mundo virtual." Paper presented at Intercom, XXXVI Congresso Brasileiro

de Ciências da Comunicação, Manaus (Brazil), 4–7 September 2013, intercom.org.br/papers/nacionais/2013/resumos/R8-1195-1.pdf.

Austin, J. L. *How to Do Things with Words*. 1962. Edited by J. O. Urmson and Marina Sbisà, Harvard UP, 1975.

Avelar, Idelber. "Transculturation and Nationhood." *Latin American Literary Culture: Subject to History*, vol. 3 of *Literary Cultures of Latin America: A Comparative History*, edited by Mario Valdés and Djelal Kadir, Oxford UP, 2004, pp. 251–57.

Badillo Pérez, César. "Las andanzas del *Quijote* en México." *Tiempos del mundo. Arte y Cultura*, 31 May 2001, pp. A10–11.

———. "El *Quijote latinoamericano*: O cómo romper el mapa de las diferencias y seguir siendo distintos." *Le Monde diplomatique/El Dipló*, vol. 85, Dec. 2009, p. 39.

Báez, Jillian M. "Mexican (American) Women Talk Back: Audience Responses to Latinidad in US Advertising." *Latina/o Communication Studies Today*, edited by Angharad N. Valdivia, Peter Lang, 2008, pp. 257–81.

Banda AfroReggae. "Iguais Sobrepondo Iguais." *Cara Nova*, Polygram International, 2006. *Letras*, letras.terra.com/afroreggae/598169. Accessed 5 October 2018.

Bary, Leslie. "Oswald de Andrade's 'Cannibalist Manifesto.'" *Latin American Literary Review*, vol. 19, no. 38, July-Dec. 1991, pp. 35–37. JSTOR, www.jstor.org/stable/20119600.

Bayliss, Robert. "What *Don Quixote* Means (Today)." *Comparative Literature Studies*, vol. 43, no. 4, 2006, pp. 382–97.

Beltrán, Cristina. *The Trouble with Unity: Latino Politics and the Creation of Identity*. Oxford UP, 2010.

Ben-Shaul, Daphna. "Critically Civic: Public Movement's Performative Activism." *Performance Studies in Motion: International Perspectives and Practices in the Twenty-First Century*, edited by Atay Citron, et al., Bloomsbury, 2014, p. 118–30.

Benassi, Carla Beatriz. "Coletivos de arte na atualidade brasileira: Panorama, apresentação e dois estudos de caso." *Anais do 18º Encontro da Associação Nacional de Pesquisadores em Artes Plásticas Transversalidades nas Artes Visuais – 21 a 26/09/2009 - Salvador, Bahia*, edited by Maria Virginia Gordilho Martins and Maria Herminia Olivera Hernández, EDUFBA, 2009, pp. 1525–40.

Bennett, W. Lance. "New Media Power: The Internet and Global Activism." *Contesting Media Power: Alternative Media in a Networked World*, edited by Nick Couldry and James Curran, Rowman and Littlefield Publishers, 2003, pp. 17–38.

Beverley, John. *Subalternity and Representation: Arguments in Cultural Theory*. Duke UP, 1999.

Bhabha, Homi K. *The Location of Culture*. Routledge, 1994.

Bishop-Sanchez, Kathryn. "On the (Im)Possibility of Performing Brazil." *Performing Brazil: Essays on Culture, Identity, and the Performing Arts*, edited by Severino J. Albuquerque and Kathryn Bishop-Sanchez, U of Wisconsin P, 2015, pp. 15–38.

Blasco, Javier. *Cervantes, raro inventor*. Centro de Estudios Cervantinos, 2005.
Boal, Augusto. "Aesthetic Education of the Oppressed." *International Theatre of the Oppressed Organization*, 2004, web.archive.org/web/20160321181523/www.theatreoftheoppressed.org/en/index.php?nodeID=83.
———. *Legislative Theater: Using Performance to Make Politics*. Translated by Adrian Jackson, Routlege, 1998.
———. *Técnicas latinoamericanas de teatro popular: Una revolución copernicana al revés*. Nueva imagen, 1982.
———. *Theatre of the Oppressed*. Translated by Charles A. and Maria-Odilia Leal McBride, Theatre Communications Group, 1985.
Bogad, L. M. *Tactical Performance: The Theory and Practice of Serious Play*. Routledge, 2016.
Bolívar, Simón. "Carta de Jamaica." 6 September 1815. *Elaleph*, 1999, www.cpihts.com/PDF/Simon%20Bolivar.pdf.
Borges, Jorge Luis. "Pierre Menard, autor del *Quijote*." *Ficciones*, Alianza Editorial, 1997.
Brewer, David A. *The Afterlife of Character, 1726–1825*. U of Pennsylvania P, 2005.
Britt Arredondo, Christopher. *Quixotism: The Imaginative Denial of Spain's Loss of Empire*. State U of New York P, 2004.
Butler, Judith. *Bodies That Matter: On the Discursive Limits of Sex*. Routledge, 2011.
———. *Gender Trouble: Feminism and the Subversion of Identity*. Routledge, 2006.
Butler, Udi Mandel. "Freedom, Revolt, and 'Citizenship': Three Pillars of Identity for Youngsters Living on the Streets of Rio de Janeiro." *Childhood*, vol. 16, no. 1, 2009, pp. 11–29.
Cabral, Izaura, and Flávia Brocchetto Ramos. "*Dom Quixote das crianças*: Uma análise comparativa do clássico e da adaptação lobatiana." *Espéculo: Revista de estudios literarios*, vol. 25, no. 22, June 2005, www.ucm.es/info/especulo/numero25/quixocri.html.
Cabral, Sérgio. *Grande Otelo: Uma biografia*. Editora 34, 2007.
Cala Buendía, Felipe. "Social Violence for Global Consumption: The Cultural Politics of *Favela Rising*." *Letral*, vol. 3, 2009, pp. 103–13.
Caldeira, Teresa, and James Holston. "Democracy and Violence in Brazil." *Comparative Studies in Society and History*, vol. 41, no. 4, 1999, pp. 691–729.
Cameron, Neil. *Fire on the Water: A Personal View of Theatre in the Community*. Currency Press, 1993.
Canavaggio, Jean. *Don Quijote, del libro al mito*. Espasa, 2006.
Castells, Manuel. *Networks of Outrage and Hope: Social Movements in the Internet Age*. Polity, 2012.
Certeau, Michel de. *The Practice of Everyday Life*. Translated by Steven Rendall, U of California P, 1984.
Cervantes, Miguel de. *Don Quijote de la Mancha*. Edited by Francisco Rico, Real Academia Española-Asociación de Academias de la Lengua Española-Alfaguara, 2005.

———. *Don Quixote de la Mancha*. Translated by Edith Grossman, Ecco, 2003.
———. *Pedro, the Great Pretender*. Translated by Philip Osment, Oberon Books, 2005.
———. *El rufián dichoso: Pedro de Urdemalas*. Edited by Jenaro Talens and Nicholas Spadaccini, Cátedra, 1986.
Chagas, Roselaine das. "O caráter performativo da linguagem dos protestos." *Cadernos da Fucamp*, vol. 15, no. 23, 2016, pp. 41–52.
Chan, Felicia, and Valentina Vitali. "Revisiting the 'Realism' of the Cosmetics of Hunger: *Cidade de Deus* and *Ônibus 174*." *New Cinemas* vol. 8, no. 1, 2010, pp. 15–30.
Chartier, Roger. "O *Dom Quixote* de Antônio José Da Silva, as marionetes do Bairro Alto e as prisões da inquisição." *Sociologia e antropologia*, translated by Estela Abreu, vol. 2, no. 3, 2012, pp. 161–81.
Checa, Jorge. "'The Play's the Thing': Teatro, poder y resistencia en las bodas de Camacho." *Revista canadiense de estudios hispánicos*, vol. 31, no. 3, 2007, pp. 473–90.
Childers, William. "Baroque Quixote: New World Writing and the Collapse of the Heroic Ideal." *Baroque New Worlds: Representation, Transculturation, Counterconquest*, edited by Lois Parkinson Zamora and Monika Kaup, Duke UP, 2010, pp. 415–49.
Chinn, Sarah E. "Gender Performativity." *Lesbian and Gay Studies: A Critical Introduction*, edited by Sally R. Munt and Andy Medhurst, Cassell Books, 1997, pp. 294–308.
CIA World Factbook. "Brazil." 2017. www.cia.gov/library/publications/download/download-2017/index.html.
Clifford, James. *The Predicament of Culture: Twentieth-Century Ethnography, Literature, and Art*. Harvard UP, 1998.
Close, Anthony. *The Romantic Approach to Don Quixote: A Critical History of the Romantic Tradition in 'Quixote' Criticism*. Cambridge UP, 2010.
Cobelo, Silvia. "Os adaptadores do *Quixote* mais publicados no Brasil." *Tradução em revista*, vol. 18, no.1, 2015, pp. 71–98. doi: 10.17771.
Cohen-Cruz, Jan, and Mady Schutzman, eds. *Playing Boal: Theater, Therapy, Activism*. Routledge, 1994.
Conrad, Diane. "In Search of the Radical in Performance: Theatre of the Oppressed with Incarcerated Youth." *Youth and Theatre of the Oppressed*, edited by Peter Duffy and Elinor Vettraino, Palgrave-MacMillan, 2010, pp. 125–41.
Cooper, Mark, and John Marx. "Humanists: Do Not Panic about Your Declining Market Share." *Humanities after Hollywood*, 29 June 2013, humanitiesafterhollywood.org/2013/06/29/humanists-do-not-panic-about-your-declining-market-share.
Cooperaacs. "Quem sou eu." *Cooperativa Cooperaacs Blogspot*, 21 September 2011, cooperativacooperaacs.blogspot.com/p/cooperaacs.html.
Coronil, Fernando. Introduction. *Cuban Counterpoint: Tobacco and Sugar*, 1940, by Fernando Ortiz, translated by Harriet de Onís, Duke UP, 1995, pp. ix–xlvii.

Costas, Ruth. "O legado dos 13 anos do PT no poder em seis indicadores internacionais." *BBC Brasil*, 13 May 2016, www.bbc.com/portuguese/noticias/2016/05/160505_legado_pt_ru.

Costigan, Lúcia Helena. "*Vida do grande Dom Quixote e do gordo Sancho Pança* by Antonio José da Silva and Miguel de Cervantes's *Don Quixote de La Mancha*: Comparative Aspects." *Signótica*, vol. 21, no. 1, Jan.–June 2009, pp. 89–102.

Courchay, Diego. "Don Quixote's Classroom: Where a 400-Year-Old Dreamer Inspires Modern Undocumented Children." *The Big Roundtable*, 28 June 2017, thebigroundtable.com/don-quixotes-classroom-80b3bfaaa2c3.

Cowie, Sam. "Inside Crackland: The Open-Air Drug Market That São Paulo Just Can't Kick." *Guardian*, 27 November 2017, www.theguardian.com/cities/2017/nov/27/inside-crackland-open-air-crack-market-sao-paulo.

de Almeida, Andreia. *Quixotes*. 2004. Unpublished play (typescript).

de Andrade, Oswald. "Cannibalist Manifesto." *Latin American Literary Review*, translated by Leslie Bary, vol. 19, no. 38, July-Dec. 1991, pp. 38–47. JSTOR, www.jstor.org/stable/20119601.

De la Campa, Román. "On Border Artists and Transculturation: The Politics of Postmodern Performances and Latin America." *Unforeseeable Americas: Questioning Cultural Hybridity in the Americas*, edited by Rita De Grandis and Zilà Bernd, Rodopi, 2000, pp. 56–84.

De la Colina, José. "As Time Goes By: 'Marcos,' or, The Mask is the Message." *The Zapatista Reader*, edited by Tom Hayden, translated by Shayna Cohen, Thunder´s Mouth Press/Nation Books, 2002, pp. 363–67.

Di Pietro, Valéria. *Num lugar de la Mancha*. Adaptation of Mário García Guillén's *Num lugar de la Mancha*. 2000. Unpublished play (typescript).

Dias, Telma. *Dom Quixote*. 2005. Unpublished play (typescript).

Didaco, Jorge. "Annotations from the Edge of an Abyss: Rogério Sganzerla's Anthropophagic Film Collages." *Senses of Cinema*, vol. 31, April 2004, sensesofcinema.com/2004/feature-articles/rogerio_sganzerla.

Dimenstein, Gilberto. "Ex-interno vira professor de teatro e ajuda na ressocialização." *Folha Online*, 21 June 2004, www1.folha.uol.com.br/folha/dimenstein/noticias/gd210604e.htm.

"*Don Quixote* gets authors' votes." *BBC News*, 7 May 2002, news.bbc.co.uk/2/hi/entertainment/1972609.stm.

"The *Don Quixote* Project." *Touchstone Theatre*, www.touchstone.org/community/the-don-quixote-project. Accessed 5 October 2018.

Dos Santos, Rosemary. "O Dom Quixote que venceu os moinhos." *Casa em revista*, vol. 1, no. 2, March 2010, pp. 12–19, www.fundacaocasa.sp.gov.br/files/efcp/revistas-casa/CASA_em_Revista_AnoI_n2.pdf.

Drew, Bernard A. *Literary Afterlife: The Posthumous Continuations of 325 Authors' Fictional Characters*. McFarland, 2009.

Dudley, Edward J. *The Endless Text: Don Quixote and the Hermeneutics of Romance*. State U of New York P, 1997.

Dunn, Christopher. *Contracultura: Alternative Arts and Social Transformation in Authoritarian Brazil*. U of North Carolina P, 2016.

Egginton, William. *How the World Became a Stage: Presence, Theatricality, and the Question of Modernity*. State U of New York P, 2003.

———. *The Man Who Invented Fiction: How Cervantes Ushered in the Modern World*. Bloomsbury, 2016.

"O enfrentamento da problemática de adolescentes e crianças nas ruas" (Interview with Dr. Auro D. Lescher). *Desenvolvimento social na cidade de São Paulo: Um trabalho em Rede*. Imprensa Oficial, April 2007, pp. 16–17.

Erasmus, Desiderius. *Praise of Folly*. 1511. Translated by Betty Radice. Penguin Classics, 1994.

Farah, Tatiana. "Movimento Passe Livre se inspira em zapatistas do México." *O Globo Brasil*. 23 June 2013, oglobo.globo.com/brasil/movimento-passe-livre-se-inspira-em-zapatistas-do-mexico-8787902.

Farias, Denis Alves, and Henrique R. A. Alves. "A linguagem dos protestos: Uma análise discursiva dos cartazes das manifestações sociais brasileiras." *RELVA (Revista de educação do Vale do Arinos)*, vol. 2, no. 1, Jan./June 2015, pp. 156–68.

Fernández de Avellaneda, Alonso. *El ingenioso hidalgo Don Quijote de la Mancha*. Edited by Luis Gómez Canseco, Biblioteca Nueva, 2000.

Ferreira, Renata Viana, et al. "Educação e transformação: Significações no pensamento de Paulo Freire." *Revista e-Curriculum*, vol. 12, no. 2, May-Oct 2014, pp. 1418–39, revistas.pucsp.br/index.php/curriculum/article/view/13856/15395.

Ferréz. *Capão Pecado*. 1999. Planeta, 2017.

Festival Cervantino. Azul, Ciudad Cervantina de la Argentina (2008–). ciudadcervantina.org.ar/v2016/secciones/festival-2018.

Festival Internacional Cervantino. Guanajuato, México (47th edition). festivalcervantino.gob.mx.

"Ficha de Texto: *A vida do grande D. Quixote de la Mancha e do gordo Sancho Pança*." Centro de Estudos de Teatro & Tiago Certal, 31 May 2007, ww3.fl.ul.pt/CETbase/reports/client/Report.htm?ObjType=Texto&ObjId=588.

Figueiredo, Eurídice. "Cross Readings: *Mestizaje*, Transculturation, Hybridism, and Creolization." *(Re)Considering Blackness in Contemporary Afro-Brazilian (Con)Texts*, edited by Antonio D. Tillis, Peter Lang, 2011, pp. 45–64.

Fish, Stanley. "The Crisis of the Humanities Officially Arrives." *New York Times*, 11 Oct. 2010, opinionator.blogs.nytimes.com/2010/10/11/the-crisis-of-the-humanities-officially-arrives.

———. "Crisis of the Humanities II." *The New York Times*, 18 Oct. 2010, opinionator.blogs.nytimes.com/2010/10/18/crisis-of-the-humanities-ii.

Flores, William V. "Citizens vs Citizenry: Undocumented Immigrants and Latino Cultural Citizenship." *Latino Cultural Citizenship: Claiming Identity, Space, and Rights*, edited by William V. Flores and Rina Benmayor, Beacon Press, 1997, pp. 255–78.

Florián Navas, Camen Alicia, and Patricia Pecha Quimbay. *El Teatro La Candelaria y el movimiento teatral en Bogotá 1950–1991*. Subdirección Imprenta Distrital, 2013.

Fordelone, Yolanda. "Vídeo 'O gigante acordou' reedita comercial da Johnnie Walker com protestos." *Radar de Propaganda Blog*, 24 June 2013, economia.estadao.com.br/blogs/radar-da-propaganda/video-o-gigante-acordou-reedita-comercial-da-johnnie-walker.

Foucault, Michel. *Abnormal: Lectures at the Collège de France 1974–1975*. Edited by Valerio Marchetti and Antonella Salomoni, translated by Graham Burchell, Picador, 2003.

———. *Discipline and Punish: The Birth of the Prison*. Translated by Alan Sheridan, Vintage, 1995.

Freire, Paulo. *Pedagogy of the Oppressed*. 1970. Translated by Myra Bergman Ramos, revised 20th anniversary ed., Continuum, 1997.

Friedman, Edward H. "Executing the Will: The End of the Road in *Don Quixote*." *Indiana Journal of Hispanic Literature*, vol. 5, 1994, pp. 105–25.

———. "Making Amends: An Approach to the Structure of *Don Quixote*, Part 2." *Vanderbilt e-Journal of Luso-Hispanic Studies*, vol. 2, 2005. doi: 10.15695/vejlhs.v2i0.3165.

Fuentes, Carlos. *Cervantes, o la crítica de la lectura*. Centro de Estudios Cervantinos, 1994.

———. "Machado de La Mancha." *Nexos: Sociedad, ciencia, literatura*, 1 July 1998, www.nexos.com.mx/?p=8927.

Fundação Telefônica. *Causos de ECA: Histórias em retrato. O Estatuto da Criança e do Adolescente no cotidiano*. Fundação Telefônica, 2006.

Fusco, Coco. *English Is Broken Here: Notes on Cultural Fusion in the Americas*. New Press, 1995

Gálvez, Andrés, and Ian Carnelli. "ESA Studies on the Don Quijote NEO Mission: Dealing with Impact Uncertainties." Advanced Concepts Team, European Space Agency, 2005, www.esa.int/gsp/ACT/doc/MAD/pub/ACT-RPR-MAD-2006-DQdealingImpactUncertainties.pdf.

Garcia, Giselle. "Entenda a crise econômica." *Agência Brasil: Últimas notícias do Brasil e do mundo*, 15 May 2016, agenciabrasil.ebc.com.br/economia/noticia/2016-05/entenda-crise-economica.

García, Santiago. *El Quijote*. 1999. *Teatro la Candelaria: Obras 4*, by Santiago García et al., Ediciones Teatro la Candelaria, 2008, pp. 11–92.

———. "El Quijote" (Interview). *Hemispheric Institute: Digital Video Library*, New York University, 9 Sept. 2000, hdl.handle.net/2333.1/z34tmpv5.

García Canclini, Néstor. *Hybrid Cultures: Strategies for Entering and Leaving Modernity*. Translated by Christopher L. Chiappari and Silvia L. López, U of Minnesota P, 1995.

García Guillén, Mário. *Num lugar de la Mancha: Edição bilíngüe*. Loyola, 1996.

Gascón, Christopher D. "At Play with Cervantes: Repertorio Español's *El Quijote*." *Comedia Performance*, vol. 4, no. 1, Spring 2007, pp. 97–123. JSTOR, www.jstor.org/stable/10.5325/comeperf.4.1.0097.

George, Anisa, and Petra Costa, directors. *The Making of Don Quixote of Bethlehem*, Touchstone Theater, 2006. DVD.

Gerli, Michael E. *Refiguring Authority: Reading, Writing, and Rewriting in Cervantes.* UP of Kentucky, 1995.

"O gigante acordou: Keep Walking Brazil." Johnnie Walker. Commercial produced by NEOGAMA/BBH, 2011. *YouTube,* 8 October 2011, www.youtube.com/watch?v=DuW1aj2s9uw.

Goffman, Erving. *The Presentation of Self in Everyday Life.* Anchor, 1959.

Gohn, Maria da Glória. "Brazilian Social Movements in the Last Decade." *Handbook of Social Movements across Latin America,* edited by Paul Almeida and Allen Corder Ulate, Springer, 2015, pp. 361–72.

Golden, Tim. "The Voice of the Rebels Has Mexicans in His Spell." *New York Times,* 8 February 1994, www.nytimes.com/1994/02/08/world/the-voice-of-the-rebels-has-mexicans-in-his-spell.html.

Goldman, Francisco. "Visiting the Real America, Where Seven-Year-Olds Translate *Don Quixote*." *Literary Hub,* 11 June 2017, lithub.com/visiting-the-real-america-where-seven-year-olds-translate-don-quixote.

Gollnick, Brian. *Reinventing the Lacandón: Subaltern Representations in the Rain Forest of Chiapas.* U of Arizona P, 2008.

Gomes Goveia, Fábio. "Imagens das rúas e das redes: Análise das jornadas de junho a partir da hashtag #VemPraRua." XXIII Encontro Anual da Compós, Universidade Federal do Pará, Belém, 27–30 May 2014, compos.org.br/encontro2014/anais/Docs/GT01_COMUNICACAO_E_CIBERCULTURA/artigo_compos_2014_compactado_200_2133.pdf.

Gómez-Peña, Guillermo. *Dangerous Border Crossers: The Artist Talks Back.* Routledge, 2000.

Green, Barbara. *Spectacular Confessions: Autobiography, Performative Activism, and the Sites of Suffrage.* Palgrave Macmillan, 1997.

Greenblatt, Stephen. *Renaissance Self-Fashioning: From More to Shakespeare.* U of Chicago P, 2012.

Gutiérrez, Bernardo. "La revuelta que sorprendió al mundo." *La Vanguardia Magazine,* 21 July 2013, pp. 38–45.

Haff, Stephen. 8 September 2018. Personal interview.

Haff, Stephen, et al. *The Serialized Traveling Adventures of Kid Quixote.* 2018. Unpublished play (typescript).

Hall, Stuart. "Foucault: Power, Knowledge and Discourse." *Discourse, Theory and Practice,* edited by M. Wetherell, S. Taylor, and S. Yates, Sage, 2001, pp. 72–81.

Hardt, Michael, and Antonio Negri. *Multitude: War and Democracy in the Age of Empire.* Penguin, 2004.

Harris, Melissa S., et al. "Community Reinsertion Success of Street Children Programs in Brazil and Peru." *Children and Youth Services Review,* vol. 33, 2011, pp. 723–31.

The Heart of the Matter. Commission on the Humanities and Social Sciences. American Academy of Arts and Sciences, 2013, www.humanitiescommission.

org/_pdf/hss_report.pdf.

Horwatt, Eli. "A Taxonomy of Digital Video Remixing: Contemporary Found Footage Practice on the Internet." *Cultural Borrowings: Appropriation, Reworking, Transformation*, edited by Iain Robert Smith, Scope, 2009, pp. 76–91.

I Am Quixote: Don Quijote de La Mancha Festival. Raleigh/Durham, North Carolina, 2015–2019, iamquixote.com.

Ibarra, Paola. "Beautiful Trash: Art and Transformation." *ReVista: Harvard Review of Latin America*, vol. 14, no. 2, Winter 2015, pp. 41–43, revista.drclas.harvard.edu/book/beautiful-trash.

IBGE Cidades. Instituto Brasileiro de Geografia e Estatística, cidades.ibge.gov.br. Accessed 11 November 2018.

Iffland, James. *De fiestas y aguafiestas: Risa, locura e ideología en Cervantes y Avellaneda*. Iberoamericana, 1999.

———. "*Don Quijote* and the Dissident Intellectual: Some Thoughts on Subcomandante Marcos's *Don Durito de la Lacandona*." *Studies in Honor of James O. Crosby*, edited by Lía Schwartz, Juan de la Cuesta, 2004, pp. 161–79.

———. "Laughter Tamed." *Cervantes: Bulletin of the Cervantes Society of America*, vol. 23, no. 2, 2003, pp. 395–435.

———. "On the Social Destiny of *Don Quixote*: Literature and Ideological Interpellation: Part I." *Journal of the Midwest MLA*, vol. 20, no. 1, 1987, pp. 17–36.

———. "On the Social Destiny of *Don Quixote*: Literature and Ideological Interpellation: Part II." *Journal of the Midwest MLA*, vol. 20, no. 2, 1987, pp. 9–27.

"Informe forense: Bolívar era mestizo y medía entre 1,64 y 1,69 centímetros." *Reportero24*, 18 December 2010, www.reportero24.com/2010/12/18/informe-forense-bolivar-era-mestizo-y-media-entre-164-y-169-centimetros.

Instituto Religare. "Instituto Religare" (original organization, since 2002). *Wordpress*, pontoculturareligare.wordpress.com/o-religaree. Accessed 11 November 2018.

———. "Instituto Religare" (current organization, since 2017). *Facebook*, www.facebook.com/religaresocial. Accessed 11 November 2018.

———. "Arte aos quatro ventos." 2009. Brochure in print.

Johnson, Nuala. "Cast in Stone: Monuments, Geography, and Nationalism." *Environment and Planning D: Society and Space*, vol. 13, 1995, pp. 51–65.

Kiefer, Sandra. "Com 15 anos de atividade em SP, Cooperifa promove saraus e espalha seu exemplo para outras cidades." *Jornal estado de minas*, 22 July 2016, www.uai.com.br/app/noticia/artes-e-livros/2016/07/22/noticias-artes-e-livros,182352/com-15-anos-de-atividade-em-sp-cooperifa-promove-saraus-e-espalha-seu.shtml.

Kozusko, Matt. "Monstrous!: Actors, Audiences, Inmates, and the Politics of Reading Shakespeare." *Shakespeare Bulletin*, vol. 28, no. 2, Summer 2010, pp. 235–51. doi: 10.1353/shb.0.0157.

Larkins, Erika Mary Robb. *The Spectacular Favela: Violence in Modern Brazil*. U of California P, 2015.

Leonard, Irving A. *Books of the Brave: Being an Account of Books and of Men in the Spanish Conquest and Settlement of the Sixteenth-Century New World*. 1949. U of California P, 1992.

Lescher, Auro Danny. "Da terra do crack ao campo de refugiados." *Estadão*, 24 April 2014, opiniao.estadao.com.br/noticias/geral,da-terra-do-crack-ao-campo-de-refugiados-imp-,1157824.

———. "Miguel de Cervantes Saavedra." *Brasileiros*, 24 July 2015, brasileiros.com.br/2015/07/miguel-de-cervantes-saavedra.

———. "Uma ilha para Sancho Pança." *Brasileiros*, 10 July 2015, brasileiros.com.br/2015/07/uma-ilha-para-sancho-panca.

Lima Barreto, Alfonso Henriques de. *The Patriot (Triste fim de Policarpo Quaresma)*. 1911. Translated by Robert Scott-Buccleuch, Rex Collings, 1978.

Lipsitz, George. "Who'll Stop the Rain: Youth Culture, Rock 'n' Roll, and Social Crises." *The Sixties: From Memory to History*, edited by David Farber, U of North Carolina P, 1994, pp. 206–34.

Lo Ré, A. G. "The Three Deaths of Don Quixote: Comments in Favor of the Romantic Critical Approach." *Cervantes: Bulletin of the Cervantes Society of America*, vol. 9, no. 2, 1989, pp. 21–41.

Luiselli, Valeria. "The Littlest Don Quixotes Versus the World." *New York Times*, 23 June 2018, www.nytimes.com/2018/06/23/opinion/sunday/the-littlest-don-quixotes-versus-the-world.html.

Maddox, John T. "AfroReggae: Antropofagia, Sublimation, and Intimate Revolt in the Favela." *Hispania*, vol. 97, no. 3, 2014, pp. 463–76.

Maestro, Jesús. "Cervantes y el teatro del *Quijote*." *Hispania*, vol. 88, no. 1, 2005, pp. 41–52.

Mancing, Howard. "Dulcinea Del Toboso: On the Occasion of Her Four-Hundredth Birthday." *Hispaniai*, vol. 88, no. 1, March 2005, pp. 53–63.

Mandel, Oscar. "The Function of the Norm in *Don Quixote*." *Modern Philology*, vol. 55, no. 3, Feb. 1958, pp. 154–63.

Maravall, José Antonio. *Utopia and Counterutopia in the Quixote*. Translated by Robert Felkel, Wayne State UP, 1991.

Marcos, Subcomandante. "The Punch Card and the Hourglass." Interview by Gabriel García Márquez and Roberto Pombo, *New Left Review*, May–June 2001, newleftreview.org/A2322.

———. *Our Word Is Our Weapon. Selected Writings*. Edited by Juana Ponce de León, Seven Stories Press, 2002.

———. *Conversations with Durito: Stories of the Zapatistas and Neoliberalism*. Acción Zapatista Editorial Collective-Autonomedia, 2005.

Mariano, Isabella, and Karolina Lopes. "Somos a rede social." *Universo UFES* (Universidade Federal do Espíritu Santo), 1 July 2013, universo.ufes.br/blog/2013/07/somos-a-rede-social.

Marín, Christina. "Ripples on the Water: Discoveries Made with Young People Using Theatre of the Oppressed." *Youth and Theatre of the Oppressed*, edited by Peter Duffy and Elinor Vettraino, Palgrave, 2010, pp. 217–28.

Maura, Antonio. "El autor y sus máscaras: Cervantes y Machado de Assis." *Revista de Estudios Brasileños*, vol. 5, no. 9, 2018, pp. 54–60, reb.universia.net/article/view/3443/autor-mascaras-cervantes-machado-assis.

Mazetti, Henrique. "Resistências criativas: Os coletivos artísticos e ativistas no Brasil." *Lugar Comum*, vol. 25–26, 2008, pp. 105–20.

McCann, Bryan. *The Throes of Democracy: Brazil since 1989*. Zed Books, 2008.

McGraw, Mark David. *The Universal Quixote: Appropriations of a Literary Icon*. 2013. Texas A&M U, PhD dissertation.

Meirelles, Fernando, and Kátia Lund, directors. *City of God (Cidade de deus)*, 2002. Miramax Films, 2004. DVD.

Meirelles, Márcio, et al. *Em defesa das causas perdidas*. 2014. Unpublished play.

Meirelles, Márcio, and Cleise Mendes. *Um tal de dom Quixote*. 1998. Unpublished play.

Melucci, Alberto. "The Symbolic Challenge of Contemporary Movements." *Social Research*, vol. 52, no. 4, Winter 1985, pp. 789–816. JSTOR, www.jstor.org/stable/40970398.

Menotti del Picchia, Paulo. "O amor de Dulcinéia." *Juca mulato*, Martins, 1965.

Mignolo, Walter, and Rolando Vázquez. "Decolonial AestheSis: Colonial Wounds/Decolonial Healings." *Social Text/Periscope*, 15 July 15 2013, socialtextjournal.org/periscope_article/decolonial-aesthesis-colonial-woundsdecolonial-healings.

Miller, Toby. "Introducing . . . Cultural Citizenship." *Social Text*, vol. 19, no. 4, Winter 2001, pp. 1–5.

Millington, Mark. "Transculturation: Contrapuntal Notes to Critical Orthodoxy." *Bulletin of Latin American Research*, vol. 26, no. 2, 2007, pp. 256–68.

Milne, Elinor, and Eloïse Di Gianni. *"Give Us the Opportunity to Change Our Story": Street-Connected Young People Speak Out (March 15–16 2016)*. Consortium for Street Children, 1 April 2016, www.streetchildren.org/wp-content/uploads/2016/05/Report-on-Brazil-consultation-April-2016-1.pdf.

Milton, John. "The Political Adaptations of Monteiro Lobato." *Cadernos de Tradução*, vol. 1, no. 11, 2003, pp. 211–27. doi: 10.5007/%25x.

Miñana, Rogelio. "*Don Quixote* among Brazilians: *Um tal de Dom Quixote* (Márcio Meirelles and Cleise Mendes, 1998)." *"Los cielos se agotaron de prodigios": Essays in Honor of Frederick A. de Armas*, edited by Christopher B. Weimer et al., Juan de la Cuesta, 2017, pp. 323–32.

———. "Don Quijote de las Américas: Activismo, teatro y el hidalgo Quijano en el Brasil contemporáneo." *El* Quijote *desde América* (Segunda parte), edited by Ignacio Arellano, Duilio Ayalamacedo, and James Iffland, Idea, 2016, pp. 247–60

———. "The 'Don Quixote of the Streets': Social Justice Theater in São Paulo, Brazil." *Cervantes: Bulletin of the Cervantes Society of America*, vol. 31, no.1, 2011, pp. 159–70.

———. "Don Quixote Never Dies in Brazil: Performative Appropriations of *Don Quixote* II.74 in Contemporary Brazilian Theater." *A Novel wihout Boundaries: Sensing* Don Quixote *400 Years Later*, edited by Carmen García de la Rasilla and Jorge Abril Sánchez, Juan de la Cuesta, 2016, pp. 199–216.

———. "Making Change Happen: The New Mission and Location of Language Departments." Anchor piece with six respondents for "Perspectives" section of *Modern Language Journal*, vol. 101, no. 2, 2017, pp. 413–23.

———. *Monstruos que hablan: El discurso de la monstruosidad en Cervantes*. North Carolina UP, 2008.

———."Righting Wrongs: *Don Quixote*'s 'Other History' in Brazilian Youth Theater." Don Quixote: *Interdisciplinary Connections*, edited by James A. Parr and Matthew Warshawsky, Juan de la Cuesta, 2013, pp. 203–22.

———. "'Veréis el monstruo': La nueva comedia de Cervantes." *Bulletin of the Comediantes*, vol. 56, no. 2, 2004, pp. 387–412.

Mochary, Matt, and Jeff Zimbalist, directors. *Favela Rising*. Thinkfilm/HBO Documentary, 2005.

Monachesi, Juliana. "A explosão do a(r)tivismo." *Folha de S. Paulo, Mais!*, 6 April 2003, pp. 4–9, www1.folha.uol.com.br/fsp/mais/fs0604200305.htm.

Monteiro Lobato, José Bento. *Dom Quixote das crianças*. 1936. Editora Globo, 2010.

Moraes, Érika de. "Brasil 're-democratizado: Um gigante que acordou? A discursivização midíatica sobre os protestos de junho de 2013." *Mídia e cotidiano*, vol. 6, no. 6, July 2015, pp. 131–51.

Morell, Arturo, director. Don Quijote, *un grito de libertad*. Fundación Voz de Libertad AC and Proyecto IntegrArte, 2006.

Morrison, Chandra. "Colouring Pollution: 'Cleaning' the City and 'Recycling' Social Values in São Paulo Street Art." *Latin American Popular Culture: Politics, Media, Affect*, edited by Geoffrey Kantaris and Rory O'Bryen, Tamesis, 2013, pp. 187–206. JSTOR, www.jstor.org/stable/10.7722/j.ctt14brt0c.13.

MV Bill. "Viver para representar!" *Causos de ECA: Histórias em retrato. O Estatuto da Criança e do Adolescente no cotidiano*, Fundação Telefônica, 2006, pp. 71–73.

Navarro Flores, Celia. "Portinari y Drummond: Dos interpretaciones del *Quijote* de Cervantes." *Cervantes y el* Quijote: *Actas del Coloquio Internacional (27–30 de Octubre, 2004)*, edited by Emilio Martínez Mata, Arco Libros, 2007, pp. 311–17.

Neate, Patrick, and Damian Platt. *Culture Is Our Weapon: Making Music and Changing Lives in Rio de Janeiro*. Penguin Books, 2010.

Neves, Letícia. "Jovens actores encantados com Márcio Meirelles." *A Nação Etc.*, vol. 358, 10–16 July 2014, pp. E1– E3. *ISSUU*, issuu.com/teatrovilavelha/docs/mate_ria_kcena.

Neves, Manoella. "Em Cartaz: O que fizeram os cartazes na jornada de junho de 2013 no Brasil." GT12: Comunicação para a Mudança Social do XII Associação LatinoAmericana de Investigadores da Comunicação (ALAIC), 2014, www.Congreso.pucp.edu.pe/alaic2014/wp-content/uploads/2013/09/GT12-Manoella-Neves.docx.

Newfield, Christopher. "Ending the Budget Wars: Funding the Humanities During a Crisis in Higher Education." *Profession*, 2009, pp. 270–84. doi: 10.1632/prof.2009.2009.1.270.

Noble, Steven E. "Mental Illness through Popular Theater: Performing (In)Sanely." *Artistic Ways of Knowing. Expanded Opportunities for Teaching and Learning*, edited by Randee Lipson Lawrence, Wiley, 2005, pp. 45–54.

Nogales Bazán, Iván, et al. *Teatro Trono: El mañana es hoy. Teatro con niños y adolescentes de la calle*. Fundación Arnoldo Schwimmer, 1998.

Olinto, Antônio. "A Brazilian Don Quixote." Introduction. *The Patriot (Triste fim de Policarpo Quaresma)*, by Alfonso Henriques de Lima Barreto, 1911, translated by Robert Scott-Buccleuch, Rex Collings, 1978, pp. vii–ix.

Oriel, Charles. "'Yo sé quién soy': How Don Quijote Does Things with Words (Part I, chaps. 1–5)." *Cervantes: Bulletin of the Cervantes Society of America*, vol. 29, no. 1, 2009, pp. 57–83.

Ortiz, Fernando. *Cuban Counterpoint: Tobacco and Sugar*. Translated by Harriet de Onís, Duke UP, 1995.

Ortiz, Arturo. Foreword. *A Study of Liberation Discourse: The Semantics of Opposition in Freire and Gutierrez*, by Roberto Rivera, Peter Lang, 2004, pp. ix–xiv.

Padilha, José, director. *Bus 174 (Ônibus 174)*, 2002, Zazon Produções, 2004. DVD.

Pardue, Derek. "Taking Stock of the State: Hip-Hoppers' Evaluation of the 'Cultural Points' Program in Brazil." *Latin American Perspectives*, vol. 39, no. 2, 2012, pp. 93–112.

———. "Reversal of Fortunes?: São Paulo Youth Redirect Urban Development." *Revista Tomo*, vol. 21, 2012, pp. 37–62.

Parr, James A. *Don Quixote: An Anatomy of Subversive Discourse*. Juan de la Cuesta, 1988.

Pasquerella, Lynn. "The Promise of Humanities Practice." *MLA Panel: Humanities in the 21st Century*. Posted by Alan Liu, 3 Jan. 2013, *4Humanities: Advocating for the Humanities*, 4humanities.org/2013/01/lynn-pasquerella-the-promise-of-humanities-practice.

Penteado, Claudia. "Gigante acorda em campanha de Johnnie Walker," *Consumo e propaganda* (blog), July 26, 2017, consumoepropaganda.ig.com.br/index.php/2011/10/10/gigante-acorda-em-campanha-de-johnny-walker.

Pérez Rodríguez, Marta. *Tras un siglo de recepción cervantina en Brasil: Estudios críticos sobre el Quijote (1900–2000)*. 2007, Universidade de São Paulo, Master's dissertation. The Digital Library of Theses and Dissertations of the U of São Paulo, www.teses.usp.br/teses/disponiveis/8/8145/tde-26052008-151439/publico/DISSERTACAO_MARTA_PEREZ_RODRIGUEZ.pdf.

Peres, Phyllis. *Transculturation and Resistance in Lusophone African Narrative*. UP of Florida, 1997.

Perlman, Janice. *Favela: Four Decades of Living on the Edge in Rio de Janeiro*. Oxford UP, 2009.

Pires, Célio. "Sou contra a redução da idade penal." *Recanto das letras*, 7 December 2006, www.recantodasletras.com.br/letras/312249.

Poblete, Juan. "US Latino Studies in a Global Context: Social Imagination and the Production of In/Visibility." *Works and Days* 47/48, vol. 24, no. 1–2, 2006, pp. 243–65.

Portinari, Cândido, and Carlos Drummond de Andrade. *Dom Quixote: 21 desenhos de Cândido Portinari*. Diagraphis, 1973.
Pratt, Mary Louise. *Imperial Eyes: Travel Writing and Transculturation*. Routledge, 1992.
Predmore, Richard L. *The World of Don Quixote*. Harvard UP, 1967.
Prengaman, Peter, and Sarah DiLorenzo. "Military Takeover in Rio Sparks Fears of Police Brutality." *Associated Press News*, 28 Feb. 2018, apnews.com/04bc31349e4847409435d74ba13bbb19.
Projeto Quixote. *Conceitos e estratégias para o atendimento de crianças e jovens em situação de risco*. Edited by Auro D. Lescher and Graziela Bedoian, Projeto Quixote, 2007.
——. *Exilados do mundão*. Directed by Daniel Rubio, Projeto Quixote, 2006.
——. *Mundo do trabalho e juventude em situação de risco*. Edited by Graziela Bedoian and Roberto Carlos Madalena, Projeto Quixote, 2008.
——. *Por trás dos muros: Horizontes sociais do graffiti*. Edited by Graziela Bedoian and Kátia Menezes, Peirópolis, 2008.
——. *Quixote: Uma outra história*. Edited by Graziela Bedoian, Auro D. Lescher, and Zilda Ferré, Projeto Quixote, 2017.
——. *Refugiados urbanos*. *YouTube*, July 2007, www.youtube.com/watch?v=orG-pEjBRgAM.
——. "Refugiados urbanos." *Projeto Quixote*, June 2010–June 2011, www.projetoquixote.org.br/wp-content/uploads/2011/10/Pesquisa-Refugiados-urbanos-2011.pdf.
——. "Resultados" www.projetoquixote.org.br. Accessed 12 November 2018.
Pueo Wood, Naomi. "A Cosmética da Fome: The Staging of Poverty in Recent Arts-Focused Documentary Film." *Brazil in Twenty-First Century Popular Media: Culture, Politics, and Nationalism on the World Stage*, edited by Namoi Pueo Wood, Lexington Books, 2014, pp. 73–90.
"Que xote é esse." *Espaço Quixote comunitário. Facebook*, 12 July 2018, facebook.com/funsaiquixote/videos/1482494708522899.
Quijano, Aníbal. "Of Don Quixote and Windmills in Latin America." Translated by Meryl Adelman, *Estudos Avançados*, vol. 19, no. 55, 2005, pp. 9–31. doi: 10.1590/S0103-40142005000300002.
El Quijote visto desde América. Edited by Jesús García Sánchez, Visor Libros, 2005.
Quiroz, Luis R., editor. *Cervantes y Don Quijote en Bolivia: Su imperecedero legado*. Proinsa, 2009.
Quixote Espaço Comunitário. "FUNSAI Unidade VII: Espaço Quixote Comunitário." *Fundação Nossa Senhora Auxiliadora do Ipiranga*, 2017, www.funsai.org.br/quixote.
Quixote Reciclado, directed by Philippe Henry, Tetra Pak Foundation, 1998, www.culturaambientalnasescolas.com.br/aluno/a-embalagem-e-o-ambiente/quixote-reciclado.
Rama, Ángel. *Transculturación narrativa en América Latina* [*Writing across Cultures:*

Narrative Transculturation in Latin America]. 1982. Edited and translated by David Frye, Duke UP, 2012.

Reed, Helen H. "Theatricality in the Picaresque of Cervantes." *Cervantes: Bulletin of the Cervantes Society of America*, vol. 7, no. 2, 1987, pp. 71–84.

Reis, Carlos. "Para uma teoria da figuração. Sobrevidas da personagem ou um conceito em movimento." *Letras de Hoje*, vol. 52, no. 2, Apr.–Jun. 2017, pp. 129–36. doi: 10.15448/1984-7726.2017.2.29161.

———. "Pessoas de livro: Figuraçao e sobrevida da personagem." *Revista de estudos literários*, vol. 4, 2014, pp. 43–68.

Reisz, Matthew. "Humanities Crisis? What Crisis?" *Times Higher Education*, 9 July 2015, www.timeshighereducation.com/news/humanities-crisis-what-crisis.

Riera, Carme. *El* Quijote *desde el nacionalismo catalán, en torno al Terrcer Centenario*. Destino, 2004.

Riley, Edward C. "*Don Quixote*: From Text to Icon." *Cervantes: Bulletin of the Cervantes Society of America*, vol. 8, 1988, pp. 103–15.

Rivera, Roberto. *A Study of Liberation Discourse: The Semantics of Opposition in Freire and Gutierrez*. Peter Lang, 2004.

Rizzini, Irene, et al. *Crianças e adolescentes com direitos violados: Situação de rua e indicadores de vulnerabilidade no Brasil urbano*. CIESPI, 2010, sistemas.tjam.jus.br/coij/wp-content/uploads/2014/06/CriancasAdolescentesDireitosViolados.pdf.

Rocha, Glauber. "Estética da Fome." *Revolução do Cinema Novo*, Cosac and Naify, 2004, pp. 63–67.

Rocha Barroso, Juliana. "Arquitetura do CRECA é inspirada em Dom Quixote e na auto-suficiência dos moinhos." *Setor3.com*, 13 July 2007, www.setor3.com.br/arquivos/10.2.0.140_7778/jsp/default979b.html.

———. "Trabalho no CRECA Moinho do Bixiga pode servir de referência para rede." *Setor3.com*, 16 July 2007, www.setor3.com.br/arquivos/10.2.0.140_7778/jsp/default7a53.html.

Rogers, Richard A. "From Cultural Exchange to Transculturation: A Review and Reconceptualization of Cultural Appropriation." *Communication Theory*, vol. 16, 2006, pp. 474–503.

Russell, Peter E. "*Don Quixote* as a Funny Book." *Modern Language Review*, vol. 64, 1969, pp. 312–26.

Said, Edward. *Culture and Imperialism*. Vintage Books, 1993.

Sandoval-Sánchez, Alberto, and Nancy Saporta Sternbach. *Stages of Life: Transcultural Performance and Identity in US Latina Theater*. U of Arizona P, 2001.

"São Paulo." *Instituto Brasileiro de Geografia e Estatística (IBGE) Cidades*, 2016, cidades.ibge.gov.br/brasil/sp/sao-paulo/panorama. Accessed 5 October 2018.

Sarmiento, Domingo Faustino. *Facundo, o civilización y barbarie en las pampas argentinas*. 1845. Siglo XXI Ediciones, 2004.

Scalona, Timothy. "The Problem with Performative Activism." *Massachusetts Daily Collegian*, U of Massachusetts at Amherst, 29 November 2017, dailycollegian.com/2017/11/the-problem-with-performative-activism.

Schmidt, Ben. "Crisis in the Humanities, or Just Women in the Workplace?" *Sapping Attention*, 26 June 2013, sappingattention.blogspot.com/2013/06/crisis-in-humanities-or-just-women-in.html.

Schmidt, Christopher. "Vik Muniz's Pictures of Garbage and the Aesthetics of Poverty." *ARTMargins*, vol. 6, no. 3, Oct. 2017, pp. 8–27.

Schmidt, Rachel. "The Performance and Hermeneutics of Death in the Last Chapter of *Don Quijote*." *Cervantes: Bulletin of the Cervantes Society of America*, vol. 20, no. 2, Fall 2000, pp. 101–26.

Sena, Ercio. "Trilhas na batalha dos cartazes." *Rumores*, vol. 15, no. 8, Jan.–June 2014, pp. 101–14.

Sneed, Paul Michael. "NGO-Action: Urban Activism in Brazilian Film and Society." *Revista Iberoamericana*, vol. 26, no. 3, 2015, pp. 23–55.

Spitta, Silvia. *Between Two Waters: Narratives of Transculturation in Latin America*. Rice UP, 1995.

Spitzer, Leo. "Linguistic Perspectivism in the *Quijote*." *Linguistics and Literary History: Essays in Stylistics*, Princeton UP, 1948, pp. 225–71.

Spivak, Gayatri C. "Can the Subaltern Speak?" *Marxism and the Interpretation of Culture*, edited by Cary Nelson and Lawrence Grossberg, Macmillan, 1988, pp. 271–313.

Stam, Robert. "Tropical Detritus: *Terra em transe*, Tropicalia and the Aesthetics of Garbage." *Studies in Latin American Popular Culture*, vol. 19, 2000, pp. 83–93.

Stavans, Ilan. *Quixote: The Novel and the World*. Norton, 2015.

Still Waters in a Storm. "I Am Don Quixote and I Want to Rescue." *Vimeo*, 21 Dec. 2016, vimeo.com/196587007.

———. "Kid Quixote Channel." *YouTube*, 19 June 2018, www.youtube.com/channel/UC8HPthZBuLK7ourDG6QH2UQ.

———. "Quixote Project." www.stillwatersinastorm.org/quixote-project. Accessed October 9, 2019.

Storey, John. *Cultural Consumption and Everyday Life*. Arnold, 1999.

Street Children: A Mapping and Gapping Review of the Literature 2000 to 2010. Consortium for Street Children, 16 June 2011. Child Rights International Network, web.archive.org/web/20180127100746/www.crin.org/en/docs/Street%20Children%20Mapping%20%20Gapping%20LiteratureStreet%20Children%20Review%20-%20FINAL%20VERSION%20-%20February%202011.pdf.

Taviani, Paolo, and Vittorio Taviani. *Ceasar Must Die (Césare deve morire)*, 2012, Adopt films, 2013. DVD.

Taylor, Diana. *Performance*. Duke UP, 2016.

———. "Transculturating Transculturation." *Performing Arts Journal*, vol. 13, no. 2, May 1991, pp. 90–104. JSTOR, www.jstor.org/stable/3245476.

The Teaching of the Arts and Humanities at Harvard College: Mapping the Future. Harvard Humanities Project, Harvard University, 2013, artsandhumanities.fas.harvard.edu/files/humanities/files/mapping_the_future_31_may_2013.pdf.

Tennina, Lucía. "Saraus das periferias de São Paulo: Poesia entre tragos, silêncios e aplausos." *Estudos de literatura brasileira contemporânea*, no. 42, July/Dec. 2013. doi: 10.1590/S2316-40182013000200001.

Torrente Ballester, Gonzalo. *El Quijote como juego*. Guadarrama, 1975.

Trigo, Abril. "Shifting Paradigms: From Transculturation to Hybridity: A Theoretical Critique." *Unforeseeable Americas: Questioning Cultural Hybridity in the Americas*, edited by R. De Grandis and Z. Bernd, Editions Rodopi, 2000, pp. 85–111.

Uribe-Echevarría, Juan. *Cervantes en las letras hispanoamericanas (Antología y crítica)*. Universidad de Chile, 1949.

Uzel, Marcos. *O teatro de Bando: Negro, baiano e popular*. Vila Velha-P555 Edições, 2003.

Valmir Gomes, José. "Transformação." *Causos de ECA: Histórias em retrato. O Estatuto da Criança e do Adolescente no cotidiano*, Fundação Telefônica, 2006, pp. 53–56.

Van Dijk, Teun A. "Principles of Critical Discourse Analysis." *Discourse and Society*, vol. 4, no. 2, 1993, 249–83.

Van Doren, Mark. *Don Quixote's Profession*. Columbia UP, 1958.

Vanden Berghe, Kristine. "Sobre armas y letras. *El Quijote* como intertexto en los relatos del Subcomandante Marcos." *Boletín AFEHC*, vol. 33, Dec. 2007, www.afehc-historia-centroamericana.org/index_action_fi_aff_id_1785.html.

Vargas, Lucila. *Latina Teens, Migration, and Popular Culture*. Peter Lang, 2009.

Velásquez Martínez, Alberto. *El Quijote en América, Colombia y Antioquia*. Taller de edición, 2018.

Vélez Sainz, José Julio. "Mutating Meninos da Rua: Teatro Religare, *Don Quijote*, and the Theater of the Oppressed." *Brasil/Brazil: Revista de Literatura Brasileira/Journal of Brazilian Literature*, vol. 32, no. 58, 2018, pp. 17–29.

"Vem pra rua." FIAT. Commercial produced by Leo Burnett Tailor Made, 2013. *YouTube*, 18 June 2013, www.youtube.com/watch?v=LKMwzMtuL9o.

Vieira, Maria Augusta da Costa. "Louco Lúcido: Dom Quixote e ou Cavaleiro do Verde Gabão." *Revista USP*, vol. 67, 2005, pp. 282–93.

———. "El *Quijote* en la prosa de Machado de Assis." *Bulletin of Spanish Studies*, vol. 81, no. 4–5, 2004, pp. 441–49.

———. "El Quijote y las huellas cervantinas en Brasil." *Actas de las Jornadas Cervantinas*, edited by Eleonora Basso and Alicia Torres, Universidad de la República, 2005, pp. 93–102.

———. "Tipología quijotesca: Presencia de don Quijote en tierras brasileñas." *Actas del XIII Congreso de la Asociación Internacional de Hispanistas, 1998. Volumen 1*, edited by Florencio Sevilla Arroyo and Carlos Alvar Ezquerra, Castalia, 2000, pp. 467–75.

Viñar, Marcelo. "Uma utopia sem lugar de chegada." Interview, *Revista Percurso*, no. 25, 2/2000, revistapercurso.uol.com.br/pdfs/p25_entrevista.pdf.

Waldron, Travis. "Brazilian Cops Are Killing More People than Ever. Somebody Tell Madonna." *HuffingtonPost*, 1 November 2017, www.huffingtonpost.com/entry/brazil-police-violence-madonna-rio_us_59f9dc68e4b0d1cf6e91f1ef.

Wasserman, Dale. "*Don Quixote* as Theatre." *Cervantes: Bulletin of the Cervantes Society of America*, vol. 19, no. 1, 1999, pp. 125–30.

Williamson, Robert C. *Latin America: Cultures in Conflict*. Palgrave, 2006.

Wood, Sara F. *Quixotic Fictions of the USA 1792–1815*. Oxford UP, 2005.

Xavier, Peterson. "Dom Quixote das ruas." *Museu da pessoa*, 28 July 2015, www.museudapessoa.net/pt/conteudo/historia/dom-quixote-das-ruas-104590.

———. "Mutatis." *YouTube*, 30 March 2007, www.youtube.com/watch?v=R5piut1W-nU.

———. "Viver para representar!" *Causos de ECA: Histórias em retrato. O Estatuto da Criança e do Adolescente no cotidiano*, Fundação Telefônica, 2006, pp. 67–70.

Yúdice, George. *The Expediency of Culture: Uses of Culture in the Global Era*. Duke UP, 2004.

Ziolkowsky, Eric J. *The Sanctification of Don Quixote: From Hidalgo to Priest*. Penn State UP, 1991.

INDEX

Bold numbers indicate photographs.

Abel, Lionel, 81
Abril Sánchez, Jorge, 63
activism
    artivism, 8, 15, 34–35, 147–52, 207n3, 217n7
    community, 3–5, 17, 20, 40–45
    expediency of cultural, 219n14, 220n17
    measuring success of, 20, 180–83, 187, 190–91, 197–99
    NGO (non-governmental organization), 4, 6, 13–32, 136–52
    Quixote-inspired, 7, 11–12, 16–17, 20, 41, 75, 82, 120, 207n1, 217n7
    See also performative activism
Adams, John, 5
Adomaitis, Kasparas, 12
aesthetics of hunger, 217n7
Afro-Brazilians, 85, 89–91, 94–97, 119
AfroReggae. *See* Grupo Cultural AfroReggae
afterlife. *See sobrevida*
agency, 40–43, 45, 189–91, 215n8
Albuquerque, Severino J., 7
Allen, John Jay, 101–2
Álvarez, Sonia, 78
Amado, Janaína, 51, 56–57

Aparicio, Frances, 38
approaches to *Don Quixote*
    Eurocentric, 3, 7, 213n1
    moralistic, 215n7
    performative, 7, 15–16, 19, 214n3
    Romantic, 99–101, 117, 120–21, 125, 214nn2–3
    satirical, 99–101, 120–21, 125
Arab spring, 132
Arciniegas, Germán, 52
Ardila, J. A. G., 48
Ariza, Patricia, 63
Arruda, Agnes de Sousa, 139
Asturias, Miguel Ángel, 53
at-risk children and youth. *See* underprivileged persons
Austin, J. L., 6–7, 129, 207n2, 218n11
Avelar, Ildeber, 209–10n2
Avellaneda, Alonso Fernández de, 47, 64, 111

Badillo, César, 66–67
Báez, Jillian, 222n7
Bando de Teatro Olodum, 89–92, 96–97, 118, 145, 213n8
Barba, Eugenio, 212n5
Bary, Leslie, 28

Index

Bayliss, Robert, 80, 101, 213n1
Belo Horizonte, 219n3, 220–21n18
Beltrán, Cristina, 216n5
Benassi, Carla B., 148
Bennett, W. Lance, 218n11
Ben-Shaul, Daphne, 129
Beverley, John, 26, 208n2
Bhabha, Homi, 37, 208n2
Bible, 73, 222n6
Bishop-Sanchez, Kathryn, 7, 128–29
Blasco, Javier, 50
Boal, Augusto, 16, 71–72, 78–81, 84, 156, 161, 202, 212nn4–5
Bogad, L. M., 129
Bolívar, Simón, 5, 24–25, 208n1
Bolsonaro, Jair, 11, 146, 217n8
Borges, Jorge Luis, 2
Brazil, 9–12, 146
    military dictatorship, 28–29, 91–93, 132
    Northeast, 12
    performing, 7
    See also Brazilian Autumn
Brazilian Autumn, 11, 126, 131–44
    Movimento Passe Livre, 132–33
    online campaigns, 133–42, 218nn11–12
    signs, 138–40, **139**, 217n9, 218n10, 219n13
    songs, 142–43
    sporting events, 132, 135, 146
    vinegar revolution, 218n12
Brecht, Bertold, 97
Brewer, David A., 48, 111
Britt-Arredondo, Christopher, 23, 214n4
Butler, Judith, 127–28
Butler, Udi Mandel, 158–59

Cabral, Sérgio, 210n4, 213n9
Cala Buendía, Felipe, 144, 220n17
Caldeira, Teresa, 145

Cameron, Neil, 87, 212n4, 213n6
Canavaggio, Jean, 73, 215n7
Candelaria, La, 62–67, 210n6
cannibalism. *See* de Andrade, Oswald
Capão pecado (Ferréz), 220n18
Cape Verde, 199–201
Carelli, Chica, 89
Castells, Manuel, 137
Castro, Fidel, 5
Castro, Guillén de, 48
Certeau, Michel de, 297n4
Cervantes, Miguel de, 1, 5, 19, 27, 73, 216n4
    Pedro de Urdemalas, 75, 211n1
    rufián dichoso, El, 75, 211n1
Césaire, Aimé, 4
Chagas, Roselaine das, 218n10
Chan, Felicia, 217n7
Chartier, Roger, 51
Chávez, Hugo, 1, 5, 208n1
Chávez-Silverman, Susana, 38
Checa, Jorge, 49
Chinn, Sarah E., 128
Cidade de Deus (Meirelles and Lund), 150, 217n7
cinema novo, 29
Circo Navegador. *See* de Almeida, Andreia
Clifford, James, 3–4
Close, Anthony, 100, 167
Cobelo, Silvia, 55
Cohen-Cruz, Jan, 212n5
Columbus, Christopher, 40, 52–53
Companhia Teatro dos Novos, 89–90
Conjunto Nacional, 14–15, 30, 36–37
Conrad, Diane, 87, 213n6
Cooper, Mark, 223–24n3
Cooperaacs, 14–15, 24, 29–39, **31**, 59, 81, 105, 173, 178, 183, 208n3, 221n1
Coronil, Fernando, 32
Correa, Thiago, 142–43
Costas, Ruth, 9

Costigan, Lúcia H., 51
Courchay, Diego, 202
Cowie, Sam, 182
Critical Discourse Analysis, 18
cultural citizenship, 216n3

D'Avellar, K., 51
de Almeida, Andreia, 16, 72
    Quixote, espaço comunitário, 127, 154–56, **170**, 171–72, 180, 201–2, 221n3, 222n5
    Quixotes, 84–85, 106–8, **107**, 113–14, 199, 212n5, 222n5
de Andrade, Oswald, 27–30, 37, 130, 151, 210n3
decoloniality, 209n4
de la Campa, Román, 25–26
de la Colina, José, 132
de Souza, José Porfirio, 56–57
Dias, Telma, 16, 72, 84–85, 104–6, 113, 212n5
Didaco, Jorge, 29
Dimenstein, Gilberto, 163–64
Dinis Rigato, Fátima, 172
di Pietro, Valéria, 16, 72, 215n1
    Instituto Religare, 17, 83, 88, 125–27, 154–55, 161–65, 169–71, 173, 199, 221nn2–3
    Num lugar de la Mancha, 83–89, 103–4, 112–13, 169–71, 199, 212n5
Dom Quixote (Dias). *See* Dias, Telma
Dom Quixote das crianças (Monteiro Lobato), 55–56
Don Quijote, un grito de libertad (Morell), 58–59
Don Quixote (Cervantes)
    adaptations, 47–49, 213n2
    in Argentina, 223n1
    birth of don Quixote, 103–8, 121
    in Bolivia, 209n1
    classic, 4, 12, 15, 19, 42
    in Colombia, 52, 62–67

death of don Quixote, 47, 65, 110–21, 215n9
    festivals, 223n1
    four hundredth anniversary, 1, 11, 23, 35–36, 193, 199
    global influence, 1, 46–47
    in Guatemala, 53
    in Mexico, 58–59, 223n1
    in Spain, 1, 27
    titles, 214n6
    in United States, 5, 223n1
    in Uruguay, 52–53
    in Venezuela, 1
    See also approaches to *Don Quixote*
Don Quixote, secondary characters
    Alonso, Pedro, 160–61, 204
    Andrés, 85, 92–93, 204
    barber, 34, 96–97
    Camacho, 49
    Carrasco, Sansón, 34, 96–97, 113, 116
    duke and duchess, 34, 47, 63
    galley slaves, 93, 204–5
    Haldudo, Juan, 85, 92–93, 204
    Mambrino, helmet of, 78, 150, 168
    Marcela, 93–94, 204
    priest, 34, 96–97
    Tarfe, Don Álvaro, 47
Don Quixote of Bethlehem (George), 58–62, **61**
Doria, João, 182
Draetta, Luciano, 84
Drew, Bernard E., 51
Drummond de Andrade, Carlos, 210n5
Dunn, Christopher, 130

ECA (Estatuto da Criança e do Adolescente), 163
Egginton, William, 211nn1–2
Em defesa das causas perdidas: Uma carta para Dom Quixote (Meirelles), 83, 199–201
Erasmus of Rotterdam, Desiderio, 169

European Space Agency, 49

Facundo, o civilización y barbarie
  (Sarmiento), 209n2
Farah, Tatiana, 132
Farias, Denis Alves, 139, 217–18n9
favela, 12, 131–32, 144–51, 185, 220nn15–18, 222n5
Favela Rising (Mochary and Zimbalist), 144–51, 220nn16–17
Fawkes, Guy, 218n12
FEBEM (Fundação Estadual para o Bem-Estar do Menor), 16, 83, 85–89, 163–65, 169–71, 185–88, 213n7
Ferreira, Renata V., 103
Ferréz (Reginaldo Ferreira da Silva), 220n18
Figuereido, Eurídice, 26
Fish, Stanley, 196
Flores, William V., 216n3
Florián Navas, Carmen A., 62
Fordelone, Yolanda, 140
Foucault, Michel, 18, 169, 215n8, 222n6
Franco, Marielle, 146
Franklin, Benjamin, 5
Freire, Paulo
  ethics and aesthetics, 176, 196
  influence, 71–72, 80–81, 211n3, 215n1
  pedagogy of the oppressed, 6, 16, 137, 149, 159
  word as praxis and transformation, 8, 76–78, 102–3, 114, 162, 176
Friedman, Edward H., 50, 111, 215n7
Fuentes, Carlos, 54, 107
Fundação Casa. *See* FEBEM

Gálvez, Andrés, 49
Garcia, Giselle, 9–10
García, Santiago, 58, 62–66, 210n6
García Canclini, Néstor, 26
García Guillén, Mário, 83, 105

Gascón, Christopher D., 210–11n6
George, Bill, 58, 59–62
Gerli, Michael, 80
Gil, Gilberto, 28, 130–31, 146
Gilrain, Jenny, 60–62
Goffman, Erving, 81, 127
Gohn, Maria da Glória, 139
Goiás, 51, 56
Golden, Tim, 41
Goldman, Francisco, 202
Gollnick, Brian, 42
Gomes Goveia, Fábio, 217–18n9
Gómez Peña, Guillermo, 132
Gordimer, Nadine, 1
Grande Otelo (Sebastião Bernardes de Souza Prata), 213n9
Green, Barbara, 8, 129
Greenblatt, Stephen, 73, 211n2
Grossman, Edith, 207n1
Grupo Cultural AfroReggae, 126, 144–52, 220n15–18
Grupo Permanente de Pesquisa. *See* Dias, Telma
Grupo Quixote, 57–58
Guevara, Ernesto "Che," 5, 18
Gutiérrez, Bernardo, 136

Haff, Stephen, 202–5, 224n4
Hall, Stuart, 18
Hamilton, Alex, 5
Harris, Melissa S., 181
hidalgo Quijano. *See* Quijano, Alonso
Horwatt, Eli, 141
humanities, 20, 196–97, 223n3
hybridism
  cultures, 4, 26, 29, 33, 37–38, 208n2
  in Latin America, 24–27, 37–38

Ibarra, Paola, 30
Iffland, James, 41, 72, 213–14n2
Instituto Religare. *See* di Pietro, Valéria

Jefferson, Thomas, 5
Johnson, Nuala, 24
Junior, José, 147–51

Kid Quixotes (Haff et al.), 202–5
Kiefer, Sandra, 220–21n18
Kozusko, Matt, 213n6

Larkins, Erica, 144, 150, 220n17
Las Casas, Bartolomé de, 53
LeCarré, John, 1
Leonard, Irving A., 50
Lescher, Auro, 156, 176–79, 183–84, 188
Lima Barreto, Alfonso H., 54–55
Lins do Rêgo, José, 210n4
Lipsitz, George, 130
Lo Ré, A. G., 214–15n2
Luiselli, Valeria, 202

Machado de Assis, Joaquim M., 54
Maddox, John T., 150
Maestro, Jesús, 49
Making of Don Quixote of Bethlehem, The (George and Costa, dirs.), 60–62
Mancing, Howard, 50, 210n3
Mandel, Oscar, 214n3
"Manifesto Antropófago" (Andrade). *See* de Andrade, Oswald
Man of la Mancha (Wasserman), 49, 58
Maravall, José Antonio, 213–14n2
Marcos, Subcomandante, 5, 41, 132, 223n2
Mariano, Isabella, 140
Marín, Christina, 80
Martí, José, 5
Matta, Roberto, 14
Maura, Antonio, 54
Mazetti, Henrique, 131, 140
McCann, Bryan, 130
MC Daleste, 143–44
McGraw, Mark, 214n3

Medea Project, 213n6
Meirelles, Márcio
 Em defesa das causas perdidas: Uma carta para Dom Quixote, 83, 199–201
 tal de dom Quixote, Um, 16, 72, 82–85, 89–97, **92**, **95**, 108–10, 114–19, 199, 212n5
Melucci, Alberto, 137–38
Mendes, Cleise, 83, 89
Menotti del Picchia, Paulo, 210n3
metatheater
 definition, 81
 in *Don Quixote*, 63–64, 103
 and marginality, 16, 66–67, 85–98, 119–20
Mignolo, Walter, 209n4
Millington, Mark, 33, 38, 43
Milne, Elinor, 157
Milton, John, 55, 202
Miñana, Rogelio, 168, 197, 211n1
Monachesi, Juliana, 145
Monteiro Lobato, José Bento, 55–56, 210n4
Montemayor, Jorge de, 160
Morell, Arturo, 58–59
Morrison, Chandra, 30
Morrison, Toni, 1
Muniz, Vik, 30
Mutatis (Xavier), 89, 162–63. *See also* Xavier, Peterson
MV Bill, 88–89

naming, 6, 63, 67, 76–78, 108–10, 137–38, 149–50, 159–67, 195, 222n5
nation-building. *See under* transculturation
Navarro Flores, Celia, 210n5
Neate, Patrick, 188
Negri, Toni, 137
neocolonial, 3–4, 37, 75, 208n2
Neves, Letícia, 199

Neves, Manoella, 218n10
Newfield, Christopher, 223n3
Niemeyer, Óscar, 83, 86
Noble, Steven E., 80
Nouvelle Vague, 29
Num lugar de la Mancha (di Pietro). *See under* di Pietro, Valéria

Olinto, António, 55
Olodum. *See* Bando de Teatro Olodum
Ômnibus 174 (Padilha), 217n7
Operación Dulcinea, 1, 5
Oriel, Charles, 6–7, 73
Ortiz, Arturo, 41–42
Ortiz, Fernando, 4, 23–25, 38
otherness, 19, 127, 155–59, 166–67, 177, 194, 203–4, 207n4, 219n13, 222n6

Pardue, Derek, 130–31
Parr, James, 101
Pasquerella, Lynn, 197
Pedagogy of the Oppressed (Freire). *See* Freire, Paulo
Penteado, Claudia, 134
Peres, Phyllis, 208n2
Pérez Rodríguez, Marta, 51
performance
    of Brazilian identity, 7–8
    of citizenship, 8, 16–17, 125–52, 155–56, 158–59
    definition, 127–29, 207n2
    performativity, 73, 127–28, 215n8
    street, 58–62, 80
    See also approaches to *Don Quixote*
performative activism
    definition, 6–8, 19–20, 128–30, 144, 151–52, 189–91, 207n3, 216n2
    in *Don Quixote*-inspired projects, 16–17, 193–205
periferia, 146, 149, 164, 180, 185, 220n18
Perlman, Janice, 148, 157
Petrovich, Carlos, 83, 90, 94–96

"Pierre Menard, author of *Don Quixote*" (Borges), 2
Pires, Célio, 162–63
Poblete, Juan, 220n17
Pontos de Cultura, 131, 161, 221n3
Portinari, Candido, 210n5
Porto Alegre, 57–58, 223n2
Pratt, Mary Louise, 36, 38, 53
Predmore, Richard, 49
Presentation of Self in Everyday Life, The (Goffman), 81, 127
Projeto Quixote, 13, 17, 127, 154–59, **175**, 221n3
    Bixiga windmill, 174–78
    Exilados do Mundão (Rubio), 155, 180, 183–89, 198–99
    programs, 165–67, 173–74, 178–79
    rematriamento, 167, 178–81
Pueo Wood, Noemi, 220n17

Quijano, Alonso
    actor, 6–7, 16, 34–35, 49–50, 63–65, 117–18, 125, 156, 215n8
    death of, 47, 110–20
    hidalgo, 2–3, 61, 77, 97–98, 108–10
    not crazy, 64, 104–8, 156
    reader, 39
    revolutionary, 73–74, 77–79, 81–82, 167–69, 184, 190–91, 214n5, 222n6
    self-transformation into Don Quixote, 99–103, 159–61, 214n6
Quijano, Aníbal, 27, 37, 208n2
Quijote, El (García), 58, 62–67
Quijote latinoamericano, El (García et al.), 66–67
Quiroz, Luis, 209n1
Quixana. *See* Quijano, Alonso
Quixote, espaço comunitário. *See under* de Almeida, Andreia
Quixote reciclado (Henry), 208n3, 221n1
Quixotes (Almeida). *See under* de

Almeida, Andreia quixotism, 6, 8

Rama, Ángel, 25
Ramos, Lázaro, 83, 90
Red latinoamericana de teatro en comunidad, 66–67
Reed, Helen H., 49, 72
Reis, Carlos, 2–3, 47–48
Reisz, Matthew, 223–24n3
Revolta de Formoso, 56–57
Riera, Carme, 23, 214n4
Riley, Edward C., 48
Rio de Janeiro, 8, 145–51, 217n6
Rivera, Roberto, 42
Rizzini, Irene, 12
Rocha, Glauber, 217n7
Rocha Barroso, Juliana, 176, 178
Rodó, José Enrique, 52–53
Rodrigues, Sandro, viii, 29, 31
Rogers, Richard A., 43, 209n5
Rousseff, Dilma, 11, 136
Rushdie, Salman, 1
Russell, Peter E., 101

Sá, Anderson, 144–51, 220n17
Sábato, Ernesto, 178
Said, Edward, 41
Salvador de Bahia, 89–91
Sandoval, Chela, 8
Sandoval Sánchez, Alberto, 103, 214n5
São Paulo, 3, 8, 11–13
 Barra Funda, 161–62
 Cidade Tiradentes, 66–67
 Crackôlandia, 174–75, 182
Sarmiento, Domingo Faustino, 209n2
Scalona, Timothy, 216n2
Schmidt, Ben, 223–24n3
Schmidt, Christopher, 30
Schmidt, Rachel, 111
Seewald, Gert, 176
Sena, Ercio, 218n10, 219n13

Serialized Traveling Adventures of Kid Quixote, The (Haff et al.), 202–5
Sganzerla, Rogério, 29
Shakespeare, William, 97
Sherman, Kim, 204
Shohat, Ella, 208n2
Silva, António José da (O Judeu), 51
Silva, Luiz Inácio Lula da, 9, 11, 131
Sneed, Paul Michael, 150
sobrevida, 2–3, 18–19, 46–49, 56–57, 65–67, 111
social roles
 definition, 127–28
 rewriting and performing, 3, 7, 81, 154–58, 161, 171–72, 189–91, 194
Spitta, Silvia, 34, 38
Spitzer, Leo, 78
Spivak, Gayatri, 40–41, 43
Stam, Robert, 29
Stavans, Ilan, 5
Still Waters in a Storm, 202–5, **203**, 224n4
Storey, John, 32, 41
street children. *See* underprivileged persons
subaltern, 25, 39–45

tal de dom Quixote, Um (Meirelles). *See under* Meirelles, Márcio
Taviani brothers (Paolo and Vittorio), 213n6
Taylor, Diana, 42–44, 78, 128, 207n2
Teatro Trono, 211n3
Teatro Vila Velha, 89–91, 117–19
Temer, Michel, 11
Tennina, Lucía, 220–21n18
theater
 in *Don Quixote*, 48–51
 social justice, 3, 78
Theatre of the Oppressed (Boal). *See* Boal, Augusto
theatricade, 60–62

250 | Index

Torrente Ballester, Gonzalo, 49–50
Touchstone Theater, 59, **61**. *See also* George, Bill
transatlantic, 3, 18, 23
transculturation
   across languages, 8, 32, 34, 75
   definition, 4, 15, 18–19, 24–27, 39–45, 208n2, 209n5, 214n5
   nation-building, 4, 15, 23–24, 32–34, 38, 52–56, 197, 209n2, 214n4
   social change, 17, 23, 33–34, 37–45, 56–67, 72, 76, 197
transformation
   of the individual and society, 6–8, 16, 18–20, 31–35, 65
   of self, 3, 7, 34, 39, 74, 87, 108–9, 149, 196
   of urban spaces, 17, 59–63, 66–67, 147–48, 151–91
trabalhadores sem terra (landless workers), 92
Trigo, Abril, 26, 42, 208n2
Triste Fim de Policarpo Quaresma (Lima Barreto), 54–55
Tropicália, 28–29, 130–31, 146
Tropicalism. *See* Tropicália
Trump, Donald J., 182, 203–4

underprivileged persons, 4, 9, 15, 19–20, 149, 152, 154, 193–95, 222n7
   material needs of, 172–74, 222n7
underserved. *See* underprivileged persons
Uribe Echevarría, Juan, 51
Uzel, Marcos, 89–90, 213n8

Valentín, Wilson, 8
Valmir Gomes, José, 164
Van Dijk, Teun A., 18
Van Doren, Mark, 49
Vanden Berghe, Kristine, 41
Vargas, Getúlio, 55–56, 130

Vaz, Sérgio, 220–21n18
Vega, Félix Lope de, 79–80
Velásquez Martínez, Alberto, 50
Vélez Sainz, Julio, 222n4
Vellado, Robson, 72, 104
Veloso, Caetano, 28, 130, 146
V for Vendetta (film; McTeigue, dir.), 218–19n12
Vieira, Maria Augusta da Costa, 54–55, 57, 102, 210n4
Viera, Ricardo, 61
Vigário Geral. *See* Grupo Cultural AfroReggae
Viñar, Marcelo, 157
visibility, 17, 88, 90, 128–29, 147–52, 165, 169–71, 174, 186–87, 195
vulnerable. *See* underprivileged persons

Waldron, Travis, 146
Walker, George F., 202
Walker, Lucy, 30
Washington, George, 5
Wasserman, Dale, 49, 58–59, 83, 101, 112, 213n9
Waste Land (Walker), 30
Williamson, Robert C., 78
Wood, Sarah F., 5
World Social Forum, 223n2

Xavier, Peterson, 86–89, 126–27, 162–65, 172, 179, 199, 222n4

Yúdice, George, 215n8, 219n14, 220n17

Zapatistas, 41, 66, 129, 132, 223n2
Ziolkowsky, Eric J., 167, 214n4
Zola, Émile, 212n4

www.ingramcontent.com/pod-product-compliance
Lightning Source LLC
Chambersburg PA
CBHW030536230426
43665CB00010B/921